Songs, Poems, and Verses.
By Helen, Lady Dufferin ...
Edited with a memoir, and some
account of the Sheridan family,
by her son, the Marquess of
Dufferin and Ava. With portrait.

Helen Selina Blackwood, Frederick Blackwood

Songs, Poems, & Verses. By Helen, Lady Dufferin ... Edited with a memoir, and some account of the Sheridan family, by her son, the Marquess of Dufferin and Ava. With portrait.

Blackwood, Helen Selina
British Library, Historical Print Editions
British Library
Blackwood, Frederick
011652.g.26.

The BiblioLife Network

This project was made possible in part by the BiblioLife Network (BLN), a project aimed at addressing some of the huge challenges facing book preservationists around the world. The BLN includes libraries, library networks, archives, subject matter experts, online communities and library service providers. We believe every book ever published should be available as a high-quality print reproduction; printed on- demand anywhere in the world. This insures the ongoing accessibility of the content and helps generate sustainable revenue for the libraries and organizations that work to preserve these important materials.

The following book is in the "public domain" and represents an authentic reproduction of the text as printed by the original publisher. While we have attempted to accurately maintain the integrity of the original work, there are sometimes problems with the original book or micro-film from which the books were digitized. This can result in minor errors in reproduction. Possible imperfections include missing and blurred pages, poor pictures, markings and other reproduction issues beyond our control. Because this work is culturally important, we have made it available as part of our commitment to protecting, preserving, and promoting the world's literature.

GUIDE TO FOLD-OUTS, MAPS and OVERSIZED IMAGES

In an online database, page images do not need to conform to the size restrictions found in a printed book. When converting these images back into a printed bound book, the page sizes are standardized in ways that maintain the detail of the original. For large images, such as fold-out maps, the original page image is split into two or more pages.

Guidelines used to determine the split of oversize pages:

• Some images are split vertically; large images require vertical and horizontal splits.
• For horizontal splits, the content is split left to right.
• For vertical splits, the content is split from top to bottom.
• For both vertical and horizontal splits, the image is processed from top left to bottom right.

SONGS, POEMS, AND VERSES

HELEN'S TOWER

Ἑλένη ἐπὶ πύργῳ

Who hears of Helen's Tower, may dream perchance
    How the Greek beauty from the Scæan Gate
    Gazed on old friends unanimous in hate,
    Death-doom'd because of her fair countenance.

Hearts would leap otherwise at thy advance,
    Lady to whom this Tower is consecrate!
    Like hers, thy face once made all eyes elate,
    Yet, unlike hers, was blessed by every glance.

The Tower of Hate is outworn, far and strange:
    A transitory shame of long ago,
    It dies into the sand from which it sprang;
    But thine Love's rock-built Tower, shall fear no change;
    God's Self laid stable earth's foundations so,
    When all the morning stars together sang.

                           ROBERT BROWNING.

April 26, 1870.

Helen, Lady Dufferin
(Countess of Gifford)

Edited, with a No
Account of the Sh...
MARQUESS OF DU...

Songs, Poems, & Verses

BY

Helen, Lady Dufferin

(COUNTESS OF GIFFORD)

Edited, with a Memoir
and some Account of the Sheridan Family, by her Son
THE MARQUESS OF DUFFERIN AND AVA

WITH PORTRAIT

LONDON
JOHN MURRAY, ALBEMARLE STREET
1894

Printed by R. & R. CLARK, *Edinburgh*

CONTENTS

A SKETCH OF MY MOTHER

A FOND desire to preserve the memory of those we love from oblivion is an almost universal sentiment, whether we build the tomb of Mausolus or carve the name of Rosalind on the forest trees in Arden. It is this motive which has led me to collect and publish the poems and songs of my mother; for a book once published has put on the robes of immortality; it becomes a κτῆμα ἐς ἀεὶ, an indestructible witness to the existence and individuality of its author. Nor need I apologise for having undertaken this pious labour, for some of the pieces have already received a warm welcome, not only in England, but also in "Greater Britain." One of them, the "Irish Emigrant," has attained to world-wide fame, and on the other side of the Atlantic is wont to bring the audience to its feet.

Another, "The Charming Woman," when it first appeared many years ago, was sung in the streets and theatres as well as in the drawing-rooms of London; while one or two of the longer poems have continued to be recognised favourites at popular recitations. Since these have pleased, I have been induced to add others to the number, and to give to what has already been published a more stable existence than belonged to the fleeting form in which my mother's verses were originally disseminated. Printed in this small volume, they will, I trust, be allowed a niche in the literature of our century.

I have had some doubts whether I should add to the others the verses addressed to myself; but it seemed to me that poems which expressed such genuine love in so direct and simple a manner would probably appeal to many a mother's heart, who would be glad to find expressed in musical language the thoughts which were struggling for utterance in her own breast. Nor have I hesitated to add the lighter and more trivial pieces which will be found at the end of the volume, because, in combination with the pathetic ones which precede them, they will convey some notion of the playful, sunny temperament which sparkled on the surface of their author's illimitable depths of feeling.

At a future time I hope to publish a selection of my mother's letters. A few amusing ones have already been dovetailed into some recently-published memoirs, and two of them I have now reproduced. She could not, indeed, put pen to paper without betraying the innocent gaiety of her disposition,—a gaiety as tender as it was witty,—for her very laughter was a caress. In accomplishing this latter task I intend giving a more elaborate account of my mother's life; meanwhile, I have thought that those who may be tempted to glance at the following pages might be glad to know a little about their writer. I have also introduced a short account of the family from which she sprung, as well as of that into which she married.

Helen, Lady Dufferin, or, to give her title in full, Helen, Baroness Dufferin and Clandeboye, was the daughter of Thomas Sheridan, and the grand-daughter of the Right Honourable Richard Brinsley Butler-Sheridan.

The Sheridans, though they fell afterwards upon evil days, were originally an ancient, affluent, and important family, possessing castles and lands in the

County Cavan, a tract of which is marked in the old maps of the period as "the Sheridan country";[1] but in Queen Elizabeth's time their property was escheated, as Thomas Sheridan bitterly complained before the bar of the House of Commons in 1680.[2] They were driven from their homes, and were forced during the next two hundred years to fight the battle of life under what were always discouraging and sometimes desperate conditions. It is, perhaps, to these persecutions of Fate that their continuous intellectual activity may be attributed.

The first of the line who laboured in the world of letters was Denis Sheridan, the son of Donald and of

[1] "In Cavan, the ancient Brefny East, the families mentioned in an old map bearing date 1607 are the Sheridans, or O'Sheridans, and the O'Reillys."—*Notes on the Sheridans*.

[2] "In clearing myself of this aspersion (*i.e.* of too great devotion to the interests of the Duke of York, afterwards James II.), I must say something, which nought but necessity can excuse from vanity, in that I was born a gentleman of one of the ancientest families and related to many considerable in Ireland. In one County there is a castle and a large demesne, in another a greater tract of land for several miles together, yet known by our name. My grandfather was the last that enjoyed our estate; and my father, left an orphan at the beginning of King James's reign, found himself dispossessed and exposed to the world, —that whole County, with five others in Ulster, being entirely escheated to the Crown."—*Thomas Sheridan at the Bar of the House of Commons*, 1680.

a daughter of the O'Neill. He must have been born about the year 1600.[1] He had quitted the Catholic fold to become a Protestant clergyman, and a devoted disciple of the saintly Bedell, Bishop of Kilmore, under whose direction he translated the English version of the Bible into Irish. Bishop Bedell died in Mr. Sheridan's house in the year 1642.

From his sister, Sarah Sheridan, descended, in the third generation, the gallant General Sarsfield, Earl of Lucan.

Denis Sheridan had four sons, three of whom were

[1] "Behind the Palace of Kilmore, where Bedell's bones repose, the traveller will come upon an intricate network of Lake scenery, among hills and wooded flats. Here is Trinity Island, where stand the remains of an old Abbey, and many legends about the Sheridans cluster round this island. It is said that the first of the family settled here from Spain, being sent over by the Pope of Rome in the fifth or sixth century, and founded a school of learning on the island, which he enriched with a library of manuscripts. This insular University was presided over from generation to generation by one of the Sheridan family, and an Irish manuscript, now in the University of Rheims, was indited by one of the name. Considerably north of Trinity Island is Cloughoughter Castle where Bedell was imprisoned. The Castle stands on a small island, and is a beautiful ruin. Here lived Donald Sheridan, the father of Denis, who translated the Holy Scriptures into Irish, which were afterwards published by Robert Boyle, and are now known as the *Irish Bible*. Donald Sheridan was married to a daughter of the O'Neill, and had two sons, Denis and another, and a daughter who was the grandmother of the gallant Sarsfield."—*Notes on the Sheridans.*

men of mark in their day, one of them, William, succeeding Bedell in the See of Kilmore; another, Patrick, becoming Bishop of Cloyne; while the third, Thomas, was the author of a very remarkable work, published in 1677, entitled *The Rise and Power of Parliaments*. It has recently been republished and edited by Mr. Saxe Bannister, who has added an interesting sketch of the author's life. Under James the Second, Thomas Sheridan was made a Privy Councillor and Secretary to the Government of Ireland, and received the honour of Knighthood, as his son did also. After James's overthrow, he adhered to the fortunes of the fallen King, and accompanied him in exile to France. " There he wrote a history of the time, which has obtained great praise from the highest authorities, Sir James Mackintosh and Lord Macaulay, both of whom have made large use of the unprinted manuscript now preserved in the Royal Library at Windsor."[1] Thomas Sheridan married a natural daughter of his Sovereign, and by her became father of the Sir Thomas Sheridan, one of " the seven men of Moidart," who followed Prince Charles to Scotland in the '45. In connection

[1] Editor's Preface to *The Rise and Power of Parliaments.*

with this fact I may mention a curious coincidence. Many years ago I accompanied the late Duke and Duchess of Sutherland, then Lord and Lady Stafford, upon a yachting cruise shortly after their marriage. We eventually reached Cromartie, the ancient seat of the attainted Earls of Cromartie, of whom Lady Stafford was the representative. One day after dinner I happened to see a large old-fashioned chest under the sideboard. I asked Lady Stafford what was in it. She said that it contained the Cromartie papers. Being fond of old-world reminiscences, I proposed that we should open it. The housekeeper having come with her key, I stretched my hand at random among the heap of documents within, and lighted on a bundle of worn and yellow letters. The very first that we opened proved to be an order, written and signed by Sir Thomas Sheridan, who acted as the Prince's Secretary, instructing the Earl of Cromartie of that day to burn down the Castle of the Earl of Sutherland. It was curious that the first time that this paper saw the light since reaching its destination, three persons so intimately connected with the original three concerned in its subject-matter, should have been alone together.

Sir Thomas Sheridan's daughter became the wife of Colonel Guillaume, A.D.C. to King William, on which occasion she received back part of the old Sheridan property. Another daughter of the house married the Marquis de Maillé de la Tour Landry, the head of one of the oldest families in France, and was the mother of the Comtesse d'Hautefort, who attended the Duchesse de Berry in prison.

The only literary remains of Thomas Sheridan's two brothers that have been preserved are some sermons and two volumes of discourses, the one published in 1704, and the other in 1720.

In the next generation we have in Thomas Sheridan an author in whom the less serious but more attractive qualities of the race were eminently apparent. Dr. Thomas Sheridan, the son of Denis Sheridan's fourth son, James, was born in 1687, and, having adopted the "profession of a Schoolmaster, he rose to great eminence both as a teacher and as a scholar."[1] But what appears to have principally endeared him to his friends were his extraordinary wit, his liveliness, his good nature, his simplicity, and an absence of worldly wisdom worthy of

[1] *Encyclopædia Britannica.*

Dominie Sampson. These were the traits which so captivated Swift, and not only Swift, but Stella, and this to such a degree that the ferocious Dean soon found life intolerable without the constant companionship of Sheridan.[1] Sheridan used to pass months in Swift's house in Dublin, and Swift in turn was a continual guest at Quilca, or rather Quilcalgh, a country house which, with a small estate, had come into Sheridan's possession. It was here that the plan of the *Drapier's Letters* was discussed between the two, that *Gulliver's Travels* received their final touches, and that, in conjunction with Swift, Sheridan edited the *Intelligencer*. Of Thomas Sheridan's attainments as a scholar it is scarcely necessary to speak; they were universally recognised at the time. But the only records of his eminence in this direction which have survived are his translations in verse of the *Philoctetes* of Sophocles, and of the *Satires* of Juvenal published in 1745.[2] Quilcalgh was also the site of Stella's Bower.

[1] People used to say that Sheridan's wit and sweet gaiety was the harp of David, that could play the evil spirit out of Saul, *i.e.* the Dean.

[2] Lord Cork says of Thomas Sheridan that "not a day passed that he did not make a rebus, an anagram or a madrigal. He was idle, poor, and gay; knew more of books than of men; and was completely ignorant of the value of money."—*Biographie Générale.*

His son, Thomas Sheridan, the fourth in descent
from Denis, was born about 1719. As his father
died a poor man, owing to his having "a better
knowledge of books, than of men, or of the value of
money," Thomas Sheridan had to gain his own living.
From early days, even at school, he seems to have
had a passion for acting, and he started by adopting
the stage as his profession, with the usual results.
But his chief claim to literary consideration rests upon
his enthusiastic efforts in favour of a better system
of education than that which was then in vogue.
To this cause he devoted a great portion of his life
and of his resources, and in recognition of his efforts
he received *ad eundem* degrees both from Oxford and
Cambridge.   He wrote a play, several works on
education, with a course of lectures on elocution,
and two dissertations on language, a biography of
Swift, and a general dictionary.   He also collected,
with a view to publication, a quarto volume of his
father's writings, but those have unfortunately disappeared.   He was the intimate friend of Garrick and
of Johnson,—for whom he was instrumental in pro-
curing a pension,—of Wedderburn, of Archbishop
Markham, and of the author of *Pamela*.   He died

in 1788, leaving two sons, Charles, who became a member of the Irish Parliament and wrote a *History of the Revolution in Sweden* in 1772, and a younger one, the author of *The School for Scandal.*

Of Richard Brinsley Sheridan, my great-grandfather, it is not necessary that I should say much. His life still remains to be written.[1]   No famous man has been more unfortunate in his biographers.   Moore planned his work upon too large a scale, and tired of his task before he had half finished it.   Moreover, though Sheridan's countryman, or perhaps for that reason, he was, as I have heard, rather jealous of him. The author of *Sheridan and his Times* says he bore a grudge against Sheridan for having, good-humouredly, twitted him with having plagiarised some of his verses.   The Prince Regent, when he read the book, said the writer had better abscond, or justice would lay him by the heels "for cutting and maiming and barbarously attempting the Life of Sheridan ! ! " Moore's subacid tone becomes more accentuated in his second volume ; but almost at the onset of the work he begins carping at Sheridan for the pains he took to refine and polish the dialogues in his plays.

[1] I understand that an eminent writer has actually taken this task in hand.

But, as is remarked in the following extract from a review of Moore's book, written, I believe, by Jeffrey, he "who was for thirty years the most brilliant talker—the greatest conversational wit of the splendid circle in which he moved—could not possibly have been a man to whom preparation was generally necessary in order to shine ; and cannot be suspected of having had a cold or sluggish fancy, which did not give its golden harvests till it was diligently laboured and manured.   His conceptions, on the contrary, seem always to have flowed from him with great copiousness and rapidity.   But he had taste as well as genius, and his labour was employed, not in making what was bad tolerable, but in making what was good better and best.   Ariosto is said to have written the first stanza of his *Orlando* ten or twelve times over."[1]

Nor does Moore seem altogether pleased at the equal terms upon which Sheridan, the son of an actor and the grandson of a schoolmaster, mingled with the smart and exclusive society of the day.   But the great houses of London have always extended a warm welcome to genius, however humble its origin, though as a matter of fact, if a claim to good birth

[1] *Edinburgh Review*, December 1826.

is dependent upon ancient descent and feudal distinction, Sheridan was as well born as Pitt, Fox, North, or any of the fine gentlemen with whom he associated; for, during the fourteenth, fifteenth, and sixteenth centuries, his direct ancestors had been as princes in the land, and his own branch of the family were the Chiefs of the Name. As for Mr. Smyth's *Memoir*, though accepted as authoritative from the fact of his having been young Sheridan's tutor, and therefore intimate with the father, I have often heard my grandmother, who was a very calm and trustworthy witness, say that it was full of exaggerations and misrepresentations. Subsequent authors have drawn their materials from these somewhat tainted sources. "Tradition, too, has attached to his name dozens of mythical anecdotes, as examples of his wit, his frolicsome humour, his habits of procrastination, his pecuniary embarrassments, and his methods of escaping from them, for which there was really no foundation. The real Sheridan, as he was known in private life, is irrevocably gone. Even Moore, writing so soon after his death, has to lament that he could find out nothing about him."[1]

[1] *Encyclopædia Britannica.*

Moreover, as has often happened with other notable persons, those who have recorded their impressions in regard to Sheridan knew him only when he was old and broken, his gaiety all quenched (though his wit still flickered in the socket), the adherent of a disorganised party, a man utterly ruined by the burning of Drury Lane Theatre, pestered by petty debts, yet still sufficiently formidable to provoke detraction at the hands of his political enemies, while his fame exposed him to the curiosity and criticism of the gossips.   These thick clouds have obscured the brightness of his early manhood and the social and political ascendency which he enjoyed during his maturer years.   It is evident that, when he had scarcely ceased to be a boy, his geniality, his good-nature, which his subsequent trials neither soured nor exhausted, his charming manners, and his handsome person,—his splendid eyes were the very home of genius,—as much as his extraordinary liveliness and wit had made him a favourite with the best English society, where he was as popular with men as with women, while his eloquence, his Parliamentary aptitude, and, above all, his solid abilities, which his more brilliant graces have thrown into the background, at once placed him on a level with the greatest orators and statesmen of that epoch.

That he had failings—when was genius without them?—cannot be denied, but their results have been absurdly magnified. He was addicted to wine,—as who was not in those days?—but in his case the nervous temperament which made him what he was, rendered its effects upon his brain and constitution exceptionally deleterious.[1] At the end of his life he was involved in pecuniary difficulties; but these arose partly from a calamity for which he was not responsible, and partly from an ineradicable and apparently hereditary inability to attend to what is called

---

[1] Byron remarks rather bitterly that the glass which half maddened Sheridan failed to affect the coarser brains of his more stolid intimates, who basked in the sunshine of his gaiety.

In contrast to Sheridan's weak-headedness, I may cite the instance of my paternal grandfather, who never had a day's illness, and lived till eighty-one. He would occasionally begin a convivial evening with what he called a "clearer," i.e. a bottle of port, and continued with four bottles of claret. He always retired to bed in a state of perfect though benevolent sobriety. He enjoyed, indeed, as President of some Social Club, the title of "The Great Benevolence of Ireland." I have reason to complain that my two grandfathers, by over-drawing the family account with Bacchus, have left me a water drinker,—a condition of degeneracy which caused, I remember, serious concern to the older friends of the family.

"business." He began life without a sixpence; he made a disinterested marriage; from a feeling of chivalrous delicacy, which won for him the admiration of Dr. Johnson, he would not allow his wife to sing in public, though in this way he might have added £2000 a year to his income; he was the boon companion and friend for forty years of men who lived in the greatest wealth and splendour; that is to say, he was surrounded with every temptation to extravagance; and yet, when after his death, his affairs were inquired into, his debts were found to amount to a comparatively trifling sum.[1]   His, too, was a gambling age, but, though fond of betting upon political events, he never touched a card or handled the dice box.

On the other hand, let it be remembered, that even when administering to the amusement of his contemporaries, and writing for a pleasure-seeking public, at a period of considerable licence, he has never sullied his pages by an impure allusion, a gross joke, or an un-

---

[1] Moore says less than £5000. Fox's debts were paid twice over by his friends, and amounted to tens of thousands, as also did Pitt's. Sheridan, on the other hand, coined from his brains an ample income, which endured in full volume until he was burnt out. Had it been but prudently administered, it would, even so, have kept him in affluence for the rest of his life.

worthy sentiment; while during his long Parliamentary career it was always on the side of justice, of liberty, and of humanity [1]—in whose sacred cause he sacrificed repeated opportunities of emolument, and some of Life's most valued prizes,[2]—that he was found fighting. Succeeding generations of his countrymen may well afford, therefore, to forget the pathetic infirmities which dimmed the splendour of Sheridan's latter years, out of respect for one of the greatest speakers that has ever entranced the House of Commons, and in gratitude for the gift his genius has bequeathed them in his two immortal Comedies, and the incomparable *Critic*.

Of Sheridan's speech against Warren Hastings,

---

[1] Sheridan opposed the war with America; he deprecated the coalition between Fox and North; he advocated the abolition of slavery; he denounced the tyranny of Warren Hastings; he condemned the trade restrictions on Ireland; he fought for Catholic emancipation; he did his best to save the French Royal Family. He was also in favour of an eight hours' day.

[2] He might at any time, had he so chosen, have " hid his head in a coronet," as he himself expressed it. On another occasion he remarked, rather pitifully, that it was easy enough for his rich and titled colleagues to exhibit a virtuous indifference to place, but for so poor a man as himself to prefer his principles to place required a different kind of heroism.

From a sense of honour towards his party he more than once refused office, especially in 1804 when offered it by Addington, with whom he agreed in opinion.—*Dict. of English History.*

Mr. Burke declared it to be "the most astonishing effort of eloquence, argument, and wit united, of which there is any record or tradition." Mr. Fox said: "All that he had ever heard, all that he had ever read, when compared with it dwindled into nothing, and vanished like a vapour before the sun." Mr. Pitt acknowledged that "it surpassed all the eloquence of ancient and modern times, and possessed everything that genius or art could furnish to agitate and control the human mind." Burke said to Fox while Sheridan was speaking, "That is the true style,—something between poetry and prose, and better than either."

Byron said: "Whatever Sheridan has chosen to do has been the best of its kind. He has written the best comedy (*The School for Scandal*); the best opera, (*The Duenna*, in my mind far before *The Beggar's Opera*); the best farce (*The Critic*); the best address (*The Monologue on Garrick*); and, to crown all, delivered the best oration ever conceived or heard in this country."

And Moore calls Sheridan:—

The pride of the palace, the bower and the hall—
The orator, dramatist, minstrel,—who ran
Through each mode of the lyre, and was master of all ;—

Whose mind was an essence compounded with art,
From the finest and best of all other men's powers;—
Who rul'd like a wizard, the world of the heart,
And could call up its sunshine, or draw down its showers;—

Whose humour, as gay as the fire-fly's light,
Play'd round every subject, and shone, as it play'd;—
Whose wit, in the combat as gentle as bright,
Ne'er carried a heart-stain away on its blade;—

Whose eloquence, brightening whatever it tried,
Whether reason or fancy, the gay or the grave,
Was as rapid, as deep, and as brilliant a tide,
As ever bore Freedom aloft on its wave.[1]

Mr. Sheridan left two sons: Thomas, whose mother was Miss Linley, and Charles, born in 1796, by a second marriage with Miss Ogle. I remember Charles very well, for he did not die till 1843. In his youth he showed great promise, but a brain fever must have injuriously affected his intellectual powers; for, though extremely amiable, he had none of the brilliancy of those who had gone before him. He interested himself, however, in Greek affairs, and in

---

[1] Though in his *Life of Sheridan*, Moore sometimes yielded to a feeling of petty jealousy, he was a good-natured man, and too clever himself not to appreciate genius, and in the above verses his truer instincts regained the mastery.

1824 he published a volume on the Greek Revolution, and in the following year a translation in verse of the Songs of Greece from the Romaic text.

Thomas Sheridan, my grandfather, seems, on the contrary, to have been endowed with all the wit of his father, and to have inherited from Miss Linley, whom he also resembled, the charm and sweet disposition which so endeared him to his friends. The author of *Sheridan and his Times* says that no man was ever more universally admired, and that such was the charm and easy grace of his wit, that, wherever he went, his presence was hailed with delight. Many of his amusing sayings have been repeated to me, of which the following is a specimen: One day his father, remonstrating with him in reference to some matter, exclaimed, "Why, Tom, my father would never have permitted me to do such a thing!"—"Sir," said his son, in a tone of the greatest indignation, "do you presume to compare *your* father to *my* father?" Unfortunately death struck Thomas Sheridan down in the flower of his manhood. Consumption, which had been fatal to his beautiful mother, displayed its baleful symptoms, and though the Government of the day gave him a small appointment at the Cape of Good Hope, where it was hoped the climate would prove propitious to his health, it was all to no purpose, for he died there in 1817. He had married Henrietta Callander, a most lovely woman. By her he left seven children, three daughters and four sons, the youngest of whom was killed when a midshipman by a fall from the fore-top of H.M.S. *Diamond* in 1826, at the age of fifteen, in the harbour of Rio de Janeiro.

Though Thomas Sheridan was a frequent writer of *vers de societé*, he published nothing. His only literary effort which has survived is a very fine poem on the loss of the *Saldanha* in Lough Swilly. This piece has recently appeared in the *Athenæum*, and I have taken upon myself to give it a permanent home at the end of this volume.

But those of the Sheridans to whom I have thus briefly referred, are not the only scions of the house who have enriched the literature of their country with works of recognised value; for it will be seen on reference to a table appended to this volume that during the last two hundred and fifty years the family has produced twenty-seven authors and more than two hundred works. Of the collateral contributors to its literary fame I will only mention two: Joseph

Sheridan Le Fanu, grandson of Brinsley Sheridan's sister Alicia, who wrote the *House by the Churchyard*, *Uncle Silas*, and some other powerful novels, as well as the delightful ballad of "Shamus O'Brien," and Sheridan Knowles, descended from Thomas Sheridan of Quilca, Swift's friend, the author of the *Hunchback*, a play that still keeps the stage, as well as of other works and poems of considerable repute.   The following short essay on the Life of Man which Joseph Le Fanu submitted, when a little boy, to his scandalised father, will show that the family wit continued to sparkle as brightly in the side channels as in the main current :—

"A man's life," writes this young philosopher, "naturally divides itself into three distinct parts—the first, when he is planning and contriving all kinds of villainy and rascality. *That is the period of youth and innocence.*   In the second, he is found putting in practice all the villainy and rascality he has contrived. *That is the flower of manhood and prime of life.*   The third and last period is that when he is making his soul and preparing for another world. *That is the period of dotage.*"

Mr. William Le Fanu, Joseph's brother, has also

recently published a charming book, entitled *Seventy Years of Irish Life*. Nor must we omit from the category of Sheridan authors the three remarkable women who became the wives of the last three Sheridans I have mentioned—Miss Chamberlaine, Miss Linley, and Miss Callander.

Miss Chamberlaine, the grand-daughter of Sir Oliver Chamberlaine, was the wife of the second Thomas Sheridan and the mother of Richard Brinsley. She was an exceptionally clever woman, and there can be little doubt it was from her that the latter obtained the divine spark which converted the mere talents he may be supposed to have inherited from his father, into the genius which made him famous. She wrote two novels which enjoyed great popularity in their day, *Sidney Bidulph* and *Nourjahad*, the latter praised both by Mr. Fox and Lord North, and two plays, *The Discovery* and *The Dupe*. *The Discovery* was one of Garrick's stock pieces, and Anthony Branville one of his favourite characters. Moore states that when *The Rivals* was running at Covent Garden, Garrick renewed *The Discovery* at Drury Lane, so that two pieces by the mother and the son were being acted at the same moment at the two great London theatres.

For Miss Linley, the wife of Richard Brinsley Sheridan, I have not words to express my admiration. It is evident, from the universal testimony of all who knew her, that there has seldom lived a sweeter, gentler, more tender or lovable human being. Wilkes said of her: "She is superior to all I have heard of her, and is the most modest, pleasing, and delicate flower I have seen for a long time." Dr. Parr said she was "quite celestial." A friend of Rogers, the poet, wrote: "Miss Linley had a voice as of the cherub choir. She took my daughter on her lap, and sang a number of childish songs, with such a playfulness of manner and such a sweetness of look and voice as was quite enchanting." Garrick always alluded to her as "the Saint." One Bishop called her "the connecting link between a woman and an angel," and another said that "to look at her when singing was like looking in the face of a Seraph." Macaulay, in his *Essay* on Warren Hastings, says of her: "There, too, was she, the beautiful mother of a beautiful race, the Saint Cecilia, whose delicate features, lighted up by love and music, art has rescued from the common decay."

Her loveliness in all its unspeakable grace is still with us in the portraits of her by Romney, Gains-

borough, and Sir Joshua Reynolds. Married to a
man who never ceased to adore her,[1] but who must
have often tried her in many ways, she clung to him,
as her touching letters attest, to the day of her death
with unfailing devotion.[2] The daughter of a musician
at Bath who had to earn his bread by the exercise of
his profession, when still little more than a child she
found herself transferred, on her marriage, to the best
society of London. But though surrounded, as a
lovely young woman in her position was sure to be,
by every sort of adulation, she neither lost her head
nor her native simplicity; and in an unpublished letter
to her husband, written only a year or two before
her death, she assures him with what glad alacrity
she would quit the blaze of social splendour in which
she was then living,—the worship of her admirers,—
and the pleasures of the world, to return with him to
the poverty and obscurity of their early life, if only he

[1] There is a touching story of a friend hearing Sheridan, who occupied
a bed-room adjoining his own, sobbing at night, weeks after his wife's
death.

[2] She writes to a friend: "Poor Dick and I have always been
struggling against the stream, and shall probably continue to do so till
the end of our lives; yet we would not change sentiments and sensations
with ——— for all his estates."

would give the signal.   As an artist she was supreme
in her day, and will go down to posterity as Reynolds's
"Saint Cecilia," and in the painted window of the
Chapel of New College at Oxford, perhaps with
even a truer application, as the fairest of the Christian
graces.

Gainsborough executed three pictures of her, one a
magnificent full length of which Lord Rothschild is
the fortunate possessor, and another of her and her
sister Maria, also full length, now in the Gallery of
Dulwich, as well as a lovely head of her with her
brother Thomas as a lad looking over her shoulder.
This last portrait is at Knole.   The brother was
drowned soon after when boating at the Duke of
Ancaster's.   Her sister Maria married Mr. Tickell,
the grandson of the poet Tickell, Addison's friend.
There exists a beautiful portrait of her by Romney
in the possession of Baron Alfred de Rothschild.
Mr. Tickell was killed by a fall from a window in
the upper story of Hampton Court Palace.   He was
in the habit of reading, seated on its outside ledge,
but no one ever knew how the accident occurred.
He was an author of some distinction, being, as was
said of him by Mathias, "one of the happiest occasional

writers of his day, and possessed of great conversational talents." In the Dulwich gallery there are portraits, also by Gainsborough, of Mrs. Sheridan's father and her three brothers, all of whom were remarkably handsome. To one of these a melancholy interest attaches. The picture represents a young man in a naval uniform. Gainsborough painted it in a few hours, just before the poor boy left home to join his ship. From this voyage he never returned.

Few things by Miss Linley have been published, but she wrote a great deal of very pretty poetry, instinct with a simple tender grace, such as resembled her own sweet self. The MSS. passed at her death into the possession of her great friend Mrs. Canning, and thence into that of the late Lord Stratford de Redcliffe, who was fond of reading her verses aloud.

The next Mrs. Sheridan, my mother's mother, was Caroline Henrietta Callander, the daughter of Colonel Callander of Ardkinglas and Craigforth,[1] by Lady Elizabeth M'Donnell, daughter of the Earl of Antrim. Mrs. Sheridan was a very beautiful woman,

---

[1] Colonel Callander, or Sir James Campbell, as he afterwards became, had an adventurous life, of which he gives an account in his memoirs published by Colburn and Bentley, 1832.

as was her sister Fanny, who married Sir James Graham of Netherby. From Lady Graham are descended the present Countess of Feversham and her not less lovely daughters the Duchess of Leinster, Lady Helen Vincent, and Lady Cynthia Graham; while by the marriage of her eldest son, Sir Frederick Graham, with his cousin, Lady Hermione St. Maur, Mrs. Thomas Sheridan's grand-daughter, the beauty of both sisters in conjunction with that of the Sheridans lives again in the present Viscountess Grimston and the Duchess of Montrose, as it did, alas! for only too brief a period in their sister the late Lady Houghton, the wife of the Lord-Lieutenant of Ireland. Mrs. Thomas Sheridan, after some years of a very happy life with her husband, whose social popularity she fully shared, accompanied him to the Cape. My mother was the only one of her children she took with her. On their return, after Mr. Sheridan's death, their ship called at St. Helena, where my mother remembered getting a sight of Napoleon walking in his garden. On her arrival in England, the King was good enough to give Mrs. Sheridan apartments in Hampton Court Palace. She was, of course, poor; but, being a woman of a firm mind and great good sense, she contrived, out of the small pension to which she became entitled at her husband's death, to pay off his few debts, and to give every necessary educational advantage to her seven children.

She also wrote several novels, one of them, *Carwell*, a story of great power. Sydney Smith admired *Carwell* very much; but, as the hero comes to be hanged, he observed that, "though he knew Mrs. Sheridan was a Callander, he was unaware that she was a Newgate Calendar!"

I now come to the seventh generation in descent from Denis Sheridan, the friend, host, and collaborator of Bishop Bedell. During more than two centuries the race had been waging a harassing and often calamitous battle with the world and fortune; but on its intellectual side it had always been eminent and occasionally triumphant. Happier days are henceforth in store for it, and, probably, no family, as regards both its men and its women, has ever blossomed out into such a glowing galaxy of beauty, wit, and talent as were concentrated in its later representatives. The Memoirs of the day, the letter writers, even the historians, have noted their preeminence in these respects. Frances Kemble, in her *Records of a Girlhood*, writes: "The Nortons' house was close to the issue from St. James's Park. I remember passing an evening with them there when a host of distinguished public and literary men were crowded into their small drawing-room, which was resplendent with the light of Sheridan beauty, male and female. Mrs. Sheridan (Miss Callander), the mother of the Graces, more beautiful than anybody but her daughters; Lady Graham, their beautiful aunt; Mrs. Norton; Mrs. Blackwood (Lady Dufferin); Georgina Sheridan (Duchess of Somerset and Queen of Beauty by universal consent); and Charles Sheridan, their younger brother, a sort of younger brother of the Apollo Belvedere. Certainly, I never saw such a bunch of beautiful creatures all growing on one stem. I remarked it to Mrs. Norton, who looked complacently round her tiny drawing-room, and said, 'Yes, we are rather good-looking people.'" Alas! only some of this brilliant group were destined to live out man's allotted span.

Charles Sheridan, the youngest and perhaps the handsomest of the men, was an enchanting companion. Even when already enfeebled by the fell disease which destroyed his father and beautiful grand-mother, I remember him sitting in one of the drawing-rooms of this Embassy, of which he was a Secretary, when a ball was going on, surrounded by a circle of men and ladies, kept away from the dancing by his sallies. He died in a room which has now been thrown into my present Chancery, when he was only twenty-eight. His nephew, Fletcher Norton, the only one of my generation who had inherited something of the same grace and liveliness in con-versation, died in the same room of the same disease, a few years afterwards.

Another brother, Frank, also died young in the Mauritius, where he was serving as Treasurer to the Government. Though of a different temperament, and not so lively as Charles, he was perhaps the cleverer and wittier of the two.[1]

[1] "In 1841, I spent many weeks with Lady Dufferin at Sorrento. The Sirens' caves along that coast are beautiful, and when poor Frank Sheridan sang in the summer evenings, his lovely voice filled the air with sounds enchanting enough to bring out the Sirens themselves. Such beauty, such talent, such wit and fascination; you could listen all day long to his songs, recitations, stories, scenes acted—some beautiful and touching, some comic beyond description,—and never tire,—his spirits never flagging nor his fund of imagination ceasing."—Letter from the Honble. Mrs. Ward.

The eldest brother, Brinsley, ran away with a great heiress, Miss Grant, the daughter of Sir Colquhoun Grant, and was married at Gretna Green—Sir James Graham having lent them Netherby for their honeymoon. Though for a time justly incensed at this proceeding, Sir Colquhoun eventually became entirely reconciled with my uncle, consulted him in all his affairs, and left him his entire personal property, in addition to that which had been entailed upon Miss Grant. Mr. Brinsley Sheridan's son, Algernon Sheridan, now lives at Frampton Court, in Dorsetshire, having married Miss Motley, the daughter of the distinguished historian; so that the Sheridans of the future will find in their beautiful home in England, and in the rolling downs and golden cornfields of Dorsetshire, a tardy compensation for the castles and territories in Cavan, of whose unjust confiscation Thomas Sheridan so bitterly complained in 1680.

Florence, Lady Poltimore, is Mr. Brinsley Sheridan's only surviving daughter.

Of my mother's two sisters, one married the Duke of Somerset, and, as Lady Seymour, was chosen to represent the Queen of Beauty at the Eglinton

Tournament.[1] She had two sons, Ferdinand, Earl
St. Maur, who died after a few hours' illness in the
prime of his manhood ; and Edward, who was killed
in India at the age of twenty-four, by a bear which he
had already mortally wounded.   Both brothers were of
the greatest promise.   Earl St. Maur had distinguished
himself as honorary Aide-de-Camp to Lord Clyde
during the Indian Mutiny, and was mentioned in
despatches, while Lord Edward had already evinced considerable intellectual vigour as a writer in the magazines.

The other sister became the wife of Mr. Norton,
a brother of Lord Grantley's, to whose title and estates
her second son succeeded in 1875.   In later life she
married Sir William Stirling-Maxwell of Keir, the
author of the *Cloister Life of Charles V.*, and other
well-known works.   He was as modest and lovable as
he was learned and accomplished, and was the only
commoner in modern times to whom the Order of
the Thistle has been given.   As already mentioned,
one of Mrs. Norton's sons, Fletcher, died at Paris.

---

[1] "In the evening came the beauty, Lady Seymour, and anything so
splendid I never gazed upon.   Mrs. Norton sang and acted, and did
everything that was delightful.   Old Mrs. Sheridan, who, by the bye, is
young and pretty, and authoress of *Carwell*, is my greatest admirer."—
Lord Beaconsfield's Letters.

The other, Brinsley (Lord Grantley), showed in early days a good deal of talent, and published, when about eighteen or nineteen, a series of poems, called *Pinocchi*. He died in 1877 at Capri, where he had made a romantic marriage, and found a very pretty bride, who made him a most loving and devoted wife. Lady Grantley, whom I had the happiness of seeing very frequently in 1890, when passing my summer holidays at Sorrento, died at Capri two years ago.

The beauty of each of the sisters was of a different type, but they were all equally tall and stately. The Duchess of Somerset had large deep blue or violet eyes, black hair, black eyebrows and eyelashes, perfect features, and a complexion of lilies and roses—a kind of colouring seldom seen out of Ireland. Mrs. Norton, on the contrary, was a brunette, with dark burning eyes like her grandfather's, a pure Greek profile, and a clear olive complexion.[1] The brothers were all over six feet.

---

[1] "Gibson, the sculptor, whom I had asked what he thought of Englishwomen, said he had seen many handsome women, but none so lovely as Mrs. Norton."—*Mary Somerville's Memoirs*, 1873.

"Though neither as perfectly lovely as the Duchess of Somerset, nor as perfectly charming as Lady Dufferin, she (Mrs. Norton) produced a more striking impression than either of them, by the combination of

My mother, though her features were less regular than those of her sisters, was equally lovely and attractive. Her figure was divine,—the perfection of grace and symmetry, her head being beautifully set upon her shoulders. Her hands and feet were very small, many sculptors having asked to model the former.[1] She had a pure sweet voice. She sang delightfully, and

poetical genius with which she alone of the three was gifted; with the brilliant wit and power of repartee which they (especially Lady Dufferin) possessed in common with her, united to the exceptional beauty with which they were all three endowed."—*Records of a Girlhood*, by Frances A. Kemble, London, 1878.

Of Mrs. Norton, Shelley writes: "I never met a woman so perfectly charming, with so variable but always beautiful expression."

[1] "Mrs. Norton's sister, Lady Dufferin, also very handsome, was delightful company and full of wit. No one else would have said, on hearing many shoes being cleaned outside her cabin door on a rough passage across the Irish Channel, 'Oh, my dear Carry, there must be centipedes on board!'"—Mrs. Ross of Bladensburg in *Murray's Magazine*, June 1890.

"Mrs. Norton and Mrs. Blackwood are looking wonderfully handsome this year. I pointed them out to Madame Sebastiani, who was in great admiration of their beauty."—*Malmesbury's Memoirs*.

"There were at this time three sisters, fairest amongst the fairest—Lady Seymour, Lady Dufferin, and Mrs. Norton—who afford the highest proofs of the transmission of hereditary qualities. Miss Linley was equally remarkable for the grace and charm of womanhood. The grandchildren possessed the united gifts which won all hearts. No one who has ever met Lady Dufferin could forget her rare combination of grace, beauty, and wit."—Lord Lamington's *In the Days of the Dandies*.

herself composed many of the tunes to which both her published and her unpublished songs were set. She also wrote the music for some of Mrs. Norton's songs. Her ear for music was so good that if she went to an opera over night, you would be sure to hear her singing the principal airs in it the next morning. Though she never studied drawing, she had a natural talent both for figures and landscape painting. I have albums full of her water-colour sketches, and the illustrations to " The Honourable Impulsia Gushington," which she did with a common quill pen, evince her intuitive aptitude for figure-drawing. She had also a charming habit, which her two sisters shared, and which has reappeared in some of my children, of illustrating her letters with the most amusing pen-and-ink scrawls and caricatures. She had mastered French before she was sixteen, as well as acquired some Latin. In after years she wrote in French as readily as in English, and she also learned German. Her talent for versifying showed itself very early. One or two of the pieces which will be found in the following pages were written while she was still a girl, or rather a child ; for she may be said to have been married out of the schoolroom. Before either of them were twenty-one, she and Mrs. Norton were paid £100 by a publisher for a collection of songs they contributed between them. As I was unable to determine the respective authorship of these compositions, none of them appear in this volume.

On her return with her widowed mother from the Cape, and until she was grown up, my mother lived uninterruptedly at Hampton Court, except on the occasion of one or perhaps two visits to Rossie Priory, the residence of Lord Kinnaird, who had been a great friend of her father.

The only other circumstance connected with my mother's childhood which may be worth mentioning, is the fact that her nurse, a Mrs. Markham, only died last year at the age of one hundred and seven. My mother was "brought out" when she was scarcely seventeen; and before she was half through the London season, my father, who was then a Commander in the Navy, and had recently returned from the China seas, met her at some ball, and fell at once in love with her. Her mother, with a large family was naturally not averse to any marriage which gave promise of a settled future for her eldest daughter. My father's family, however, took a different view of the matter, and by no means approved of what they not unreasonably considered a very imprudent match.

The Blackwoods originally came from Fife in Scotland. They passed over into Ulster in the reign of Queen Elizabeth, at the same time that James Hamilton, the first Lord Clandeboye, "settled" the northern half of the County of Down. Up to that time they seem to have been a family of no importance, though some high-sounding epitaphs of the time of Queen Mary claim for them a rank and distinction which no documents are extant to justify. But their coats of arms are displayed as early as 1400. The only persons of the name mentioned in history are William Blackwood, who died fighting against the English at the battle of Pinkie in 1547;[1] and his son, Adam, who was a trusted servant of Mary Queen of Scots, a member of her Council, and her representative in Poitou (the Province from which she drew her revenues as Queen Dowager of France). This Adam Blackwood was a man of learning and ability, as were also his sons. He settled permanently

[1] This William is referred to in his son's epitaph as, "inclytorum majorum serie in Caledoniâ notus," but their fame has not stood the wear and tear of time.

in France, and married a French wife, having been granted "titres de noblesse" by the French king. One of the sons became a distinguished Professor in the University of Paris; another was killed at the assault of St. Paul l'Amiate, near Castres in Languedoc. Another of the name, Maximilian, commanded Mary Queen of Scots' guard on her journey from Paris to Calais, where she embarked for Scotland. Adam Blackwood wrote the Life of Mary Queen of Scots in French, and thus became the earliest of her biographers. He was a fervent Catholic, and, I regret to say, composed a Latin ode congratulating Charles IX. upon the massacre of St. Bartholomew. This indiscretion, however, he in part redeemed by presenting another complimentary poem in the same learned language to Henri IV. on his arrival in Poitiers. The male line of the French Blackwoods is now extinct, the last of the name, a Mademoiselle Scholastique, dying in 1837.

The dispersal of both branches of the family, the one to Ireland and the other to France, was probably the result of straitened circumstances, and of the troubles engendered by Queen Mary's unhappy fate; and each retained a treasured memorial of their dethroned

Sovereign, my own ancestor having brought away with him a beautiful miniature of the Queen; and the French Blackwood a *Livre d' Heures* which she herself had given him. The latter is also now in my possession; and, to show how Providence watches over the sacred guild of bibliomaniacs, I may mention how it came there. Being engaged in collecting all the works ever written by members of my family, I had made a list of those published by the French Black-woods, many of which, in spite of the assistance of the eminent Mr. Quaritch, I had failed to acquire in London. Business calling me to Paris some thirty years ago, I put this list in my pocket, and repairing to the Quai d'Orsay, which is the home of old curiosity and book shops, I entered the first that took my fancy. When he saw my list, the bookseller shook his head; these sixteenth-century books, he said, were difficult to come by. However, he had one, and he added, "I know of another which, though not on your list, will interest you." He then routed out from his stores a small square volume of Latin prayers by Adam Blackwood, and told me that the originals had been written out and signed in the author's own hand on the fly-leaves of a Mass book which Queen Mary had given him, and which contained a further inscription to that effect. This missal had come recently into his hands, and he had sold it only a few days ago. It was from its purchaser that, some time afterwards, I acquired it.

The Ulster Blackwoods sat in the Irish Parliament continuously throughout the best part of the last century. They were created Baronets in 1763, and were advanced to the Peerage in 1800 as Barons Dufferin and Clandeboye, in consideration of my great-uncle, James Lord Dufferin, having raised a regiment of horse during the French war. My great-grand-father, Sir John Blackwood, was strongly opposed to the Union, and on two occasions had refused an Earldom with which the Government of the day had proposed to gratify him ;[1] but his eldest son was a personal friend and neighbour of Castlereagh's, and of a different way of thinking. Through his mother he was the heir-general of the Hamiltons, Viscounts Clandeboye, Earls of Clanbrassil, on which account

[1] On another occasion a Government emissary, who was a guest at Clandeboye, in admiring the crest upon the silver observed that it would be much improved were a coronet placed above it. "But how," said Sir John, "would that agree with the motto below?" The motto was "Per vias rectas."

the second title of Clandeboye was conferred upon him, or rather upon her.

And here I am tempted to relate an old-world story which I have always thought would furnish a novel writer with one of those critical turning-points in his plot, which are so difficult to invent. James, second Viscount Clandeboye, who lived in the time of Charles the First, had married Lady Annè Carey, daughter of Henry Earl of Monmouth, and grand-daughter of the Sir Robert Carey to whom, when Queen Elizabeth breathed her last, the ring was thrown out of the window, with which he posted off to James the First at Edinburgh. By this lady, Lord Clandeboye, who subsequently became the first Earl of Clanbrassil, had a son, Henry, who married Lady Alice Moore, sister of the Earl of Drogheda. In his will Lord Clandeboye left all his estates in the County of Down, which were then considerable, to this only son; but, should this son have no children, everything was to go to his next of kin. When Alice, Lady Clanbrassil, saw that she was not likely to have children, she suggested to her husband that he should make a will leaving the estates to herself and her brothers. Her husband objected that such a will would be waste paper, as the property had been already entailed by his father on his cousin. The lady, however, persisting, Lord Clanbrassil, who is represented in his portrait with a handsome but weak face, consulted his mother as to what he should do. His mother warned him that if he made such a will, he would be sleeping within a month in the family vault at Bangor. Lady Alice, however, eventually prevailed, and, on the sudden death of her husband, whom she is supposed to have poisoned, her father-in-law's will, which settled the estate on the collaterals, was nowhere to be found, she having destroyed it. There then ensued for twenty years a double contest, —a contest of armed bands representing the defrauded heirs on the one side, and Lady Alice and her friends on the other, in the County ; and an interminable lawsuit between the same parties in the Courts at Dublin. One day, however, a little maid was sent by her mistress, the old dowager Countess, the mother of Henry, the last Earl, to dust out the Charter Room in the Castle of Killyleagh,[1] which then served as a dower house. The family deeds lay upon shelves

---

[1] This Castle is probably one of the oldest inhabited houses in Ireland, dating from the days of Henry the Second. Lord Clandeboye bought it and the lands of Dufferin from the Le Blancs or Whites.

fitted into a recess in the wall, and the lower shelf
was only a few inches from the ground. Being tidier
than any of her predecessors, this admirable young
woman (whose name I regret not being able to
immortalise) pushed her broom underneath the lowest
shelf, and brought out, with an accumulation of dust,
a large oblong envelope on which was written " The
Last Will and Testament of James, Earl of Clanbrassil,"
—a paper which proved, indeed, that the missing will
had existed, but nothing more.   On its inner side,
however, it was observed to be covered with writing
in the cramped legal hand of the time, though much
soiled and defaced, which on a further scrutiny
proved to be a perfect and valid copy, duly executed
and signed, of the lost will.   Then the whole story
came out.   The wicked Lady Alice, as soon as she
had got her husband to make a will of his own,
obtained access to the Charter Room at Killyleagh,
where she knew her father-in-law's will was kept.
Seeing the superscription on this envelope, she tore it
open, and, finding within it the paper of which she
was in search, she allowed the envelope to fall to the
ground, where by some accident it got swept under
the lowest shelf in the recess.   But, as it happened,

when the old Earl lay on his deathbed he had wished
to make an alteration in his will. The document
was accordingly taken for the purpose into the adjoining
apartment. In making the alteration, during the
hurry and confusion of the moment, a bottle of ink
was upset over it. When it was brought back to
the dying man, he said, "This is too important an
instrument to be left in this blotted condition. I will
sign it in the meantime, but let a fair copy be made,
and if I am still alive I will sign that too." This was
accordingly done, and the blotted copy was used as an
envelope for the fair copy, a fact which, in her natural
agitation when she was committing the theft, the Lady
Alice had failed to perceive.

But though the rightful heirs were thus reinstated
in their property, a strange consequence ensued from
the foregoing circumstances; for the last Earl's cousin,
who was his next heir, had died while the ownership
of the estates was still in dispute,—consequently he
was unable in his own will to designate, item by item,
the property of which he had to dispose. He therefore
declared broadly that one half of whatever castles, lands,
tenements, mills, islands, and other rights he might
die possessed of, should go to his only surviving child,

a daughter, who was my own immediate ancestress, and the other half to his nephew, who was the ancestor of my wife and of Colonel Gawen Hamilton, the actual head of this branch of the family of Hamilton. When, therefore, the contest with Alice was concluded, every parcel of the property had to be cut in two, and for seven generations, until my own accession, half the estate, half the islands, half the village of Killyleagh, and even half the Castle and half the Castle garden (the division running down the middle of a garden walk), belonged to my wife's father, and the other half to me. The inconvenience of this arrangement, as far as the Castle of Killyleagh is concerned, has since been obviated, though not through the intervention of my wife, as might be imagined, for at the time I speak of she was a child of six years of age.

In 1814 a second Baronetcy was conferred on the family in the person of Admiral Sir Henry Blackwood, my father's uncle, who was a fine seaman. He commanded Nelson's squadron of frigates at Trafalgar, and brought his body home. He also had the honour of conducting Louis XVIII. and his family back to France, and of conveying the Allied Sovereigns to England. One of his principal achievements during the war was his engagement in the *Penelope*, a 36-gun frigate, with the *Guillaume Tell*, an 80-gun line-of-battle ship, carrying the flag of Admiral Decrès. The English fleet was blockading Malta, at that time in the possession of France. Knowing that they must shortly surrender, the French authorities were anxious to save the *Guillaume Tell*, one of the two ships which had escaped from the Battle of the Nile, and the following stratagem was resorted to: As night fell, a frigate was ordered to put on the appearance of getting under way, but, as soon as it was dark, the *Guillaume Tell* slipped out in her place. The English Admiral, deluded by this device, detached the *Penelope* in pursuit. About nine o'clock, being the faster ship of the two, she had overhauled her opponent. According to the account given to me by an officer who was on board, the Master stepped up to my great-uncle and said, "We can rake her now, sir?" Sir Henry replied, "No, lay me alongside of her." But a few minutes later the huge quarter of the line-of-battle ship, looming high above them in the darkness, revealed the real nature of the situation. Thus forced to fall back upon his seamanship, Sir Henry Blackwood passed the rest of the night in manœuvring in such a way as to pour alternate broadsides into his antagonist's stern, without allowing the bigger vessel to get a chance of sinking him, which she could have readily done with her lower deck guns alone. By daylight the *Guillaume Tell* had lost her mizzen-top-mast, her main-top-mast and her main yard, and was lying a wreck on the water. In the meantime the English Admiral, hearing the heavy guns of the French ship, guessed what had happened, and detached three two-deckers in pursuit; but when the *Lion* engaged the Frenchman, her gallant Admiral gave the English vessel such a reception as completely to disable her. Eventually, however, he was compelled to surrender to superior numbers, but he asked permission to deliver his sword to the Captain of the frigate, who was the real cause of his capture.[1]

[1] His nautical skill had been already even more signally evinced when, in July 1798, in the *Brilliant*, a 28-gun frigate, he beat off the attack of two French 44-gun ships, a feat which the French, with their usual generosity, have not failed to applaud :—

"Sa haute capacité et sa bravoure éclatèrent de nouveau dans le combat qu'il soutint contre deux frégates françaises, *la Vertu* et *la Régénérée*, chacune de quarante-quatre canons : il leur causa d'assez grands dommages, et parvint à leur échapper."—*Biographie Générale.*

Admiral Decrès afterwards became Napoleon's Minister of Marine, and met with his death, as was related to me by the late Lord Willoughby de Eresby, who was staying in the same hotel, in the following singular manner :—A sudden explosion was heard proceeding from the Admiral's room. It was then found that his Swiss servant, who had been with him for a number of years, had put a keg of gunpowder under his bed, and blown him up. Immediately afterwards the valet threw himself from an upper window, and was killed on the spot, thus obliterating every clue to the cause of the crime. The present representative of Sir Henry is Sir Francis Blackwood, and the late Sir Arthur Blackwood, the Secretary of the Post Office, was his great-grandson.

My father was the youngest of the three sons of my grandfather, Hans, Lord Dufferin, by his marriage with Mehetabel Temple, second daughter and co-heir of Robert Temple, Sir John Temple's elder brother. One of my father's brothers died of fever at Naples ; and the other, Robert, the eldest, was overtaken by a very sad fate either at Waterloo or Quatre Bras. He was an officer in the 52nd, and had been all through the Peninsular War. He was severely wounded at Badajoz ;

E

and, being still an invalid, after the war was ended by
the abdication of Napoleon, he was induced by his
uncle, James, Lord Dufferin, who was anxious that
the heir of the family should remain at home, to
resign his commission. He accordingly sent in his
papers, but, before all the formalities were completed,
Napoleon's escape from Elba, and the prospect of fresh
fighting, prompted him to rejoin the army, in spite of
his disabled arm. He bought a couple of horses, and
reached Brussels the very morning that our troops had
marched out. Arriving on the field, he was looking
for his regiment, when a general officer, wanting to
send a message, said, "Oh! here's Blackwood, he'll
do." My uncle put spurs to his horse, and a few
minutes after was destroyed by a round shot.

This misfortune made my father the heir to the title
and the estate; but, as his father had not yet succeeded
his elder brother, he himself at this time had little
more than his pay to live upon. It is not surprising,
therefore, that his friends should have objected to his
marrying a penniless young girl, who had appeared
for the first time that season at a few London parties,
and who apparently had nothing to recommend her but
her beauty. In spite of their opposition, however, my

parents were married at St. George's Church on the 4th of July 1825, and started the same day for Italy, in order, as I gather from my father's letters, to spare my mother the mortification of the cold reception which she would probably have met at the hands of his own relations. I have in my possession a diary my mother kept on this journey, exhibiting an almost child-like wonder (for, as I have already stated, at this time she was only just out of the schoolroom) at the new world which was opening around her.

Within a few months after her arrival in Florence her health became very delicate, and had it not been for the kindness of two ladies, to whose memory it is a delight to me to offer this tribute of gratitude, she would undoubtedly have died in her confinement, which took place at Florence, at No. 1916 Via Maggio, in the following June 1826, eleven months after her marriage. One of these ladies was the Marchioness of Normanby, and the other Mrs. Balfour, the wife of General Balfour of Balbirnie, and mother of the Mrs. Ellice of Glenquoich to whom one of the pieces in the following pages is dedicated, who was herself a most charming and remarkable woman, and whom my mother loved like a sister.

At one moment the danger was so great that the doctors held a consultation as to which they were to preserve, the mother or the child, which my mother overhearing, cried out, as a person who was present relates in a letter, " Never mind me ! save my baby ! " and the feelings which prompted this exclamation remained ever after the ruling sentiment of her life.

Previous to her illness, in order to escape the heat of the early summer, my father had hired a suite of rooms in a house in Siena ; and as when a child I had often heard my mother talk of the life she led in this desolate old Tuscan city, I determined to pay it a visit during my stay in Florence in 1890. I never dreamt of being able to find the lodging which, more than sixty years before, an English naval officer and his wife had occupied for a short period ; but it so happened that Sir Dominic Colnaghi, our Consul-General at Florence, at a dinner he was giving, happened to mention my proximate arrival, on which a lady said, "Oh ! that is very interesting, for Lord Dufferin's parents lived in my father's house. I was then a slip of a girl about fourteen, and I shall never forget the impression made upon me by the angel of beauty and sweetness who came to stay with us. She took a great fancy to me; used to tell me stories, and sing to me, so that I perfectly adored her." This lady was no other than Mrs. Maquay, whose grand-daughter married my poor friend Colonel the Hon. George Villiers, who was my military attaché at St. Petersburg. Mrs. Maquay was a daughter of the house of Gigli, a distinguished Sienese family, and as the municipality had placed a marble tablet on the front of their mansion in Siena in honour of one of its former members, I had no difficulty in identifying the house, nor indeed the actual rooms in which my parents had lived, for the house had only two stories, and it was the upper one, as Mrs. Maquay explained, which they had inhabited. I may here mention that my mother's playful, caressing way in singing or talking to children was enchanting. She was also a wonderful reciter of poetry, especially of Shakespeare. As Mercutio, Benedick, Touchstone, and the Clowns, she was inimitable. But Falstaff was the part in which she excelled. To hear her on such occasions was to live with very indifferent company in Eastcheap. On another occasion, when I myself was dining with Sir Dominic Colnaghi, he informed me that there was a lady in the room who had long wished to make my acquaintance. On being brought up to the person who had done me this honour, she said to me, "Yes, Lord Dufferin, for many years I have wanted to know you; indeed, ever since when, at a play at Lord Normanby's, I was sitting behind a lovely young English lady, whose beauty and grace had quite fascinated me, and whom I took for a girl until I heard her consulting with a friend as to whether her baby's ribbons should be pink or cherry-coloured. And you were the baby!"

As soon after her illness as my mother was able to be moved, my father carried her off to an old castle in the Apennines, called Barberino di Mugello, the property of the Marchese Guido Mannelli Riccardi, which I also visited—a most romantic little place, with its grey towers and battlements, crowning an isolated eminence which rises in the middle of a smiling valley formed by the adjoining hills. A river winds round its foot, and a little feudal town nestles not far off in one of its bends, the whole place being rich with gardens, vines, fig trees, and mulberry leaves. Barberino is about forty miles distant from Florence, and I do not remember a day which made a greater impression upon me than that which I spent in wandering about the deserted and evidently unaltered rooms and courtyards of this old castle, where perhaps my mother passed some of the happiest moments of her life, as she slowly regained her strength, and wandered about the old-fashioned gardens with her new-found treasure in her arms.

Although it is probable that my mother, in consenting to marry my father, who was neither exceptionally brilliant nor exceptionally good-looking, when she herself was so young, and after so short an acquaintance, rather yielded to the advice of her friends than to the impulse of a sudden passion, the union proved a most happy one; and, though superior to her husband in the quickness of her intelligence and in her literary acquirements—for in those days young naval officers were but poorly educated—his deep affection for her, his strong sense of duty, his sterling good-sense and high-minded character, soon won for him her respect, devotion, and love. While still abroad, the news of her sister Caroline's proposed marriage to Mr. Norton reached her, and, in an earnest and intimate letter, she describes her own happiness as a wife in the most enthusiastic terms, and urges her sister to follow her example. The same feeling runs

through all her correspondence with her husband during
their only too brief married life—a correspondence
which is unusually voluminous, in consequence of my
father's absence at sea during a considerable part of
the time. I have inserted amongst her poems one
which was addressed to him when he was on his way
back from China, illustrating the tender ties by which
my parents were bound to one another.

After two years spent in Florence and its neighbourhood, my father and mother returned to England, and
took up their abode in a small cottage at Thames-
Ditton, which they chose on account of its proximity
to my grandmother at Hampton Court. The cottage
was situated in the grounds of the late Mr. Corkran,
between whose daughters and my mother a life-long
friendship ensued, one of them, Mrs. Broughton, the
mother of Mr. Lewis Broughton, who was Adminis-
trator-General of Bengal when I was Viceroy, having
helped me to nurse her during her final illness. It was
while living in this little cottage in Ditton that my
first recollection of my mother fixed itself for all time
in my memory, as her loving, radiant face, which was
my childhood's Heaven, as indeed it never ceased to
be, bent over my cradle. It was also here that I

celebrated my mother's "coming of age" by nearly poisoning myself with some laburnum seeds. It is not every son that can remember his mother's twenty-first birthday; but my own discomfort and my mother's subsequent reproaches for having disturbed the serenity of so august a celebration impressed the date upon my memory.

In this manner three tranquil and happy years passed away, their monotony being occasionally varied by visits to London, where both my mother's sisters were settled—the one, Lady Seymour, at 18 Spring Gardens, and the other, Mrs. Norton, in a little house just within Story's Gate. Her brother Charles was also a clerk at the Admiralty, and it was in his honour that she wrote "The Fine Young English Gentleman," which will be found at page 119. By this time Mrs. Norton had become famous both as an author and as a member of a brilliant literary society, to which my mother was introduced for the first time. Her wit, grace, charm, and beauty soon won for her numerous friends, amongst whom, in the literary world, were the two Miss Berrys, Rogers, Henry Taylor, Lord Brougham, Lockhart, Sydney Smith, Fanny Kemble, Theodore Hook, and, a little later, Mr. Disraeli, at whom, however, it was then rather the fashion to laugh. Under his eccentricities, however, my mother was quite quick enough to discover his remarkable talents, while Mr. Disraeli, who was already a devoted adherent both of Lady Seymour's and of Mrs. Norton's, conceived an equal amount of admiration for my mother. The date of his first acquaintance with Mrs. Norton and her sisters happens to be noted, Lord Rowton tells me, in Mr. Disraeli's diary as in 1832-33. Lord Rowton was also good enough to give me a few letters written by my mother at this time to the author of *Contarini Fleming*, thanking him for the gift of some of his books, including the *Wondrous Tale of Alroy*. In one of them she laughingly adds, "I am certain you will not sit down with your hands before you, contented with a paltry Premiership." These letters I hope to publish with my mother's other correspondence. In the meantime I may mention the following amusing circumstance :—The elder Mr. Disraeli being as yet more celebrated than his son, my mother had expressed a desire to see him. But the introduction could not be managed, inasmuch as at this particular moment Mr. Disraeli had quarrelled with his father. One fine morning, however, he arrived with his father in his right hand, so to speak, in Mrs. Norton's drawing-room at Story's Gate. Setting him down on a chair, and looking at him as if he were some object of *vertu* of which he wanted to dispose, Mr. Disraeli turned round to my mother, and said in his somewhat pompous voice, "Mrs. Blackwood, I have brought you my father. I have become reconciled to my father on two conditions: the first was—that he should come and see *you*; the second—that he should pay my debts."

Though in after life I did not meet Mr. Disraeli more than a very few times, and only once dined at his house, he always treated me with great friendliness, no doubt in remembrance of his early admiration for my mother and her sisters—an admiration which he recalled very shortly before his death, in a touching conversation of which Lord Ronald Gower has given an account in his interesting *Reminiscences*.[1] One of my earliest encounters with Mr. Disraeli was in Brook Street, the afternoon of the day he had won his

[1] "Lord Beaconsfield spoke of his early friendship with the three Sheridan sisters, all beautiful women. He described how delightful were the dinners in old days at Mrs. Norton's, and the wit and humour that flowed more copiously than did the claret. Lady Dufferin was his chief admiration."—Lord Ronald Gower's *Reminiscences*.

Buckinghamshire election.   I stopped to congratulate
him on his successful campaign, when he said to me,
"Yes, I said rather a good thing on the hustings
yesterday.   There was a fellow in the crowd who kept
calling me 'a man of straw without any stake in the
country,' and asking 'what I stood upon,' so I said,
'Well, it is true I do not possess the broad acres of
Lord So-and-So, or the vast estates of the Duke of A.,
but if the gentleman wants to know upon what I
stand, I will tell him—I stand upon my head!'"   Many
years after, I passed him again, as he was strolling up
hatless from the House of Commons to speak to
some colleague in the House of Lords.   Happening
to inquire whether he had read a certain novel, he
said, "Oh! I have no time for novel-reading now.
Moreover, when I want to read a novel—I write
it!"

Of all these new acquaintances, there was no one to
whom my mother became more attached than to the
two Miss Berrys, one of whom, it will be remembered,
had received an offer of marriage from Horace Walpole
after he became Lord Orford.   As an illustration of
this intimacy, as well as of my mother's charming style,
I subjoin, though written at a later date, the following

letters to the eldest sister, in which she gives an account of the trial at the Old Bailey of certain burglars who had broken into Mrs. Sheridan's apartments at Hampton Court Palace, and at which, to her dismay, Mrs. Sheridan was summoned as a witness :—

FRAMPTON, *Saturday, October* 1846.

Your kind little note followed me hither, dear Miss Berry, which must account for my not having answered it sooner. As you guessed, I was obliged to follow my *things* (as the maids always call their raiment) into the very jaws of the law ! I think the "Old Bailey" is a charming place. We were introduced to a live Lord Mayor, and I sat between two Sheriffs. The Common Sergeant talked to me familiarly, and I am not sure that the Governor of Newgate did not call me "Nelly." As for the Rev. Mr. Carver (the Ordinary), if the inherent vanity of my sex does not mislead me, I *think* I have made a deep impression there. Altogether, my Old Bailey recollections are of the most pleasing and gratifying nature. It is true, I have only got back three pairs and a half of stockings, one gown, and two shawls; but that is but a trifling consideration in studying the glorious institutions of our country. We were treated with the greatest respect, and ham sandwiches; and two magistrates handed us down to the carriage. For my part, I could not think we were in the *criminal* court, as the law was so uncommonly *civil.* But I will reserve any observations I may have made in those pleasant and polite regions until we meet.—Yours very truly,

NELLY.

HAMPTON COURT, 22nd October 1846.

MY DEAR MISS BERRY—I began a little line to you the other day, to thank you for coming so far to see me; but my note, in the agitating agonies of packing up, disappeared, and I had not strength of mind to begin another. My mother and I have returned to this place for a few days in order to make an ineffectual grasp at any remaining property that we may have in the world. Of course you have heard that we were robbed and murdered the other night by a certain soft-spoken cook, who headed a storming party of banditti through my mother's kitchen. window; if not, you will see the full, true, and dreadful particulars in the papers, as we are to be "had up" at the Old Bailey on Monday next for the trial. We have seen a great deal of life, and learnt a great deal of the criminal law of England this week—knowledge cheaply purchased at the cost of all my wardrobe and all my mother's plate. We have gone through two examinations in court; they were very agitating affairs, and I had to kiss either the Bible or the magistrate, I don't recollect which, but *it* smelt of thumbs. The magistrates seemed to take less interest in my clothes than in my mother's spoons—I suppose from some secret affinity of which they were conscious.

I find that the idea of *personal property* is a fascinating illusion, for our goods belong, in fact, to our country and not to us; and that the petticoats and stockings which I have fondly imagined *mine* are really the petticoats of Great Britain and Ireland. I am now and then indulged with a distant glimpse of my most necessary garments in the hands of different policemen; but, "in this stage of the proceedings," may do no more than wistfully recognise them. Even on such occasions, the words of justice are: "Policeman B 25, produce *your* gowns." "Letter A 36, identify *your* lace." "Letter C, tie up *your* stockings." All that is harrowing to the feelings, but one cannot have *everything* in this life! We have obtained *justice*, and can easily wait for a change of linen. Hopes are held out to us that at some vague period in the lapse of time we may be allowed to *wear* out our raiment,—at least, so much of it as may have resisted the wear and tear of the law; and my poor mother looks confidently forward to being restored to the bosom of her silver tea-pot. But I don't know! I begin to look upon all property with a philosophic eye, as unstable in its nature, and liable to all sorts of pawnbrokers. Moreover, the police and I have so long had my clothes in common, that I shall never feel at home in them again. To a virtuous mind, the idea that "Inspector Dowsett" examined into all one's hooks and eyes, tapes and buttons, etc. etc., is inexpressively painful. But I cannot pursue that view of the subject. Let me hope, dear Miss Berry, that you feel for us as we really deserve, and that you wish

me well "Thro' my clothes" on Monday next. If I were
sure you are at Richmond still, I might endeavour to
return your kind visit; but at present our costumes are too
light, and our hearts too heavy, for the empty forms and
ceremonies of social intercourse. I hope, however, to see
you ere very long; and with very kind remembrance to your
sister, believe me, yours very truly,

HELEN S. DUFFERIN.

It was also in these early days that my mother wrote
"The Charming Woman," "The Mother's Lament,"
and some of the other humorous pieces in this volume.

The quiet and happy existence of my parents at
Ditton was, however, suddenly interrupted by the
appointment of my father to the *Imogene*, a 28-gun
frigate. As up till then he was only a commander
in the navy, and still very poor, it was necessary
he should pursue his profession, and he had ardently
desired a ship. At the same time, the idea of separat-
ing himself from his wife and only child at this
early period of their married life for four long years
was a dreadful trial to him, and in one of the first
entries in the journal which he kept during the whole
period of his absence he writes at Spithead: "In the
morning I was most unexpectedly ordered to accompany the squadron to the Downs, and had to take

leave of my dear wife and lovely boy almost on the instant. None can tell, except those who have been similarly situated, the poignancy of grief the heart feels when, in your loneliness, you think of all you have parted with. Then comes the reflection of the uncertainty of this life, and the numberless casualties that may occur to both, previous to the expiration of your three, or perhaps four, years of service." My mother and I had stayed with my father at Portsmouth while the *Imogene* was being fitted out. Though I was only about five years old, I remember only too well the misery of the leave-taking between my parents, and my mother's irrepressible grief as we returned together to the empty lodging after the *Imogene* had got under way.

My father reached Rio on the 14th of January 1832, where he mentions meeting Captain Hamilton, my wife's grandfather, who was then in command of the *Druid*, and who had greatly distinguished himself at the Battle of Navarino and in the war of Greek Independence.[1] On the 16th of February 1832, he arrived at the Cape of Good Hope, where he

---

[1] In gratitude for his services, a street in Athens is called after Captain Hamilton, and his bust has been placed in the Museum.

visited the room in which my grandfather died. He then proceeded to Calcutta, where he was the guest of Mr. Cockerell, whose son I afterwards had the pleasure of knowing when I was myself the tenant of Government House. In his journal he mentions being run away with in Mr. Cockerell's carriage on the Maidan; and on returning to the anchorage at Kedgeree, where he had left the *Imogene* only a fortnight before, he notes the death from fever of three handsome young ladies, after a short illness, and within a few days of each other. On 16th June he again got under way. On the 21st of the same month I find this further entry:—" At sea. This is the anniversary of my little boy's birthday—now six years old. Drank his and his poor mother's health." A day or two afterwards he himself was down with fever, probably contracted in the Hooghly, which nearly cost him his life. From Calcutta the *Imogene* sailed to Australia, New Zealand, and the Friendly Islands. The bracing climate of the latter soon restored my father's health; but returning on the 29th of November 1833 to Bombay, he was prostrated by a sunstroke on his way up to Poonah, which was followed by a fever of a still more critical character than that which had attacked him a year and a half before. Indeed, his illness obliged him to surrender the command of his ship for a few weeks. On his recovery he sailed to the China seas. On the 7th of September 1834, in company with the *Andromache*, Captain Chads, he engaged the Chinese Bogue Forts, and forced the passage of the Bocca Tigris, a short time before the death of Lord Napier, of which he gave a very melancholy and interesting account. On the 7th of March 1835 he left Bombay for the Cape of Good Hope, and sighted the coast of England on the 11th of July 1835, having been absent nearly four years.

During this interval my mother had lived alternately with Mrs. Sheridan at Hampton Court Palace, or at Clandeboye with my great-uncle, James, Lord Dufferin, who after her return from Italy had conceived the deepest affection for her, as indeed had all the other members of my father's family, including the person who had originally most opposed the marriage, namely, my father's father. My father's half-sister, Mrs. Hamilton Ward, who still, I am happy to say, survives, has often told me what sunshine my mother's advent brought into the somewhat dull and common-place existence of the quiet North of Ireland family of which she had become a member. Her beauty, her liveliness, her musical talents, and her loving, playful, and affectionate ways proved a never-ceasing delight to all of them.

After the death of my great-uncle, my father's circumstances as the eldest son of Hans, Lord Dufferin became somewhat easier, though still sufficiently straitened, for there were five half-brothers and sisters to be provided for. Soon after his return from sea he took a very pretty cottage called Bookham Lodge, in the parish of Stoke, half-way between Cobham and Leatherhead, where my mother lived a very quiet life, varied by occasional visits to London, to Ireland, or to English country houses, until the autumn of 1839, when my grandfather died. Unfortunately, however, my mother's health, which had always been delicate, became so seriously affected at this time that the doctors ordered her to proceed to Italy without delay; nor would they allow her to return during the two succeeding years. This was a serious trial to my father, who, instead of being able to take possession at once of his home in Ireland, was obliged to postpone attention to his affairs in order to nurse his wife during these anxious months. He therefore contented himself with a hurried visit to Clandeboye, and started, shortly afterwards, for Rome and Naples. In the summer of 1841, business again requiring his presence in Ireland, he left my mother at Castellamare under the care of two friends, of whose sympathy and affection she was destined soon to stand in dire need. At this time I was a boy at Eton. On the 25th of June my father came down to see me after our long separation, and I at once called upon him to become "sitter" in our eight-oar, accompanied by the hamper of champagne which is the recognised attribute of that privilege. He left me the next day, having arranged that, on Election Saturday, in the following July, the beginning of the Eton holidays, I was to join him in Ireland, a prospect to which I was looking forward with unspeakable pleasure. On the afternoon, however, before the appointed day, I remember standing on the little bridge overhanging the stream which forms the boundary of the College precinct, watching the willows waving in the wind, and saying to a friend, " It is very odd, I have every reason to be happy ; to-night we have the boats, and to-morrow the holidays begin, and I am going over to my father in Ireland, and yet I feel quite wretched ! " The next morning as I was packing my clothes, my tutor, Mr. Cookesley, sent for me. He looked very grave, and said, "I have got bad news for you; your father is very ill; what would you like to do?" I said I would like to go to him—"No, my poor boy, your father is dead."

During the interval which had elapsed since I had last seen him, he had stood a contested election at Chatham, which he lost. He then started for Liverpool, and had given a lift in his carriage to General the Honble. Sir St. George Foley, who was travelling in the same direction, and was the last of his friends who saw him alive. On arriving at Liverpool he went on board the steamer; but, being fatigued and heated with his journey, and upset probably by the excitement of the election, he sent his servant to a chemist's situated on the quay just before the steamer started, with a prescription for some morphine pills, which, ever since his illness in India, he had been accustomed to take, when feeling out of sorts. While the servant was in the shop he heard the steamer's bell ringing, and he called upon the chemist to make haste. The chemist seems to have lost his head and to have compounded the pills into a fatal dose. As soon as they had cleared the river, my father retired to bed.

He was heard during the night to be breathing very heavily, and when the ship arrived at Belfast it was discovered that he had died. This happened on the 20th-21st July 1841.

I was sent out to my mother, as soon as the necessary arrangements could be made, in company with my uncle, the late Captain Henry Blackwood, my father's half brother, and his half sister, Mrs. Hamilton Ward. Fortunately, her brother, Frank Sheridan, was staying with her when the news of this terrible calamity arrived. The Duchess of Montebello and Mrs. Nugent had been like sisters to her in her grief, and my arrival was also a great consolation. The shock, nevertheless, greatly affected her health, and eventually brought on a critical illness; nor would the doctors allow her to return to England, as had been previously arranged. Some months later, her brother-in-law and her sister, Lord and Lady Seymour, joined her in Naples, whither she had removed in the autumn, having taken a small apartment in the Casa Parieté on the Pizzofalcone.

Having now been for six months away from school, my mother, though still ill and weak, felt it her duty to part with me. The day before I started there was to be a dance at the Accademia, to which my aunt, Lady Seymour, was going; and, as she thought it would amuse me, she suggested that I should come with her. Though I was only a boy in a jacket, she induced a very pretty young lady, who having lately had a fever wore her hair cropped and consequently looked herself like a school-girl, to dance with me. She was the daughter of a great but impoverished house, and, having no dower, was soon to enter a nunnery. Being much impressed by her beauty, and still more by her sweet condescension, I remember deeply regretting that, instead of returning to my lessons at Eton, I could not stay to rescue her from impending celibacy. Twenty years afterwards I happened to be again in Naples, and on the morning after my arrival I met the late Duke di Sant' Arpino on the Chiaja. The Duke, who was about my own age, had been a playfellow of mine in Naples at the period I have mentioned. I consequently began inquiring about some of our mutual acquaintances. While we were talking, a great military funeral rolled past. Referring to my pretty partner at the Accademia, I asked whether she had gone into a convent, or whether she had married. At this very moment the catafalque, with the exposed body of the dead man, an ex-Governor of Sicily, arrayed in uniform with all his orders, had reached the spot where we were standing. "Yes," said the Duke, "she married."—"Whom?" asked I. "That man," said he, pointing to the bier! When, many years later, I returned to Naples as Ambassador, I again inquired for my little partner, who had come to be well known as one of the great beauties of the south of Italy, and I learnt that she had married again, but had died the year before.

My mother, having recovered her health, in the course of some weeks moved with her sister to Rome; and in Mary Somerville's [1] *Personal Recollections* there is the following description of her appearance (1842):—

"There was much beauty at Rome at that time. No one who was there can have forgotten the beautiful, brilliant Sheridans. I recollect Lady Dufferin, at the Easter ceremonies at St. Peter's, in her widow's

---

[1] Mary Somerville was an extraordinarily clever woman, and was possessed of great scientific acquirements. She translated Laplace's *Mécanique Céleste*, and he paid her the compliment of styling her the only woman who understood his works. She was elected a member of the Royal Astronomical Society; and her bust by Chantrey was placed in the hall of the Royal Society in London. She died at Naples in 1872, and her *Personal Recollections* were published the year after.

cap, with a large black crape veil over it, creating quite a sensation. With her exquisite features and oval face, anything more lovely could not be conceived; and the Roman people crowded round her in undisguised admiration of 'La bella monaca inglese.' Her charm of manner and her brilliant conversation will never be forgotten by those who knew her."

At the conclusion of her visit to Rome, my mother returned straight to England, and took a small house in London, No. 29 Lower Brook Street; but my father having in his will left the entire direction of my education to his widow, and having expressed a desire that I should reside a good deal in Ireland, and my mother herself taking the same view, I spent my summer holidays, and after leaving Eton, the greater part of the following years, at Clandeboye. Excepting my father's relations, who occasionally passed a few weeks with us, my mother saw very little company; and this tranquil interval which preceded my going up to Oxford were years of great happiness, though to a beautiful woman, only a little over thirty, possessed of so many accomplishments, and delighting in social intercourse, it must have been no little sacrifice to pass so many of the best years of

her life in the solitude of an Irish country house. The
gain, to me, however, was incalculable. The period
between seventeen and twenty-one is perhaps the most
critical in any man's life. My mother, in spite of the
gaiety of her temperament and her powers of enjoyment,
or perhaps on that very account, was imbued with a
deep religious spirit,—a spirit of love, purity, self-
sacrifice, and unfailing faith in God's mercy. In spite
of her sensitive taste, keen sense of humour, involuntary appreciation of the ridiculous, and exquisite critical
faculty, her natural impulse was to admire, and to see
the good in everything, and to shut her eyes to what
was base, vile, or cruel. Nowhere is this instinctive
benevolence more apparent than in her letters, for
among the hundreds which I possess, addressed in
the most intimate confidence to her sisters and myself,
and in which she discusses the current events of the
day, and the men and women of her time, with the
utmost freedom, there is scarcely one that could not be
published as it stands, without causing the slightest
pain to any human being.[1] The intensity of her love

[1] In the lines already quoted, Moore emphasises this harmlessness as
the characteristic of Sheridan's humour—

> Whose wit in the contest, as gentle as bright,
> Ne'er carried a heart-stain away on its blade.

of Nature was another remarkable characteristic. I never knew any one who seemed to derive such exquisite enjoyment as she did from the splendours of earth and heaven, from flowers, from the sunshine, or the song of birds. A beautiful view produced in her the same ecstasy as did lovely music. But the chief and dominant characteristic of her nature was her power of loving. Generally speaking, persons who love intensely are seen to concentrate their love upon a single object; while, in my mother's case, love seemed an inexhaustible force. Her love for her horse, for her dog, for her birds, was a passion, and the affection she lavished on her own mother, on me, on her brothers, sisters, relations, and friends was as persistent, all-embracing, perennial, and indestructible as the light of the sun. However little, as I am obliged to confess to my shame, I may have profited by these holy and blessed influences, no one, I am sure, has ever passed from boyhood to manhood under more favourable and ennobling conditions.

As soon as I had attained my majority, we gave up the little house in Brook Street, and took a somewhat bigger one, 39 Grosvenor Place. This was a great comfort to my mother, as it enabled her to have my grandmother to stay with her, especially when the latter's health began to fail, which it did at the end of 1850. Here she was also able in some degree to repay the kindness shown her seven years before by the Duchess of Montebello; for, when the Revolution of 1848 broke out, the Duc de Montebello, who was one of Louis Philippe's ministers, was compelled to fly from Paris with his family, and it was under my mother's roof that they took refuge for some weeks until their affairs were settled.

In 1849, I became a Lord in Waiting to the Queen, and lived the pleasant social life which is open to a "young man about town," with this difference, that after a round of gaiety or country visits I had always the delightful society of my mother and a happy fireside to fall back upon. My mother also went a good deal into the world, and we paid many visits together to country houses both in England and Scotland; and, through their intimacy with my mother, I became acquainted with all the remarkable literary men of the day, including Dickens, Thackeray, Stirling-Maxwell of Keir, Carlyle, the late Mr. Venables, Charles Buller, Macaulay, Kingsley, Proctor, and others. But the three places where my mother spent her happiest hours were, I think, at Dunrobin, as the guest of Harriet, Duchess of Sutherland, the sister of the late Lord Carlisle, a house which was then full of the loveliest bevy of children that ever was collected under one roof; Glenquoich, with its charming hostess, Janie Ellice; and the Grange, where Lord and Lady Ashburton were in the habit of commingling the most delightful elements both of the fashionable and of the literary world. Between Lady Ashburton and my mother there was formed a very close friendship, and it was my mother who nursed her during her last illness. She was also very much attached to the late Lady Cowper, in whose charming house at Wrest she spent many happy hours. Another of my mother's oldest and most intimate friends was William, the late German Emperor, whom she had long known as Prince of Prussia. She had made his acquaintance originally at Baden, and whenever he came to England His Royal Highness never failed to honour her with several visits, and he became one of her constant correspondents. My mother was also very much attached to the Comte de Sainte Aulaire, who was for many years French Ambassador in London, and to his charming wife. She frequently visited them both at Etiolles and at their old *château* of Fumel in Perigord, where they lived surrounded by a delightful circle of sons and daughters. Amongst the most lovable of the latter was the Marquise d'Harcourt, who has only recently died, to the great grief of every one who knew her.

After living a few years in London my mother began to feel that the air of Grosvenor Place did not agree with her. She was always a bad sleeper, and she thought that a purer atmosphere might give her better nights. She accordingly hired a tiny toy cottage in the Vale of Health at Hampstead, where she occasionally passed a day or two. This did her so much good that the next year we took a bigger cottage in the same neighbourhood, and eventually, getting rid of the house in London, we established ourselves in a charming villa at Highgate. I subsequently acquired some adjoining grounds from Mr. Crawley, and in this way my mother became mistress of a very enviable possession, which soon became the resort of a great number of distinguished and agreeable people. The view from Dufferin Lodge, as my mother's villa was called, was lovely. Beyond a pretty garden in front of the house, descended some undulating lawns, with the woods of Lord Mansfield's park on the right, and a corresponding wealth of stately trees and shrubberies opposite. The only buildings in sight were a church spire or two in one direction, and the dome of St. Paul's in the other, while beyond the mist which overhung the valley of the Thames rose the beautiful Surrey hills. Anybody sitting on the terrace on a summer's day might have convinced himself that he was in some remote country district. Even in winter it was a most pleasant and healthy place.

My mother always accompanied me to Ireland during the months we continued to spend at Clandeboye, until the year 1858, when she joined me on board the *Erminia*, a comfortable yacht of 220 tons, which I bought from the late Lord Ellesmere, and fitted with a high pressure auxiliary engine, for a cruise in the Mediterranean. She enjoyed this trip very much, especially an expedition we made up the Nile, where she acquired the reminiscences which afterwards saw the light through the medium of the Honourable Impulsia Gushington's virgin pen. From Egypt we passed along the coast of Asia Minor, anchoring in every little creek and old Greek harbour between

Rhodes and the Dardanelles. We spent the summer of 1859 at Constantinople, where I left my mother in order to visit Mount Athos and Syria. During my absence she unfortunately fell very ill at Therapia, but was most kindly watched over by Madame Baltazzi, who subsequently became the wife of Sir Charles Alison, our Minister in Persia. Having finished my tour through the Holy Land, I rejoined her at Athens, which had been made very pleasant to her by the genial kindness and companionship of the late Sir Thomas Wyse, returning to England by Marseilles. The next year I was appointed Commissioner to Syria; and after some months, having heard that I was suffering from an attack of fever, my mother came out to Beirût, where we again spent many happy months together. Beirût at this time had become the residence of a number of men who subsequently became very distinguished, — General Chanzy, one of my life-long friends, who for a time so nobly retrieved the fortunes of France on the Loire, and who eventually became my brother Ambassador at St. Petersburg; General Ducrot, who headed the famous sortie through the gates of Paris; Cardinal Lavigerie, M. Renan, and M. Waddington, the late French Ambassador to England. During the ensuing spring, while I was still occupied with the affairs of the Druses and Maronites, my mother, under the auspices of the present Sir Cyril Graham, who knew every inch of the country, and was a master of Arabic, rode right through the Holy Land on her Arab mare "Jerida," filling a sketch-book with views of the scenery through which she passed.

On my return to England, I became Under-Secretary of State for India, and was shortly afterwards offered the government of Bombay by Sir Charles Wood, then Secretary of State for India; but, though a tempting appointment for so young a man, I felt bound to decline it, as entailing a separation from my mother, whose health would have never stood the climate. In 1862 I married, and on no occasion did my mother's unselfishness and nobility of character declare itself more triumphantly than by the way in which she took to her heart of hearts the woman that was thenceforth to share with her the adoration and affection which had hitherto been solely her own. If my wife had been her own daughter, she could not have welcomed her with greater tenderness, or taken a deeper interest from first to last in all that con-

cerned her. Nor can words express the passionate
delight and joy she took in her grandchildren, of
whom she lived to see three born.

The time, however, had now approached when her
tranquil and comparatively happy life at Highgate was
darkened by the shadow of a great sorrow.

It may readily be supposed that a lady so young,
bright, and charming as my mother, should be often
asked in marriage, when once she had put aside the
weeds of her early widowhood. Indeed, so much was
this the case that, had she chosen, she might have
become the mistress of more than one princely home,
with all the advantages which wealth and the highest
rank in the English Peerage can add to the lustre of
a beautiful woman's social position ; but these proposals
she steadily declined, preferring to make a home for
me as long as I myself remained unmarried. Amongst
those who entertained for her a deep and enthusiastic
admiration was the late Earl of Gifford. He was the
son of George, eighth Marquess of Tweeddale, a most
gallant officer who had served with the highest distinction under Wellington during the Peninsular War.
He had been a remarkable benefactor to Scotch agricul-
ture, and had also discharged, with the greatest credit

to himself and advantage to his country, the responsible duties of Governor of Madras. Lord Gifford's eldest sister had married the Marquess of Dalhousie; another was the Duchess of Wellington; while a third had become the wife of the present Sir Robert Peel.

Lord Gifford first made my mother's acquaintance when he was quite a lad studying with a tutor in Italy, preparatory to entering Cambridge. His health at this time was not very good, or rather, from work or from other causes, his nervous system had got into a depressed and morbid condition. Without there being any fault, perhaps, on either side, he was not happy at home. His tutor worried him; and he was still further beset by a most unfounded sense of his own mental deficiencies. By some accident he became acquainted with my uncle, Frank Sheridan, who at once conceived the greatest liking for him, and, in this way, with my mother. As in reality he was one of the most amiable and intelligent of human beings, and, as the result proved, was possessed of talents of a very high order, my mother at once extended to him a cordial welcome. She was touched by his forlorn condition, as well as by his gratitude for her kindness. In a little while he confided to her all his misgivings, as well as his fancied wrongs. She did her best to soothe his somewhat unreasonable irritation, and to make him conceive a juster idea of his own abilities; in short, advising, reproving, and encouraging him in the same spirit as she was accustomed to talk to me, who was but a few years younger. Under these wise and sunny influences Lord Gifford's character soon acquired strength and fibre, his disposition became more mellow, his views of the future more hopeful and ambitious, while my mother's intelligent and appreciative sympathy, the first of the kind that had ever been shown him, acting on an acutely sensitive nature, at once inspired him with that kind of chivalrous veneration which every generous-hearted young man feels for a beautiful and clever woman, who, being older than himself, takes a considerate interest in his welfare. The remarkable thing, however, in Lord Gifford's case, was that the feelings thus early generated, instead of gradually changing or decaying, grew stronger and stronger with the lapse of time, in spite of absences and the various changes and chances of life, and after an existence of more than twenty years were only extinguished by death.

At the conclusion of a successful career at Cambridge, during the course of which he impressed his instructors with his mathematical ability, Lord Gifford joined his father in India. On his return to England, after travelling in Italy and visiting Rome, where he developed a remarkable talent for sculpture and executed several good busts, he became, through the influence of the Duke of Somerset, member of Parliament for Totnes ; which borough he continued to represent for many years. Though his constitutional diffidence, which my mother was always trying to overcome, prevented him from speaking except on one or two occasions, his industry, his sound judgment, and his intellectual power soon gained for him the admiration and respect of those of his colleagues with whom he came into contact. And through his work upon various Commissions and on Committees in the House of Commons, he was rapidly creating for himself a position of great influence and authority in the political world. Nor have I ever known any one take more pains to fit himself for the discharge of the new duties to which he was called. From the outset he had an idea that his early education had been unduly neglected ; and after he left Cambridge he set himself to learn Latin and to acquaint himself with classical literature. To every other subject to which accident turned his attention he applied himself with equal ardour. As a mathematician he had naturally a good head for figures; and, when appointed to serve on a financial Commission, he placed himself in an Accountant's office with the view of learning the mysteries of book-keeping. He was fond of the sea, and an excellent navigator, having taken several cruises along the coasts of Norway and Scotland, as well as through the Mediterranean, on which latter occasion he joined us in our trip up the Nile. Having a tenacious memory, he used to astonish people by the extent of his information, which he had the art of retailing in the most charming manner, his simplicity and evident modesty disarming the jealousy of his hearers. As a consequence, he was as popular in fashionable circles as he was amongst his political friends; while his strong taste for music—the theory and history of which he had specially studied; his skill on the violin, and his love of Art, still further enlarged the field of his friendships. But, as too often happens in this world, these lovable qualities which seemed so certain to assure him a happy as well as a distinguished career in the service of his country, were blasted just as they had arrived at full maturity. One day he was superintending the clearing away of some earth and stones that had accumulated round the base of the old castle of Gifford, which still rears its legendary battlements amid the beautiful woods of Yester. Lord Gifford was on the top of a wall, and was giving directions to some men who were working with their pickaxes at its base, when he saw that one of the large stones with which it was coped was about to fall with fatal consequences upon the people below. He exerted, therefore, all his strength to maintain it in its position until they should have time to escape from under. In doing so, the effort was so great that he lacerated several internal muscles. At first he paid no attention to the inconvenience arising from what he considered a mere strain, but eventually he came to feel so unwell, with so much fever, that he thought it better to come up to his London lodgings. We were in Ireland at the time, and as in his letters he made very little of the incident, we did not anticipate any serious consequences ; but when, a few weeks later, we returned to England, and found him still suffering, my mother persuaded him to allow himself

to be removed to our house at Highgate. Here he
lingered on for nearly the space of a year, one week
better, the next week worse; the doctors still hopeful,
and unable to determine the exact nature, or rather
the extent of the injury. It was a very weary and
miserable time for us all, and it was heart-breaking to
see a fine strong man in the very prime of life, reduced
to this pitiable extremity of weakness. It is needless
to say that my mother nursed him with the tenderest
solicitude, and, if loving care and watchfulness could
have prevailed, his life would have been saved. But
it was all in vain. In the first week of October
1862, there was a final consultation, and the doctors
pronounced the case hopeless. On one or two occasions in happier days, when the flight of time had
obliterated the disparity of years between himself
and my mother, who maintained an extraordinarily
youthful appearance, and changed the admiring boy
of eighteen into the strong firm friend of thirty-
five, Lord Gifford had asked my mother to marry
him; but to these proposals she would never listen.
When, however, on his deathbed he repeated the
same prayer, she could not refuse him this last satisfaction; but, in justice to herself, to him, and to

his parents, she thought it necessary to obtain from the doctors a formal assurance that his recovery was impossible. This being given without any hesitation, the marriage ceremony was performed in Lord Gifford's bedroom on the 13th of October 1862, and immediately after they took the Sacrament together. On the same day my mother wrote the following letter to Lord Tweeddale :—

Private.

My dear Lord,—As Gifford's father, I cannot allow you to remain an hour longer than I can help in ignorance of an important and painful step which I have just taken. I believe you are aware of the strong attachment Gifford has borne me for more than twenty years, and no doubt you have understood and appreciated the reasons which have hitherto led me to consider a marriage between us utterly out of the question ; the difference of our ages, the great and rational dread I entertain of conflicting duties, the deep affection I bear towards my son, and the fear of diminishing (by an unsuitable union) the respect he owed me ; lastly, and not least, the consideration of what was best and wisest for Gifford's own prospects and position. These causes combined to make me refuse to grant what has long been his earnest wish. Could I have foreseen, years ago, that his attachment was of the strong and enduring nature it has proved to be, I might perhaps have wavered in my strong determination ; but I judged him by the common experience of life, and I did what I considered just and right by all concerned, and believed it was for the best.   My views (or rather the circumstances) have changed ; his long sad illness, the constant alternations of hope and fear which I have gone through, above all, his angelic patience and cheerful courage, have inexpressibly endeared him to me, and, had God so willed, I would have gladly devoted the rest of my life to his happiness.   This was not to be, but at least I can have the satisfaction of ful-filling his last wish.   About seven months ago, when he was very ill (though not hopelessly so), I gave him a half promise that if ever my son married, I would then consent to our union.   This promise he has constantly adverted to with a degree of anxiety and earnestness that has had a deep effect upon my mind, and the consideration that now no one's future interests or happiness can be influenced by the act, has brought me to the determination of complying with his request, made under circumstances that add an almost sacred character to his wishes.   He was anxious that his sister, the Duchess of Wellington (whose presence and constant affectionate care have been lately a great comfort to him), should be present at this ceremony, but I have shown him that it was not right to ask her to share in the responsibility of an act of an unusual character, in which she had no voice, and had not even been consulted. You are the only person, except my son and my brother, to whom I have yet made the circumstance known. We were married a few hours ago in the presence of my brother and another witness. It has given ease and satisfaction to my dear Gifford's mind; it gives me the right to devote every hour and every day that God spares him to his comfort and relief, and (if my worst anticipations are realised) the right to mourn him openly, whose loss I shall never cease to deplore as the dearest and most faithful of friends.

To-morrow, or rather this day, he is to take the Sacrament with me. This is in itself an inexpressible happiness to me, as he has not always thought on this subject as he now does. His mind is in the calmest, most happy state, at peace with the whole world, submitting himself entirely to God's will, and resigned to what I fear must be the end. He is quite aware of his danger, and heard of it with perfect composure.

Believe me, my dear lord, yours very truly,

HELEN DUFFERIN.

P.S.—As I am a peeress, there is no absolute necessity for any change of name.[1]   I shall do as Gifford wishes on that point.

The foregoing simple words sufficiently explain the motives which led to my mother's second marriage, of which I have thought it well to give a detailed account,

---

[1] My mother herself did not want to change her name.

in order that its circumstances may not be misrepresented hereafter by any casual retailer of contemporary gossip. As long as Lord Gifford was a strong hale man, with the best part of his life still before him, while so much of hers was spent, she had for him the frank and loyal affection of a friend of many years' standing, mingled with a feeling of pride in the powerful intellect and lovable qualities which had blossomed so richly under her fostering care; and their relations, which in the early years were almost those of a mother and a son, had, as time flew by, merely changed into those of a clever elder sister towards a younger brother. Now, however, the sad condition to which she saw her friend reduced, the patience, fortitude, and resignation with which he bore his sufferings, themselves the result of a most heroic act,

> The often feeling of the helpless hands,
> The wordless broodings on the wasted cheek,

gave birth to such a passion of pity in my mother's breast, that there was no sacrifice she was not ready to make, if it could bring her poor patient some little comfort or consolation.

Lord Gifford's taking the Sacrament was a great

satisfaction to her, for in early days, though his life was blameless and honourable, he leant rather towards what is now called agnosticism; but eventually, under the influence of my mother's gentle teaching, his doubts and difficulties disappeared, and on the 22nd of December 1862, holding the hand of her to whom he had clung for sympathy, comfort, and support from boyhood, and in the peace of God, he passed painlessly away. Among those whom I have admired, respected, and loved, I have never known any one more sweet-tempered, more truthful, or more modest, and very few more highly endowed; nor have I ever met a more agreeable companion. Shortly after his death, Mrs. Norton, who knew him well, wrote the verses in his memory which I have appended to this volume. He is buried in the churchyard of Friern Barnet.

Unfortunately, during the whole of this tragic period I was unable to be at Highgate, my own marriage having taken place but a few days before Lord Gifford's case was declared hopeless.

As soon as all was over, my great object was to get my mother to Clandeboye; but grief, and the physical exhaustion of nursing Lord Gifford, had completely prostrated her. Nothing, however, could be more tender, loving or considerate than the way in which Lord Gifford's brothers and sisters did what they could to support her in this terrible time of trial. The late Lord Walden, the present Marquess of Tweeddale, and Lord John Hay showed her the greatest sympathy, as did also the Duchess of Wellington ; but it was in the presence of Lady Emily Peel, to whom she had been long united by the most sisterly affection, that she found the greatest comfort. Eventually, however, she was able to move, and the peace and rest of her old home in Ireland, and the gentle and loving ministrations of my wife, gradually restored her to health and to some degree of happiness ; but, until the day of her death, the memory of all that she had gone through continually weighed her down, and the loss of so dear a companion and friend at the very moment when she had ceased to become the sole object and preoccupation of her son brought a great blank into her life, and deprived her existence of what had become one of its chief interests. But her nature, except when broken down by ill health (and here I may say I do not think there was a day of her life which she passed quite free from pain), was naturally joyous and elastic. Eventually her old gaiety returned, and her insatiable instinct to love something and to forget herself in others found a new outlet in my children. Highgate again became, for a period, alas! too brief, a bright and happy dwelling, the resort of clever men and charming women, and for many months in the year the home of its mistress's grandchildren.

This tender after-glow was destined, however, to be soon overshadowed. In 1866 my mother was attacked with cancer in the breast, brought on, she fancied, by a blow. This was a malady which she had always dreaded. Suspecting the premonitory symptoms, she consulted an eminent surgeon. As soon as he had given his verdict, it was she herself who, with the utmost composure, and far more preoccupied with its effect upon me than with her own fate, made me the dreadful announcement. An operation was performed at Highgate, which she bore with her usual fortitude, and when, after many weary weeks, she was sufficiently recovered, we went over to Ireland, where we passed together the happiest months perhaps that we ever spent in our lives. The doctors had given her good hopes that the torture to which she had submitted would produce a permanent cure; and though I suspect she knew too much of the nature of the disease to put implicit faith in their predictions, a reaction from her recent sufferings seemed to take possession of her soul: she had passed through the valley of the shadow of death, and its horrors had in some degree obliterated the recollection of what she had previously undergone; her general health became a good deal better than it had been for many years, and she was filled with the delight of living. Her love of Nature had always been intense; but now the earth, the sky, the trees appeared invested in her eyes with a new and magical beauty. She enjoyed the loveliness of the world, the fragrance of the hay, the song of the birds, the scent of flowers, as though she had been again a child, and her wit, gaiety, and playfulness, which had the rare and divine quality of always shining more brightly in her own home than even in the most brilliant company, were never more delightful. But one morning I went into her room while she was still in bed, and she told me "she thought she would go to London a little sooner than she had intended. In fact, she would like to set out at once. She knew it was nothing, but she had a slight pain in her shoulder, and she would be happier showing it to the doctor." Though she said all this in a light,

H

cheerful way, I knew its purport was a sentence of almost immediate death, and that she knew too that the fatal symptoms had returned. A few days afterwards we were back at Highgate, where we remained till the end came about seven months afterwards. The intervening period was not all uninterrupted misery and suffering. Though she was seldom without pain, she bore it with such cheerful patience, and exerted herself so much to take her usual share in our daily life, that all of us, including herself, often forgot the doom which was hanging over us. Every day friends and relations came to see her. Lord Gifford's brothers and sisters were unremitting in their attentions, while Mrs. Broughton, the playfellow of her early married life at Ditton, and Mrs. Nugent, who had comforted her in her sorrow after the death of my father, with infinite kindness helped me to nurse her. Nor was her conversation less full of the sweet tender humour which always enlivened it, more especially as she fondly imagined that I did not fully realise the inevitableness of the result. Under this impression, on the 1st of January 1867, she commenced a journal, from which I transcribe a few of the opening sentences :—

MY DEARLY LOVED AND MOST LOVING SON—I shall keep this little record of my thoughts and inmost feelings for you, as something to speak to you when I am no longer with you, and because there are many things that come into my mind which I am forced to keep from you now (to spare your kind warm heart), but which would, I think, comfort you could I share them with you. They shall be posthumous confidences, and will lose nothing in your eyes by that condition. I believe that, although you are ignorant of my real state, the gracious God—who has shown us both so many mercies—is teaching you by secret instincts that I am soon to leave you. I felt that so strongly the day we left Clandeboye. Do you remember coming through the gallery where Hariot and I were sitting waiting to see you start, and opening your arms to me, embracing me so tenderly, as if we were parting for a long time, though we were really to meet in an hour and to cross over together? May peace and innocent joy grow up around you, and my dear good Hariot to be the same comfort and support to you that you have been to me. May no evil (no real evil!) ever come nigh your dwelling; and when the temporary sorrows and anxieties—inseparable from even the happiest existence—come upon you, may God bless them to you, and turn them into good.

That last day at Clandeboye was full of sweet and bitter thoughts to me. I walked round the lake, and took leave of all the old (and new) places! I sat upon the fallen tree at "the mother's seat," and looked long at the Tower, the monument of your love. May all those objects be pleasant memories to you. I had a poignant thought of regret in thinking I should see them no more (at least with my earthly eyes), for I have occasional happy fancies of some sort of spiritual presence with those we love that may be permitted after death, and, if so, how continually I shall be with my darling—alone, or in company—in your walks, or by your fireside,—the fervour of my love, my blessing, my whole soul, will surely encompass you!

The last entry was on the 15th of the next month, when increasing weakness and pain forced her to discontinue writing. She was attended by Mr. Hewett, as kind a friend as he was a great surgeon, who manifested wonderful skill in mitigating the agony which she endured. Though compelled to take to her bed, she still received many visitors; but what perhaps chiefly evinced her courage and utter forgetfulness of self was the intense interest she took in some letters which at this time I was writing to the *Times* on the Irish land question. These letters generally filled five columns of the *Times*, but before sending them I always submitted them to her, and she took great interest in examining and criticising them, and was very proud the next morning to see her son occupying so large a space in so powerful a journal. I had the further satisfaction, as soon as they were published in a volume, of placing it in her hands, but by this time she was too weak to do more than read the title and fondle the book a little, as though she were stroking the head of a child. At last, on the 13th of June, at a quarter to five, on a beautiful summer's afternoon, she breathed her last in the presence of myself and of two nurses. Latterly, she had been kept a good deal under the influence of morphia, but there was an hour every morning and every evening, before each fresh dose was administered, when she was perfectly conscious and comparatively free from suffering. On the morning of her death, she must have had some presentiment that she would not live throughout the day, for when she awoke she sent for my wife and children to her bedside, and, kissing them one after the other, bade them good-bye in the same fond, cheerful way in which she was in the habit of wishing them good-night, with many a little tender joke and loving word of endearment. She is buried in the quiet churchyard of Friern Barnet, where, four years before, she had laid Lord Gifford, and where a child of my own is resting.

Thus there went out of the world one of the

sweetest, most beautiful, most accomplished, wittiest, most loving, and lovable human beings that ever walked upon the earth. ᾽There was no quality wanting to her perfection; and I say this, not prompted by the partiality of a son, but as one well acquainted with the world, and with both men and women. There have been many ladies who have been beautiful, charming, witty, and good, but I doubt whether there have been any who have combined with so high a spirit, and with so natural a gaiety and bright an imagination as my mother's, such strong unerring good sense, tact, and womanly discretion; for these last characteristics, coupled with the intensity of her affections to which I have already referred, were the real essence and deep foundations of my mother's nature. Her wit, or rather her humour, her gaiety, her good taste, she may have owed to her Sheridan forefathers; but her firm character and abiding sense of duty she derived from her mother, and her charm, grace, amiability, and lovableness, from her angelic ancestress, Miss Linley. ᾽

A very few concluding words in reference to the contents of this little volume will suffice. Some of the pieces were written, as I have stated, when my mother was under two or three and twenty. Amongst these may be reckoned "The Charming Woman," "The Fine Young English Gentleman," "The Mother's Lament," etc. "The Irish Emigrant" came later, as did also "The Nuns of Minsk." The dates of her verses to myself are noted in their titles. Her last poem was "The Dead Language." The play of "Finesse" was finished just before Lord Gifford's accident, and she never saw it acted. "Lispings from Low Latitudes by the Honourable Impulsia Gushington" she wrote during his illness, with the view of amusing him.

The portrait placed as a frontispiece is after a crayon drawing by Swinton,[1] and is an excellent likeness.

Browning's Sonnet to my mother, opposite the title-page, he sent me as a dedication to Helen's Tower, for which Tennyson also composed a poetical inscription. This tower I built on a hill at Clande-

---

[1] One day my mother and Mrs. Norton were engaged to dine with this admirable artist, whose studio was situated in what at that time was a remote district of Belgravia. The two ladies arrived very late, and Mrs. Norton, to excuse herself, cried out on entering, "Why, Mr. Swinton, coming here is like a pilgrimage to Mecca!"—"You mean," added my mother, "to Medina (my dinner)!"

boye, overlooking a lovely view of land and sea, in order to contain the verses which my mother wrote to me the day that I came of age, which will be found on page 159. The little skit on the weather was written when she returned from Italy, and was simply a letter in verse dashed off on the spur of the moment to her brother-in-law, Lord Seymour. Most of the lighter pieces were written about the same period.

' With these few words of explanation, I commit to the stream of Time these slight and inadequate tokens of the existence of an adorable woman. ,

THE IRISH EMIGRANT

I'M sitting on the stile, Mary,
    Where we sat, side by side,
That bright May morning long ago
    When first you were my bride.
The corn was springing fresh and green,
    The lark sang loud and high,
The red was on your lip, Mary,
    The love-light in your eye.

The place is little changed, Mary,
    The day is bright as then,
The lark's loud song is in my ear,
    The corn is green again ;

I

But I miss the soft clasp of your hand,
    Your breath warm on my cheek,
And I still keep list'ning for the words
    You never more may speak.

'Tis but a step down yonder lane,
    The little Church stands near—
The Church where we were wed, Mary—
    I see the spire from here;
But the graveyard lies between, Mary,—
    My step might break your rest,—
Where you, my darling, lie asleep
    With your baby on your breast.

I'm very lonely now, Mary,—
    The poor make no new friends;—
But, oh! they love the better still
    The few our Father sends.
And you were all I had, Mary,
    My blessing and my pride;
There's nothing left to care for now
    Since my poor Mary died.

Yours was the good brave heart, Mary,
    That still kept hoping on,
When trust in God had left my soul,
    And half my strength was gone.
There was comfort ever on your lip,
    And the kind look on your brow.
I bless you, Mary, for that same,
    Though you can't hear me now.

I thank you for the patient smile
    When your heart was fit to break ;
When the hunger pain was gnawing there
    You hid it for my sake.
I bless you for the pleasant word
    When your heart was sad and sore.
Oh ! I'm thankful you are gone, Mary,
    Where grief can't reach you more !

I'm bidding you a long farewell,
    My Mary—kind and true !
But I'll not forget you, darling,
    In the land I'm going to.

They say there's bread and work for all,
   And the sun shines always there;
But I'll not forget old Ireland,
   Were it fifty times as fair.

And when amid those grand old woods
   I sit and shut my eyes,
My heart will travel back again
   To where my Mary lies;
I'll think I see the little stile
   Where we sat, side by side,—
And the springing corn and bright May morn,
   When first you were my bride.

SONG[1]

APRIL 30, 1833

I

WHEN another's voice thou hearest,
    With a sad and gentle tone,
Let its sound but waken, dearest,
    Memory of *my* love alone !
When in stranger lands thou meetest
    Warm, true hearts, which welcome thee,
Let each friendly look thou greetest
    Seem a message, Love, from *me !*

---

[1] These lines were written to the author's husband, then at sea, in 1833, and set to music by herself.

2

When night's quiet sky is o'er thee,
 When the pale stars dimly burn,
Dream that *one* is watching for thee,
 Who but lives for thy return !
Wheresoe'er thy steps are roving,
 Night or day, by land or sea,
Think of her, whose life of loving
 Is but one long thought of thee !

THE CHARMING WOMAN

So Miss Myrtle is going to marry ?
    What a number of hearts she will break !
There's Lord George, and Tom Brown, and Sir
      Harry,
    Who are dying of love for her sake !
'Tis a match that we all must approve,—
    Let gossips say all that they can !
For indeed she's a charming woman,
    And he's a most fortunate man !

Yes, indeed, she's a charming woman,
    And she reads both Latin and Greek,—
And I'm told that she solved a problem
    In Euclid before she could speak !

Had she been but a daughter of mine,
    I'd have taught her to hem and to sew,—
But her mother (a charming woman)
    Couldn't think of such trifles, you know !

Oh, she's really a charming woman !
    But, perhaps, a little too thin ;
And no wonder such very late hours
    Should ruin her beautiful skin !
And her shoulders are rather too bare,
    And her gown's nearly up to her knees,
But I'm told that these charming women
    May dress themselves just as they please !

Yes, she's really a charming woman !
    But, I thought, I observed, by the bye,
A something—that's rather uncommon,—
    In the flash of that very bright eye ?
It may be a mere fancy of mine,
    Tho' her voice has a very sharp tone,—
But I'm told that these charming women
    Are inclined to have wills of their own !

She sings like a bullfinch or linnet,
    And she talks like an Archbishop too ;
Can play you a rubber and win it,—
    If she's got nothing better to do !
She can chatter of Poor-laws and Tithes,
    And the value of labour and land,—
'Tis a pity when charming women
    Talk of things which they don't understand !

I'm told that she hasn't a penny,
    Yet her gowns would make Maradan stare ;
And I feel her bills must be many,—
    But that's only her husband's affair !
Such husbands are very uncommon,
    So regardless of prudence and pelf,—
But they say such a charming woman
    Is a fortune, you know, in herself !

She's brothers and sisters by dozens,
    And all charming people, they say !
And several tall Irish cousins,
    Whom she loves in a sisterly way.

O young men, if you'd take my advice,
    You would find it an excellent plan,—
Don't marry a charming woman,
    If you are a sensible man !

THE MOTHER'S LAMENT

SHOWING HOW A FAMILY RESEMBLANCE IS NOT ALWAYS DESIRABLE

I

IT is now nearly forty years, I guess,
Since I was a girl coming out,
And Spriggins proposed—and I said, yes,
At old Lady Mumble's rout
My match was reckon'd by no means bad,
Take the marrying world as it goes—
But then I must own—Mr. Spriggins had
A remarkably ugly nose !

2

Now the length or shape of your husband's nose
Is a thing that don't signify—

As long as your mother and aunts suppose
There's enough to lead him by !
But I own it often has made me sigh,
At the time of our honeymoon's close—
To hear the folks who were passing by
Remark on my Spriggins's nose !

3

It wasn't round—nor was it square—
Nor three-corner'd as some noses be !
But upon my conscience I do declare
'Twas a mixture of all the three !
And oh ! how painful it was to hear,
When our son was in swaddling clothes,
The nurses exclaim—"Oh, sweet little dear,
He has got his papa's own nose ! "

4

Five daughters besides were born to me
To add to my woe and care—
Bell, Susan, Jemima, and Dorothee,

And Kate—who has sandy hair ;
But it isn't the number that makes me grieve,
Tho' they cost me a mint in clothes,
—Five gawky girls !—but you'd hardly believe—
They have all got their father's nose !

5

They've been to Brighton for many years past,
And a season in London too,
And Bell nearly got a proposal at last—
But we found that it wouldn't do !
And oh ! 'tis a grievous thing, I declare,
To be told, wherever one goes,
" I should know the Miss Sprigginses—anywhere—
They've all got the family nose ! "

6

No beau will be seen in our company,
Do all that we possibly can,
Except Mr. Green—who is fifty-three—
And Gubbins—the Doctor's young man !

There's Captain Hodson and Admiral Bluff,
I wonder they don't propose—
For really the girls are well enough—
If they hadn't their father's nose!

THE FINE YOUNG ENGLISH GENTLEMAN

DEDICATED TO CHARLES SHERIDAN, ESQ. AND HIS FELLOW CLERKS AT THE ADMIRALTY

I'LL sing to you a fine new song, that was made by a
    mad young pate,
Of a fine young English gentleman, who lives on no
    estate,
But who keeps up appearances at a very dashing rate,
As well as his old landlady, by coming home so late,
Like a fine young English gentleman, one of the
    present time !

He has a lodging smart and new, up rather a narrow
    stair,
And the furniture is fine enough, though growing
    worse for wear,

For two or three fine friends of his are fond of smoking
    there,
And though the carpet may be spoilt, this brave young
    man don't care,
For he's a fine young English gentleman, one of the
    present time !

His habit of an afternoon, for he's something of a
    swell,
Is lounging on a borrowed horse to chat with some
    Park belle,
He dines with two or three young friends at the
    Clarendon Hotel,
Where the turtle soup is excellent, and they ice the
    champagne well,—
Like a fine young English gentleman, one of the
    present time !

He takes his glass of Curaçoa, gets up and walks
    away,
Surprised that common folks should ask such a fine
    young man to pay,

The waiter gets an oath or two as he drives off to the
    play,
Where he spends an hour peaceably, admiring
    Duvernay,
Like a fine young English gentleman, one of the
    present time !

And then, as he's not settled yet where next he means
    to go,
He just drops in at Crockford's Club for half an hour
    or so,
But finding only Lord A-ll-n and some fogies he don't
    know,
The Cider Cellar sees him sup, though it's reckoned
    rather low
For a fine young English gentleman, one of the
    present time !

What happened as the night grew late, I really cannot
    say,
Save that the punch was excellent and the company
    was gay,

K

And that he challenged three men friends, though they
    settled it next day,
And he doesn't quite remember how or when he came
    away,
For he's a fine young English gentleman, one of the
    present time !

Now, instead of being seen next day, at his desk at
    half-past ten,
He doesn't go till one o'clock, perhaps not even
    then ;
His head aches so, his hand shakes so, he can hardly
    hold a pen,—
But such small accidents occur to the steadiest of
    men,
Says this fine young English gentleman, one of the
    present time !

But the senior clerk's a grim old ‹man, as strict as he
    is sly,
And he calls up this young gentleman and asks the
    reason why,

And this good young man replies to him, for "he
    scorns to tell a lie,"
He'd sat up with a poor sick friend—to the best of his
    memory !
Like a kind young English gentleman, one of the
    present time !

Then back he goes to his brother clerks, if naught else
    intervenes,
And they're neither wise as judges, nor quite as grave
    as deans,
And a deal is talked of " flaring up " ;—"going it like
    bricks and beans ; "
And they call each other "slap up trumps " ;—I'm
    told the expression means
A fine young English gentleman, one of the present
    time !

NOTE.—This parody has been republished in *Parodies of the Works of
English and American Authors*, London, 1887, Reeves and Turner, and is
given as anonymous. It was sung by the beautiful Mrs. Honey in
the Comedy of *Catching an Heiress*, at the Adelphi Theatre.

THE BAY OF DUBLIN

Oн, Bay of Dublin ! how my heart you're troublin',
Your beauty haunts me like a fever dream ;
Like frozen fountains, that the sun sets bubblin'
My heart's blood warms when I but hear your name ;
And never till this life's pulsation ceases,
My early, latest thought you'll fail to be,—
Oh ! none here knows how very fair that place is,
And no one cares how dear it is to me.
Sweet Wicklow mountains ! the soft sun-light sleepin'
On your green uplands is a picture rare ;
You crowd around me, like young maidens peepin'
And puzzlin' me to say which is most fair,
As tho' you longed to see your own sweet faces
Reflected in that smooth and silver sea.
My fondest blessin' on those lovely places,
Tho' no one cares how dear they are to me.

How often when alone at work I'm sittin'
And musing sadly on the days of yore,
I think I see my pretty Katie knittin',
The childer playin' round the cabin door,
I think I see the neighbours' kindly faces
All gathered round, their long-lost friend to see ;
Though none here knows how very fair that place is,
Heav'n knows how dear my poor home was to me.

TERENCE'S FAREWELL TO KATHLEEN

So, my Kathleen ! you're goin' to lave me
    All alone by myself in this place !
But I'm sure that you'll never decaive me,
    Oh no ! if there's truth in that face !

Tho' England's a beautiful country,
    Full of illigant boys, och ! what then ?
You wouldn't forget your poor Terence,
    You'll come back to ould Ireland again.

Och ! them English, decaivers by nature !
    Tho' may be you'd think them sincere,
They'll say you're a sweet charmin' creature,
    But don't you belave them, my dear !

No, Kathleen agrah ! don't be mindin'
    The flatterin' speeches they'll make ;
Just tell them a poor boy in Ireland
    Is breakin' his heart for your sake !

It's a folly to keep you from goin',
    Tho' faith ! it's a mighty hard case,
For, Kathleen, you know there's no knowin'
    When next I may see your sweet face !

And when you come back to me, Kathleen !
    None the better shall I be off then ;
You'll be spakin' sich beautiful English,
    Sure I won't know my Kathleen agen !

Eh now ! where's the need of this hurry !
    Don't fluster me so in this way !
I've forgot, 'twixt the grief and the flurry,
    Every word I was manin' to say !

Now just wait a minute, I bid ye !
    Can I talk if you bother me so ?
Och, Kathleen ! my blessin' go wid ye,
    Every inch of the way that you go !

KATEY'S LETTER

Och, girls, did you ever hear,
    I wrote my love a letter,
And altho' he cannot read,
    I thought 'twas all the better.
For why should he be puzzled
    With spellin' in the matter,
When the manin' was so plain
    I loved him faithfully,
      And he knows it—oh, he knows it—
    Without one word from me.

I wrote it, and I folded it,
    And put a seal upon it,
It was a seal almost as big
    As the crown of my best bonnet ;

For I wouldn't have the postman
 Make his remarks upon it,
As I'd said inside the letter
 I loved him faithfully,
  And he knows it—oh, he knows it—
 Without one word from me.

My heart was full, but when I wrote
 I dared not put the half in,
For the neighbours know I love him,
 And they're mighty fond of chaffin',
So I dare not write his name outside,
 For fear they would be laughin',
But wrote, "From little Kate to one
 Whom she loves faithfully,"
  And he knows it—oh, he knows it—
 Without one word from me.

Now, girls, would you believe it
 That postman so concaited,
No answer will he bring me,
 So long as I have waited?
But maybe—there mayn't be one,
 Because—as I have stated—

My love can neither read nor write,
But he loves me faithfully,
And I know, where'er my love is,
That he is true to me.

SWEET KILKENNY TOWN

I WAS workin' in the fields near fair Boston city,
    Thinkin' sadly of Kilkenny—and a girl that's there,
When a friend came and tould me—late enough—
        and more's the pity !—
    " There's a letter waitin' for ye, in the postman's
        care ! "
Oh ! my heart was in my mouth all the while that he
        was spakin',
    For I knew it was from Katey !—she's the girl
        that can spell !
And I couldn't speak for cryin', for my heart had
        nigh been breakin',
    With longin' for a word from the girl I love so well.
Oh ! I knew it was from Katey. Who could it be
        but Katey ?
    The poor girl that loves me well, in sweet Kilkenny
        Town.

Oh! 'twas soon I reached the place, and I thanked
them for the trouble

  They wor takin' with my letter, a-sortin' with
such care;

And they asked "Was it a single?" and I tould them
'twas a double!

  For wasn't it worth twice as much as any letter
there?

Then they sorted and they searched, but somethin'
seemed the matter,

  And my heart it stopped beatin' when I thought
what it might be:

Och! boys, would you belave it? they had gone and
lost my letter,

  My poor Katey's letter that had come so far to
me.

For I knew it was from Katey. Who could it be
but Katey?

  The poor girl that loves me well, in sweet Kilkenny
Town.

I trimbled like an aspen, but I said, "'Tis fun you're
makin'

  Of the poor foolish Paddy that's so aisy to craze;

Och, gintlemen, then look again, maybe you wor
  mistaken,
  For letters, as you know, boys, are as like as
    pase!"
Then they bade me search myself when they saw my
  deep dejection,
  But, och! who could be searching when the tears
    blind the sight?
Moreover (as I tould them) I'd another strong
  objection,
  In regard to never learnin' to read nor to write.
For I wasn't cute like Katey, my own darling Katey,
  The poor girl that loves me well, in sweet Kilkenny
    Town.

Then they laughed in my face, and they asked me
  (tho' in kindness),
  What good would letters do me that I couldn't
    understand?
And I answered, "Were they cursed with deafness
  and with blindness,
  Would they care less for the clasp of a dear loved
    hand?"

Oh ! the folks that read and write (though they're so
    mighty clever),
  See nothin' but the words, and they're soon read
    through ;
But Katey's unread letter would be spakin' to me
    ever
  Of the dear love that she bears me, for it shows she
    is true !
Oh ! well I know my Katey, my own darling Katey,
  The poor girl that loves me well, in sweet Kilkenny
    Town.

SONG

FROM HER LOVER TO A LADY WITH A BEAUTIFUL NOSE [1]

I

If, after all, thou still wilt doubt and fear me,
And think this heart to other loves will stray—
And I must swear—then, lovely doubter, hear me :—
By all the pangs I feel, when thou'rt away—
By all the throbs I feel, when thou art near me—
I love but thee ! I love but thee !

2

By those dark eyes, where light is ever playing,
And love, in depth of shadow, holds its throne ;—
By those sweet tones, which give whate'er thou'rt
    saying,
Or grave or gay, a music of its own—
A music far beyond all minstrels playing—
I love but thee ! I love but thee !

[1] A skit on her sister's (Mrs. Norton) Grecian profile.

3

By that dear brow, where innocence reposes,
As soft as moonlight sleeping upon snow ;—
And by that nose, the model for all noses
Which dignify the human face below,
And only fit to smell the sweetest roses,—
I love but thee ! I love but thee !

DISENCHANTED!

SHE hath her wish—for which in vain
    She pined in restless dreams—
"O mother! is this home again?
    How desolate it seems!
Yet all the dear, familiar things
    Look as they did of yore,
But oh! the change this sad heart brings,-
    This is my home no more!

"I left thee!—like the dove of old
    I left thy parent breast
But on life's waste of waters cold
    My soul hath found no rest!
And back the weary bird is come,
    Its woes—its wanderings o'er
Ne'er from the holy ark to roam—
    Yet this is home no more!

L

"O mother ! sing my childhood's songs
They fall like summer rain
On this worn heart, that vainly longs
To be all thine again !
Speak comfort to me ! call me yet
'Thy Mary'—as of yore,
Those words could make me half forget
That this is home no more !

"Sit near me !   Oh this hour repays
Long years of lonely pain ;
I feel—as if the old bright days
Were all come back again !
My heart beats thick with happy dreams
Mine eyes with tears run o'er !
Thou'rt with me, mother !   Oh it seems
Like home !—our home once more !

"O home and mother ! can ye not
Give back my heart's glad youth ?
The visions which my soul forgot—
Or learnt to doubt their truth !

Give back my childhood's peaceful sleep
    Its aimless hopes restore !—
Ye cannot ?—mother let me weep—
    For this is home no more !"

Thou mourner for departed dreams !
    On earth there is no rest
When grief hath troubled the pure streams
    Of memory in thy breast !
A shadow on thy path shall be
    Where sunshine laugh'd before ;
Look upwards—to the happy sky !
    Earth is thy home no more.

FAME

It was a wild and wayward stream
    From the lone hill's secret springs,
It wandered like an infant's dream
    'Mid fair and fairy things ;
The woodland knew its happy voice
    A song both sweet and wild,
Its music made the heart rejoice
    Like laughter in a child.

And thus it wander'd to the plain
    Where, curbed 'tween bands of stone,
Its waters swelled with wild disdain,
    But made no useless moan !

Fair towers rose upon its side—
    And castles proud and gay—
But the music of that prison'd tide
    For ever died away !

Young Bard ! whose genius hath outpour'd
    Its treasures like that stream—
Its burning thoughts, in silence stored,
    Its pure love's holy dream !
Rest now ! thy feet have reached the goal,
    Fame's weary search is o'er
But the voice of joy within thy soul
    Must cease for evermore !

Rest now—and weep—thou praised of Earth !
    And own, when all is done,
A world's false worship is not worth
    The deep tried love of one !
Weep ! for the cheated heart must yearn
    For youth's first hopes,—in vain !
The torrent cannot back return
    To its first home again !

OH SING NO MORE!

Oh sing no more that sadd'ning strain,
Tho' sweet thy mournful numbers flow!
I would not hear those sounds again,
Which I have loved so long ago!
The lips are mute,—the hand is cold,
That made that lay belov'd of old!
'Tis like the sound of Sabbath bells,
To guilty souls that dare not pray!
'Tis like the faint, sweet breeze that tells
Of perfumes which have past away!

Oh sing no more!   Those thrilling notes
Wake sad remembrance in my brain!
And in my dizzy ear there floats
A voice earth may not hear again!

For she on whose loved tones I hung
Is gone—like that sad lay she sung !
I know not if her fingers fair
Made melody as sweet as thine ;
I only know her heart breath'd there,
And that young, faithful heart was mine !

THE CHANGE

LIKE pilgrims old and weary,
We have wandered back once more,—
To the pleasant home of childhood
Where we liv'd and lov'd of yore !
The same old roof is o'er us—
The same hearth bright again—
The same dear friends before us—
Are we glad as we were then ?

We are list'ning to the flowing
Of the same sweet mountain rill !
And the flowers we left growing,
Are blooming round it still.

The ev'ning sun is shining
On the lone hill's side again,—
Where we sat at day's declining,—
Can we laugh as we did then ?

The morn's fresh breeze of gladness,
Brings no freshness to our hearts—
And the ev'ning's holy sadness,
No calm when it departs !
Does the smile of yon fair heaven
Bring grateful tears again ?
We are changed to all, and even
Cannot weep—as we did then !

AND HAVE I LOST THEE?

And have I lost thee?   Is thy love a dream of other
    days?

Can act of mine no longer move thy censure or thy
    praise?

I miss. thee from the lonely earth—I miss thy quiet
    smile!

Thy voice with its melodious mirth! thy lips that
    knew not guile!

I gaze on thine accustom'd place, but strangers fill it
    now;

Alas! and is there left no trace of one so lov'd as
    thou?

And have I lost thee?   Must I learn to live through
    lonely years?

To seek for love in eyes that turn all coldly from my
tears !

Thy silent home ! none greet me there, none speak to
me of thee !

Our ancient haunts no longer wear familiar looks to
me !

Restore, thou silent tomb ! restore, the young hopes
thou hast slain !

Give back the lov'd and lost once more ! give me mine
own again !

I AM WEARY

I AM weary !   I am weary of the green earth and the
    sun,
They are joyful things to look upon when life is but
    begun !
In the young days when a flower's breath or wild
    bird's thrilling tone,
Or the sweet, fresh air of heaven were happiness
    alone !

But the green earth in its beauty, hath a mournful
    look to me,
And a dream of sadness dwells within the voice of
    stream and tree.

The kindly looks are vanished that made home
    Paradise,
The glorious sunshine is not worth the light of loving
    eyes !

I am weary ! I am weary, but the long night comes
    at last !
And the sleep that brings no 'wild'ring dreams, no
    voices from the past !
The peaceful sleep ! when vain regrets and vainer
    hopes are o'er,
And the looks and tones of other days shall haunt my
    soul no more !

Who calls thee lone and dark, thou grave ! thou art
    the quiet home,
The holy tryst, where parted friends shall meet no
    more to roam !
Where the sad ones left on this dim earth, their long-
    lost dead shall see !
And ye, my well beloved, ye will be there with me !

CHACTAS' LAMENT FOR ATALA

ATALA ! my lov'd and lost, to these lone woods I
    flee—
And call on thy dear name and dream, thy sweet tones
    answer me !
Alas ! the woods are silent now—thou mad'st so oft
    rejoice,
The desert echoes have forgot the music of thy voice!

I hear it still—that voice uprais'd in wild appealing
    prayer !
The fond impassion'd tones that spoke thy love and
    thy despair !
Still, still I watch the failing light, thine eyes expiring
    shed—
The smile of love that linger'd there, when light and
    life had fled !

Can I forget thee, Atala, e'en I who lov'd thee so !

Forget thy patient tenderness,—thy beauty and thy
woe !

No ! tho' in fairer lands than these, thy Chactas' steps
may roam,

He'll sigh for that lost loveliness, that bless'd his desert
home !

They tell me that the wreathed shell—torn from the
deep's lorn caves,—

Far from its ocean home still keeps the music of its
waves—

So in this sad heart's inmost core, deep, deep, thy love
shall dwell,

For ever mourning, like the sound within that broken
shell !

THEY BID ME FORGET THEE

They bid me forget thee; they tell me that now
The grave damp is staining that beautiful brow!
They say that the sound of thy gay laugh is o'er!
Alas! shall I hear its sweet music no more?

I cannot forget thee, thy smile haunts me yet,
And thy deep earnest eyes, bright as when we first
  met!
Thy laughter returns in the silence of sleep;
And I start from my slumbers, to listen! and weep!

The spring of the desert in darkness flows on,
When the hand that has seal'd its pure waters is gone!
And the eye of the stranger in vain seeks to know
Where the Arab's bright fountain is sparkling below!

So this fond heart has closed o'er the source of its
      tears—
O'er the love it has lived on deep hidden for years !
Thou art gone and another's rude hand seeks in vain—
To bring that chok'd fountain, to daylight again !

ON MY CHILD'S PICTURE

ALAS ! those pictured eyes may keep
    The light of earlier years,
When thine perchance have learnt to weep,
    And thou—to hide thy tears !
This mimic smile may still retain
    Its fresh and sunny youth,
When none of thy sweet looks remain
    To witness for its truth,
As wandering flower-scents still live on,
When flowers themselves are dead and gone.

It has thine own dear playful look—
    Thy smile ! thy sun-bright hair !
Thy brow—so like a holy book
    With sweet thoughts written there !

The full, soft lids, half-raised above
    Those blue and dreamy eyes,
Within whose gaze of trusting love
    No fear—no falsehood lies !
Like lonely lakes of Heaven's pure rain,
Reflecting only Heaven again.

Thy face is turned, with farewell bright,
    Like some sweet flowers at eve,
Unto thy mother's eye,—that light
    Thou art so loth to leave ;
Lift up that brow, which never yet
    Hath sin or shame defil'd ;
No wasting care, no vain regret
    Hath wrung thy heart—my child !
Look up ! God's holy earth and skies
Bring thee no saddening memories.

Thy sleep is soft ; thy dreams, fair boy,
    Are of some joyous thing,
And thine, the hope—the causeless joy,
    That light and morning bring ;

Thou hear'st not in thy calm repose
    The mother's murmur'd prayer;
The sob, the stifled voice of woes
    Thou art too young to share;
Thy cheek,—that rose so newly blown,
Is wet with tears,—but not thine own!

Perchance, in future years, some word,
    Some low and loving tone
Of her's, who wept by thee unheard,
    Shall haunt thee when alone;
And thou wilt turn from lips that pour
    False counsel,—hollow praise,—
And vainly yearn to hear once more
    That voice of other days;
And none will answer!   Death has wove
A mightier chain than Woman's love!

Then think of her—not mournfully!
    She owes thee many days
Of tranquil joy; she blesses thee
    For all thy gentle ways—

Thy laugh,—that music prized above
    All happy sounds of earth,—
The eternal riches of thy love
    Thou light of her lone hearth,
Whose presence made this sad life be
Too dear to lose—in leaving thee!

LINES ON A CLOCK GIVEN TO MY SON

I AM come from one who holds thee
Dearer than all earthly things,
With a blessing that enfolds thee
Like an angel with its wings ;—

With a wish that every hour
Might, for thee, be fraught with bliss ;
With a sigh that all her power
Lies in wishes, vain as this ;—

With a prayer that, howsoever
Dark or bright thy future be,
God may help thine own endeavour,
God may bless thy time and thee.

PARIS, *New Year's Day*, 1845.

TO MY DEAR SON

ON HIS 21ST BIRTHDAY, WITH A SILVER LAMP, ON
WHICH WAS ENGRAVED "FIAT LUX"

How shall I bless thee ?   Human love
Is all too poor in passionate words ;
The heart aches with a sense above
All language that the lip affords :
Therefore a symbol shall express
My love,—a thing not rare or strange,
But yet—eternal—measureless—
Knowing no shadow and no change.
Light ! which, of all the lovely shows
To our poor world of shadows given,
The fervent Prophet-voices chose
Alone as attribute of heaven !

At a most solemn pause we stand,
From this day forth, for evermore,

The weak but loving human hand
Must cease to guide thee as of yore.

Then, as thro' life thy footsteps stray,
And earthly beacons dimly shine,
"Let there be light" upon thy way,
And holier guidance far than mine!
"Let there be light" in thy clear soul,
When passion tempts and doubts assail;
When grief's dark tempests o'er thee roll,
"Let there be light" that shall not fail!
So, Angel guarded, may'st thou tread
The narrow path which few may find,
And at the end look back, nor dread
To count the vanished years behind!
And pray that she, whose hand doth trace
This heart-warm prayer,—when life is past—
May see and know thy blessed face,
In God's own glorious light at last!

TO MY SON

JUNE 21, 1848

WHEN this sweet summer month brings back
    The day which gladdened all my days,
My soul retreads life's shining track,
    And with thy childish image strays.

Yet not for that past hour it pines,
    When—proud of all thy baby charms—
Far off—beneath Italian vines—
    I held thee in my girlish arms.

Nor could that hour's enchanting toy
    E'er rival the dear friend of this ;
Thy life was then an untried joy,
    Thy love is now a certain bliss !

The grateful song this day demands
    Is not unmingled joy alone,—
Love fears to turn the golden sands,
    Which mark what blessèd hours are flown.

And mine is grown a coward heart
    Since those bright days of early youth,
For grief has held too large a part
    In all its oracles of truth.

I strive to quench the coward fear
    In that blest hope to Christians given,
That, should I leave or lose thee here,
    Thou yet shalt be my own in Heaven.

But earth lies heavy on my heart,
    So strong to feel, so weak to bear,
It cannot choose " the better part,"
    Thus cumbered with its passionate care,

And, weary with that inward strife,
    Clings sadly to its human bliss,
And asks no Heav'n, no better life,
    But only thy dear love in this !

Only to sit in silent peace
    Beside thee thro' the pleasant day,
And mark thy glad voice sound or cease,
    Obedient to thy fancy's play;

Or trace in those clear, honest eyes
    The half-formed purpose, thought, or dream,
(Pure thoughts! that love the light and rise,
    Like lilies, to the surface stream);—

And onward thus, thro' months and years,
    To share thy lot, wherever cast,
No chance, no change, no with'ring fears,
    Such life were Heav'n, did life but last.

Oh, dream! oh, heathen dream! at length
    My soul hath burst thy slavish bond,
One thought, one word, hath given strength
    To triumph in a life beyond.

The "perfect love that casteth out
    All fear" hath kept its promise true;—
Whose love is strong, can never doubt
    That love to be immortal too.

TO MY SON

WITH A SHABBY PRESENT

This 21st of June 1852

THOU know'st that love,—(whose secret heart
Is ever sad and full of fears,—
As conscious of how small a part
Time grants him in the coming years!)
Still seeks by flippant smile and jest,
And mad device and fancy strange,
To dull the warning in his breast,
And mock his own drear sense of change;
He coins his earnest soul in words
Of playful import—light and vain,—
Because the treasure which he hoards
Has grown a burden,—e'en to pain!

So I, that fain would have thee crowned
With life's best gifts and endless joy,
But bring thee—when this day comes round,—
An empty wish—a worthless toy;
Yet no! the day that gave thee birth,
Endears the worthless token given,
E'en as the wish—so vain on earth—
Becomes a solemn prayer—in Heaven!

TO MY DEAR SON

GOING TO SEA IN THE "FOAM"

June 21, 1854

WHAT seeks thy restless heart across the seas ?
    Dwells not the eternal beauty everywhere,
Dim seen thro' softening haze on England's leas,
    Or with sharp outline steeped in Orient air ?

Nature—sweet mother Nature !—can but show
    New combinations of the same fair things !
Morn's freshened glory, or Eve's purple glow
    To stranger shores familiar beauty brings.

And the lone traveller sees with startled eye—
    Duped by some fancied form of mount or stream—
His highland hills against a southern sky,
    Whose splendour mars the likeness, breaks the
    dream.

Sighing, he turns away with sudden start,
     Blurs the bright landscape with regretful tears,—
As lo ! before that image in his heart
     The far-sought wonder fades and disappears.

So I, in Fancy's realm, seek newer thought
     And fresher words to mend the imperfect song
That hails thy birthday !   Yet, alas ! find nought
     But the same old, fond " blessing " on my tongue !

The pen drops idly down ! the mocking lines
     Swim in my tearful eyes, and melt in air—
And the love-burdened spirit inly pines
     To take safe refuge—in a voiceless prayer !

TO MY SON

RONDO

*To be sung on the 21st of all Junes, but more especially
on this Thursday, 1855*

At the summer's advent,
Sweet recurrent song
Greets her glorious footsteps
As she moves along,—
Bird, and breeze, and insect
Swell th' exultant hymn,
From the purple sunrise
Until evening dim.
On her ear it palls not—
Music loved so long,
(Since to earth's first summer
Sang the starry throng,)
"Love, and joy, and welcome,"
Still the old, old song!

Yet the Bird of Evening—
—Who loves summer best,—
Thro' the sunny hours
Sings not with the rest,—
Waits until the Day-star
Sinks into the West,—
Keeps her thankful music
Deep within her breast.
But in quiet hours,
Which to Night belong,
Pours upon the silence
Anthems rich and strong—
"Love, and joy, and welcome,"
Still the old, old song!

"Joy" is full of trembling—
"Love" is full of fears—
"Welcome" oft is uttered
With a gush of tears.
And—tho' all of gladness
Which my fond heart knows,
Thy dear presence brings me,
Thy dear love bestows,—
Still—when round thee pressing

Comes the friendly throng—
Fervent blessings linger
Mutely on my tongue,—
And alone I join not
In the old, old song !

But, at Eve's sweet closing,
Mounts my heart to Heaven,
Grateful for that gladness
Which the Dawn has given ;
(Dawn !—to me the dearest
Of all summer days,
Memory's holiest Sabbath
Hailed with prayer and praise),
Like that Bird of Evening,
Quiet shades among,
Pours my soul its music
With unfaltering tongue,—
On thine ear it palls not,
Though the old, old song !

TO MY DEAREST SON

WITH A CHAIN MADE FROM MY HAIR

June 21, 1860

GREAT love doth keep a Royal state
  In those true hearts wherein he reigns ;
Laws, language, coinage, value, rate
  Of meaner monarchs he disdains.

Love hath a language for all years—
  Fond hieroglyphs, obscure and old—
Wherein the heart reads, writ in tears,
  The tale which never yet was told.

Love hath his meter too, to trace
  Those bounds which never yet were given,
To measure that which mocks at space,
  Is deep as death, and high as heaven.

Love hath his treasure hoards, to pay
　　True faith, or goodly service done,—
Dear priceless nothings, which outweigh
　　All riches that the sun shines on.

And from that treasure house he brings
　　E'en such a gift, this morn, for thee—
The best of those poor precious things
　　He hoards within his treasury.

A slender chain and yet more sure
　　Than steel to bind, than gold to sway—
A fragile thing—that shall endure
　　When life and love have passed away.

THE GATES OF SOMNAUTH

WHEN Sultan Mahmud in 1024 sacked the Hindu shrine of
Somnauth on the north-west coast of India, he carried off with its
treasures the temple gates, and set them up in his capital of Ghazni.
After the occupation of Cabul by the British troops under Pollock and
Nott in 1842, Lord Ellenborough ordered these gates to be brought with
great pomp and solemnity to India, and he issued a proclamation,
in which he referred to the recapture of the gates as having "wiped
out an insult of 800 years' standing, inflicted on the Indian people."
As, however, a great proportion of the Indian people were the co-
religionists of the Prince who carried them off, the proceeding was considered all the more inappropriate. What added to the ridicule of the
business was that the gates in question were not the original gates, but
reproductions of them, to which the Ghazni Moulvi colony clung as
a source of income from the faithful visitors to the old conqueror's
tomb. They are now hidden away in the Citadel at Agra.

Macaulay denounced the whole proceeding in a speech in the House of
Commons on the 9th of March 1843, on the motion of Mr. Vernon
Smith, that "the proclamation respecting the restoration of the gates of
the temple of Somnauth was unwise, indecorous, and reprehensible."
During the course of his speech, Macaulay said, "We have sometimes
sent them Governors whom they loved, and sometimes Governors whom
they feared, but they never before had a Governor at whom they laughed.

Now, however, they laugh, and how can we blame them for laughing when all Europe and all America are laughing too. You see, sir, that the gentlemen opposite cannot keep their countenances."

Though betrayed by his too fervent imagination into this mistake, Lord Ellenborough was a man not only of great ability, but of genius, and a great portion of his Indian administration was eminently successful. He was a most beautiful speaker, and his singularly noble presence and burning words always left the deepest impression on the House of Lords.

My friends and my brothers ! our army victorious
A deed has accomplished as useful as glorious !
You remember that insolent fellow Mahmud,
Who, a very few thousand years after the flood,
Ran away with the sandal-wood gates of Somnauth,
To your utter disgrace and our infinite wroth ?
Well, some folks might think that this terrible blow
(Falling rather far off and a long time ago)
Might have slipped through a very great Nation's
        great mind,
If our notions of honour had been less refined !
And that, as you'd contrived in a sort of a way
To rub on—unavenged until this time of day—
The matter might still be hushed up for the present,
Nor ended in anything very unpleasant !
But amongst the great names that with us cut a
        figure,

Is the great Irish Khan called Sir Lucius O'Trigger,
Whose strict code of honour appoints and commands
That "so pretty a quarrel" should "keep as it stands,"
And, in fond imitation of him, we all try
That Great Britain's finger should be in each pie !
To return to the facts,—we've revenged you at last !
The disgrace (of eight hundred years' standing !) is
      past !
We have put all those horrid Afghans to the rout,
And turned Sultan Mahmud's old tomb inside out,
And, if it had eyes, how 'twould chuckle to see
The ridiculous figure we've made of Ghuznee !
Perhaps you imagine that this is the sum
Of our deeds and exploits ? but the best is to come !
—You surely have heard how, a short time ago,
Our Government shook from its top to its toe,
At the daring exploit of a Khan of ability,
Who headed great part of the English Nobility
In a series of dreadful Municipal wars,
Where the "spolia opima" were knockers off doors ? [1]

---

[1] It had become rather a fashion about this time for the smart young
men of the day, of whom a former Lord Waterford was a very popular
leader, to amuse themselves by twisting the knockers off the doors of
the houses in London.

Some envious wretches at home there may be
Who may think young Khan Waterford equal to
    me !
But this answer I fling in the teeth of such mockers,
—My trophies are doors carried clean off their
    knockers !
Receive then, my brothers and friends, undefiled
Your sandal-wood gates, which in fact may be styled·
(As a Statesman once said who the truth ne'er
    infringes)
" The feature on which the whole question now
    hinges."
Take your doors ! but allow me to hint, if you
    please,
That your sextons henceforth take good care of the
    keys,
For should such an accident happen again—
England might be unwilling (I say it with pain)
To waste blood and treasure—Pooh ! what do I say ?
A few million pounds may be spared any day ;
And what can it matter how much blood is spilt ?—
In the cause of religion, economy's—guilt !
And we feel, my dear friends, to our very hearts'
    cores,

What errors creep into a church—without doors !

My brothers and friends, I conclude with a prayer,

That Providence still may have me in its care—

And still may inspire—for the good of all Nations—

My series of super-sublime Proclamations !

May defend English arms from all checks and
    disgraces,

And (above all) keep India and me in our places !

ON A PICTURE OF ELIZABETH

DAUGHTER OF SIR WILLIAM AND LADY SOMERVILLE,[1]
PLAYING ON THE PIANO

Sweet elf! with fingers soft and round,
Wild wandering o'er the shifting keys,—
With gay eyes glistening at the sound,
As conscious of thy power to please:
The gracious form that Love will take,
How well this "graven image" shows!
Since fond idolatry can make
E'en discord sweet,—for thy sweet sake,—
And yet no miracle disclose!

Thy smile, and playful gestures, tell
Glad tales of a most happy lot
And pleasant Home; wherein there dwell
Good Angels,—though thou seest them not!
That Patience, Zeal, and watchful Love

---

[1] Not to be confounded with Mary Somerville, the astronomer.

Are ever near thee,—night and day,—
A thousand nameless trifles prove :—
The grace with which those small hands move,—
Those eyes at once so good and gay !

God grant, dear child ! thy smile may long
Adorn and bless that happy home;
And to those lips—so formed for song—
May nought but mirth and music come.
No wonder that the painter took
Thy fair, round face, thus turned, this way—
(Unconscious of the music book !)
Such harmony is in thy look,
We would not hear,—but see thee play !

And when, perhaps, in after days,
Grown learnèd in thy lovely art,
Thy graceful skill shall challenge praise
More smooth in word,—less warm in heart ;
Still value most the fond applause
That greets thy infant efforts now ;—
For now, thy skill is not the cause
That tears of fond affection draws !
Thy music charms us not,—but thou !

CONSULTING THE "STICKS OF FATE"[1]

CONTENT thee, sad mortal !
Were the future discerned,—
Could we read in Life's volume
The page yet unturned—
So blurred with errata
The writing appears,
Who would finish the chapter,
Or wish for long years ?

[1] Suggested by a picture of a Chinese lady consulting the "Sticks of Fate."

Occasions of applying to the "Sticks of Fate", are sometimes of moment; such as undertaking a journey, building a house, purchasing a new wife, or burying a deceased relation. The devotee, having paid the bonze in advance, takes up a vase and continues to shake it with becoming timidity until a pair of sticks fall out. The priest then examines the inscriptions, and, comparing them with the pages, or paragraphs, or number in the prophetic volume, declares whether the applicant is likely to succeed in his undertaking. The German mode of ascertaining the will of Fate was almost identical with that practised by the Chinese.

Could we know that the Friendship
Which gladdened our youth
With its measureless fervour,
Its candour, and truth,—
Built of light, like the rainbow,—
In tears, too, shall end ;
Who would trust the sweet falsehood,
Or wish for a Friend ?

Could we know that the warm Love
Which follows us now,
Like our shadow at noontide,—
More deep for that glow,—
Shall fade like that phantom,
And leave us at last,
When the glow, and the glory
Of *our* noon is past,

Oh, where breathes the Mortal
Whose heart would not cry,
In the depth of its anguish,
" Enough ! let us die !

o

Cold earth ! cruel Mother !
Of thy gifts, we but crave
Our place in thy bosom—
Our birthright, the Grave ? "

Could we count, ere the battle,
The dear lives it cost ;—
Could we know, ere the struggle,
The good cause is lost ;—
Who would strike the oppressor
Enthroned in his might ?
What hand would be lifted
For Honour—or Right ?

In the thought of life's sadness
No heart would have peace ;—
In the sense of its vainness
All action would cease ;—
Love, Honour, and Friendship,
And Hope would but seem
The visions of madmen—
A Lie—or a Dream !

Accurst be such knowledge !
Misled by its light,
Shall the hand lose its cunning,
The heart lose its might ?
From the blight of such foresight,
Oh, Father ! defend ;
And the sheep of Thy pasture
Lead on—till the end !

THE EMIGRANT SHIP

"Cead Mille Phailte!" [1]

"A flight of Swallows passed us to-day. Some one said, 'If those birds had but sense to take news of us home, they'd be the welcome birds in Connaught this day!' I stood and watched them out of sight, and God knows my heart went with them."—*Extract from the letter of an Irish Emigrant.*

OH, happy, happy Swallows! the Spring is come
    again;
And *ye* are bound for Summer homes beyond this
    weary main!
Fly on! fly on! your Summer nests our roofs may
    shelter still;
But the poor turf-fire is out at last, and our hearths
    are black and chill;
There is no life; there is no sound; the old man sits
    no more

[1] "A hundred thousand welcomes."—*Erse.*

Within the shadow of the thatch, beside the cottage
   door ;
The child has ceased its playing in the shallow brook
   close by ;
No kindly smoke is climbing up the grey and empty
   sky ;
Few eyes shall watch your coming ; few and sad our
   friends remain ;
But the " hundred thousand welcomes " shall be said
   to you again !

For us alone (poor exiles !) those words of kindly
   cheer
Shall fall no more, in Irish tongue, upon the longing
   ear !
None wait for us, none welcome us, beyond the
   moaning wave ;
Small space—to labour in and die—is all the exiles
   crave !
But tell our friends in Ireland that we talk of them by
   day,
And dream of them the livelong night, and waken
   up to pray ;

In sleep we feel the pressure of the eager, trembling
    hand,
And hear the fervent accents of that cordial-spoken
    land ;
And we'll teach them to our children,—even on that
    alien shore,
Where the "hundred thousand welcomes" shall be
    said to us no more !

O blessed words ! the very sound takes back the
    heart again,
Like a glad bird, a thousand miles across this dreary
    main !
We hear no more the plashing wave beneath our
    vessel's prow ;
The dear green fields lie round us (which another
    labours now !)—
The sunny slopes, the little paths that wound from
    door to door,
So worn by friendly steps which ne'er shall tread those
    pathways more !
Dear faces, gathered round the hearths ; dear voices
    in our ear ;

And neighbour-hands that press our own, and spread
    their simple cheer ;
The scanty meal so hardly earned, yet shared with
    such good-will ;
And the " hundred thousand welcomes " that made it
    sweeter still !

Is the cabin still left standing ?   Had the rich man
    need of all ?
Is the children's birthplace taken now within the new
    park wall ?
The little field, that was to us such source of hopes
    and fears,
An unregarded harvest to the rich man's barn it
    bears !
Oh, could he know how much to us that little field
    has been ;
What heart-warm prayers have hallowed it, what
    dismal fears between ;
What hopeless toil hath groan'd to God from that
    poor plot of ground,
Which held our all of painful life within its narrow
    bound ;

'Twould seem no common earth to him,—he'd
    grieve amidst his store
That the " hundred thousand welcomes " can be said
    to us no more !

But tell our friends in Ireland that, in our far-distant
    home,
We'll think of them at that glad time, when back the
    Swallows come ;—
The time for hopeful labour, when the dreary winter's
    past,
And you see the long brown furrows are growing
    green at last !
And tell our friends we pray them to be patient in
    their pain,
The dear God knows our sorrows, and His promise
    is not vain !
A little toil,—a little care,—and in a world of bliss
We shall forget the poverty that parted us in this.
How small a thing 'twill seem to us upon that blessed
    shore,
Where the " hundred thousand welcomes " shall be
    ours for evermore !

DONNA INEZ'S CONFESSION

Donna Inez Consuelo
    De Ascunha y Belvor
Kneeleth by the patient friar,
    Saying her " Confiteor."
Greatly puzzled is the Father—
    At the truth he can but guess—
Donna Inez being rather
    Apt to wander and digress
With transitions instantaneous—
    (Which in ladies seldom fail),—
Mingling matters quite extraneous
    With her interesting tale.
" Well, good daughter, pray continue ;
    Candour doth repentance prove :—

How did this *Don Pedro* win you
    First to listen to his love ?"
"Father, yes !—as I was saying—
    I was prudent and reserved,
All his flattering vows repaying
    With the scorn they well deserved :
'Sir !' I said—and I was going
    To say something still more strong—
By my distant manner showing
    That I thought him—really—wrong !
When, at this important minute,
    Looking toward the chamber door,
Who should put her head within it
    (So unlucky ! such a bore !)
But my cousin Natalita,
    With her hair all out of curl !
I confess I could have beat her—
    Horrid, flirting, odious girl !
'Twas the greater inconvenience,
    For, of course, Don Pedro caught
From my accidental lenience,
    More assurance than he ought.
Well, next day (a great bull-baiting
    Was arranged the night before)

Natalita kept us waiting
    Full two hours, I'm sure, and more !
Nothing could be more annoying—
    Really now I wished for wings—
Pedro all that time employing
    Saying fifty foolish things.
Nothing could have been discreeter
    Than my answers—quite sublime ! —
Still I think that Natalita
    Might have dressed in proper time !
But you know, when people's faces
    Are by nature but so-so,
It takes time, in certain cases,
    Just to make them fit to show !
Not that some folks' estimation
    Of their charms is very just—
Had you seen that girl's flirtation,
    'Twould have filled you with disgust !
Such vile ogling, and coquetting—
    Staring in Don Pedro's face ;
All propriety forgetting
    Due to every public place !
He (to do him justice) merely
    Showed great sense of what was right,

And, to prove his meaning clearly,
 Only danced with me that night.
If, since that time, Holy Father,
 My forbearance has been more ;—
If his visits have been rather
 Longer than they were before ;—
Why, indeed, it is for this chief
 Reason—as all Seville knows—
Just to keep him out of mischief."
 (Here the Father rubbed his nose.)
"Not much more than half a dozen
 Visits has he paid this week ;
But, of course, my charming cousin
 To a dozen more would speak.
Every kind of base invention
 She maliciously has spread ;
But I don't think fit to mention
 All the odious girl has said.
As for me, a temper sweeter
 Job himself could hardly keep !
But my cousin Natalita "——
 (Here the Father dropped asleep.)
Back again, in time for dinner,
 In her chair fair Inez goes ;

At each vile pedestrian sinner
  Turning up her ivory nose ;
Comforted beyond expression
  (See what peace such candour wins !)
By her full and true confession
  Of all—Natalita's sins !

TO JANIE ELLICE

ON QUITTING GLENQUOICH WHERE MY SON HAD LAIN ILL OF A DANGEROUS FEVER

THE Morn rises dim in its mantle of mist,
    And the sad wind is burdened with snow,
Yet one gleam of sunrise streams red in the East,
    And the calm lake reflects it below.
The storm-wearied traveller lifts his worn eyes
    When that reflex of morn meets his sight,
To seek in the depths of those lowering skies
    The source of that heart-cheering light.

Oh ! 'twas thus in my hour of darkness and care,
    When my coward heart spoke but in sighs,
The Hope I scarce sought seemed to answer my praye
    In the light of thy comforting eyes ;

And Peace from their calm depths my heavy heart
    drew,
    And thus their sweet lesson was given.
When friends here on earth are so tender and true,
    Who doubts of His mercy in Heaven?
Oh! glorious the gift, by true friendship possest,
    To read, as a token and sign,
Like that reflex of morn on the lake's tranquil breast,
    A Light and a Love more divine!

TO MR. SAMUEL ROGERS

FROM MY BED THIS IST OF JANUARY 1843

I murmur'd 'mid my waking hours,
    As on a feverish couch I lay,
How barren is Life's path of flowers,
    How sadly dawns my New Year's day!

But, as I breathed th' impatient thought,
    Lo! there thy fragrant gift appeared;
At the glad augury I caught,
    The sad and sullen heart was cheered!

And doubly shall thy gift be dear—
    (Of New Year's joys the seal and sum),
An omen for the present year,
    A memory for all years to come!

THE NUNS OF MINSK

THE following poem was written in reference to a report which had obtained general credence throughout Europe of the treatment to which the Roman Catholic Nuns of Minsk had been subjected, at the . instigation of the Russian Orthodox Archbishop of the locality, whose cruelties were said to have occasioned the death of a number of the ladies of the Convent. The facts were, probably, exaggerated ; but at the time the story aroused a storm of widespread indignation. The Abbess repaired to Rome to throw herself at the feet of the Pope. About the same time the Emperor of Russia himself visited Rome.

"THE GATES OF ROME—THE GATES OF HEAVEN"

FLING wide thy solemn gates, O Rome !
 A Kingly guest draws near,
Whose slightest frown in his far home
 Sad millions watch and fear !
He cometh not in pilgrim guise,
 To bow before thy shrine ;
The blessing which his faith denies
 He will not ask from thine.

P

He cometh—as a King should come !
    With pomp and rich array,
With sound of trump and beat of drum,
    A conqueror on his way ;
He looketh—as a King should look—
    Proud step and lofty eye,—
And gestures of command that brook
    Nor peer, nor rival nigh :

The memory of one lost and dear
    Hath touched that brow of pride,[1]
The shadow of a human fear
    Yet stalketh by his side ;
But strength to that stern spirit comes
    The weight aside to fling ;—
He bears him nobly—as becomes
    A warrior—and a king.

Again fling wide thy solemn gates,
    O Rome ! without there stands
A pilgrim, who in patience waits
    With meek and folded hands ;

[1] The death of his daughter.

A woman, travel-stained and worn,
    Thy portal tottereth thro',
Alone, unfriended, weak, forlorn,—
    And yet a Conqueror too!

O noble heart! whose faith upbore
    The faint and feeble frame,
Thro' hopeless years of travail sore,
    In torture, doubt and shame;
The good fight hast thou fought; and now
    Thy promised rest is near,—
Why sinketh down that noble brow,
    That knew nor guilt nor fear?

She cometh, as the poor do come,
    With bated breath and sigh,
To ask a boon, O mighty Rome!
    Thy leave in peace to die.
Of all thy wealth's uncounted sums
    She asks but this—a grave;
And craves it meekly, as becomes
    A suppliant and a slave!

O ! holy city ! art thou dumb
    When, as in days of yore,
The oppressor and his victim come
    Thy judgment seat before ?
Shall the old thunders wake again
    The echoes of thy hills ?
Speak—to a listening world !   In vain :
    No voice the silence fills !

Shall he, who guiltless life destroys,
    Have sanction at thy shrine ?
And, deaf to a wronged nation's voice,
    Hear " Welcome " now from thine ?
A voice, as of a mighty flood,
    Shall drown that " Welcome " sound ;
The cry of blood ! the guiltless blood,
    That crieth from the ground !

When henceforth at the gates of Heaven
    Those pilgrims both shall stand,
In His dear name—to whom is given
    To sit at God's right hand ;

No rags shall hide, nor purple screen
    The deeds by either done ;
For God Himself shall judge between
    The Emperor and the Nun !

THE GERMAN TEACHER

THE long day's done and she sits still,
And quiet, in the gathering gloom :
What are the images that fill
Those absent eyes—that silent room ?
Soft winds the latticed casement stir ;
The hard green rosebuds tap the pane,
Like merry playmates, beckoning her
To join them at their sports again ;
And from the hill, a pleasant chime
Of bells comes down upon the ear,
That seems to sing—" The evening time
Is passing sweet ! come forth !—come here."
But she sits still, and heedeth not
The sweet bell, nor the fading light :
Time, space, earth, heaven, are all forgot
In one dear dream of past delight.

Oh, letter! old and crushed and worn!
Yet fresh in those love-blinded eyes
As on that first delightful morn,
Which gave thee to her patient sighs;
How hoped for—dreamed of—dear, thou art!
What earnest of like joys to come!
How treasured near her simple heart,
That first fond letter from her Home!
Poor child! so early com'st thou forth,
Like Ruth, to glean in alien fields?
Cold welcome greets thee, on this earth,
And poor the harvest that it yields!
Thy thoughts, lone, wandering where they list,
Still seek that village on the Rhine,
Where thou art longed for, loved and missed,
With yearnings as intense as thine :—
No wonder that thy young heart burns,
And, with such aching sense of love,
To that dear sheltering ark returns
That sent thee forth—poor wandering dove!
The hour will come—tho' far it seems—
When, schooled by pain, and taught by time,
Thou'lt lose no more, in idle dreams,
The good hours of thy golden prime :

Each day, with its appointed care,
Shall bring its calm and comfort too :
The power to act, the strength to bear,
What Duty bids thee bear, or do :
And when the eve's repose shall come,
Thy tranquil thoughts shall then be given—
Not back to that lost earthly home—
But forwards—to thy home in Heaven !

TO MY LITTLE FRIENDS

("Done out of my heart," as Ian says!)—*September 22, 1852*

THE DUNROBIN GARLAND[1]

Oh Flowers! oh lovely, living Flowers!
That bloom in fair Dunrobin's Hall,
How Memory oft in future hours
Your guileless beauty shall recall,
And paint you—gathered at my side—
Fair, golden heads of every shade—
With dimpled fingers raised to chide
The sounds your own sweet lips had made;

[1] "Ian," Marquis of Lorne; "Archie," Lord Archibald Campbell; "Mary," Hon'ble Mary Stuart; "Albert," Lord Albert Gower; "Ronald," Lord Ronald Gower; "Evelyn," Lady Evelyn Campbell; "Ellen," Hon'ble Ellen Stuart; "Geraldine," Lady Geraldine Fitzgerald; "Earl of Kildare"; "Gertrude," Hon'ble Gertrude Stuart; "Gower," Earl Gower; "Edith," Lady Edith Campbell (now Countess Percy).

With eyes that widened as they shone,
And fair cheeks—flushing with delight—
As flowed the wondrous story on
Of Goblin Dwarf, or Fairy Sprite!—
Or, in the garden's sheltered ground,
Ethereal forms—ye wander by—
Your laughter mingling with the sound
Of the wild surf, or seagull's cry!
On Fancy's airy tablets drawn
Bright Archie's fervid glance beams now,—
Or, like the star that heralds dawn—
Young Ian's calm, seraphic brow!
Sweet Mary's shy and pensive face,
Half hid in Naiad locks the while!
Kind, gentle Albert's courteous grace,
And lovely Ronald's side-long smile!
And Evelyn, with her locks of gold,
Fair Ellen, merry Geraldine,
And then—with brow so bright and bold—
The noble son of Leinster's line!
And Gertrude, with her violet eyes,
And rosy Gower—so fresh and·fair!
And one sweet, *nameless* bud, that lies
Close folded from the curious air!

And thou, young Lily! pride of Lorn!
The garland's gem, the crowning flower!
Whose cheek—fresh as that hour of morn
That but foretells the day-beam's power,—
E'en now such promised bloom can breathe,
As shall to future years make known,
How fair the flower that could bequeath
Such beauty, yet retain its own!
Wear meekly that transmitted dower,
Lest future times compare with scorn
Thy fairness with th' ancestral flower,
Thy sweetness—with our Rose of Lorn!
Grow like them, Edith! seek to charm
By more than beauty's dangerous spell,
So bloom like them, secure from harm,
Honoured as much, and loved as well!
Oh, human blossoms! may ye long
Grow up in beauty, side by side,—
No canker do your beauty wrong—
No storms your fellowship divide!
Oh, keep those promises of worth
That shine in your angelic eyes,
And—like your fragile types on earth—
Look upwards—to the constant skies!

Live long on earth ! a lovely band !
To men as bright examples given,—
And—garnered by the Eternal Hand—
Be not one blossom miss'd in Heaven !

September 22, 1852.

MRS. HARRIS'S SOLILOQUY

WHILE THREADING HER NEEDLE

AH, deary me! what needles—well really I must say,
All things are sadly altered—(for the worse too) since
    my day!
The pins have neither heads nor points—the needles
    have no eyes,
There's ne'er a pair of scissors of the good old-
    fashioned size,
The very bodkins now are made in fine new-fangled
    ways,
And the good old British thimble is a dream of other days!
Now that comes of machinery!—I'm given to under-
    stand,
That great folks turn their noses up at all things
    " done by hand,"

Altho' it's easy proving to the most thick-pated dunce,

That things aren't done the better—for all being done
  at once.

I'm sure I often ponder, with a kind of awful dread,

On those bold "spinning jennies," that "go off of
  their own head"!

Those power-looms and odd machines—those whizzing
  things with wheels,

That evermore "keep moving";—besides one really
  feels

So superannuated-like, and laid upon the shelf—

When one sees a worsted stocking get up and knit
  itself!

Ah! that comes of those Radicals! why, Life's a
  perfect storm,—

A whirlwind of inventions! with their "Progress"
  and "Reform"!

The good old days—the quiet times, that calmly used
  to glide,

Are changed into a steeple-chase,—a wild cross-
  country ride!

A loud view-holloa in our ears—away! away! we
  go;

A-levelling all distinctions, and a-mingling high and
    low :
All spurring on, with seats so tight, and principles so
    loose,
Whisk ! over this old prejudice ! slap-bang ! thro'
    that abuse !
No matter why,—no matter where ! without a stop
    or hitch,
And nobody has time to help his neighbour in the
    ditch !
And then, what turns and changes !   Why, good
    lack ! I'd rather be
A joint-stool in a pantomime,—than some great folks
    I see !
Because in pantomimes, a stool may turn to anything,
You're not surprised if chairs step out to dance a
    Highland fling !
A coffee-pot perhaps becomes a mitre by and by,—
And everything is something else—and nobody asks
    why.
But there's a rage for questioning, and meddling now-
    adays ;
And what one does don't matter half so much as
    what one says.

A Minister can't change his mind, without such stir
    and fuss,

That one would think the "public voice" was some
    huge omnibus,

Which takes you to a certain point, whereat you must
    remain,

Until the same old 'Bus may choose to take you
    back again !

For (odd enough) in all this change, they keep some
    order still, .

And when they turn—turn all at once—like soldiers
    at a drill :

But won't allow a public man a private pirouette,

When once his part of Harlequin or Pantaloon is set.

And that's what makes their pantomime so dull and
    such a bore,

That their joint-stool must still remain—a joint-stool
    evermore.

Now that comes of newspapers ! I know in my
    younger days,

"Least said and soonest mended," was a maxim
    worthy praise ;

But were I to give counsel to the Public—as a friend,

"Little say, and nothing write," is the rule I would
    commend.

Such snapping up—and setting down! Reporters left
    and right!

All bent on pinning down a man to lie, in black and
    white!

Such raking up of Hansard! And such flinging in
    one's face,

The little "lapsus linguae" that may once have taken
    place!

Such a-fending and a-proving,—and a-calling over coals,

As if it really mattered to our poor immortal souls,

That Thingumbob should think or say, on question
    so and so,

The foolish things he thought and said, some forty
    years ago!

There's one thing in those papers, tho', I'm very glad
    to see,

That many more old women think extremely much
    like me:

I'm even told that certain Dukes, will echo back my
    groan,

And sigh for those dear golden days, when we "left
    well, alone"!

Q

ON A PICTURE OF A CHINESE
PROCESSION

"GOING OUT TO MEET THE SPRING"

THE assurance of some persons !   Just conceive so bold
    a thing,
As those horrid Chinese monsters, going out to meet
    the Spring,
With their lanthorns and their banners, and their
    tom-toms and their drums ;
Why, they'll frighten back the flowers, long before
    the Summer comes !
Are their roses like young ladies, that there need
    be such a rout—

Such confabs and monster meetings at their time of
      "coming out"?

Or has the Chinese Empire some Celestial Doctor
      Reid,[1]

Without whose ventilation the warm weather can't
      proceed?

Do Imperial edicts sanction, that it shall be hot
      at noon?

Have the gas-contractors orders to "turn on" the sun
      and moon?

Do the mandarins imagine—without laughing in their
      sleeves—

That the very Tea-trees cannot bud, without their
      Worships' leaves?

What should such folks know of Nature? what should
      Nature know of them?

Are such slant-eyed creatures worthy, e'en to kiss her
      garment's hem?

No! she sends them some mock goddess—some tawdry,
      painted thing,

And it's "Hail fellow well met!" with their own
      peculiar Spring.

[1] A great authority on ventilation; he superintended the system of ventilation for the Houses of Parliament.

I have never been to China, and, I trust, I never can
Be chosen as Ambassador to Pekin or Chusan ;
But I know the sort of place it is—as well as wiser
      pates,
From different "Works on China"—illustrated by
      some plates.
The colour of the country is a kind of dirty blue,
With chaotic sky and water, here and there, appearing
      through ;
Interspersed with little bridges, and paths that seem
      to guide
To—nothing in particular—upon the other side.
The scenery's monotonous—but singularly grand—
And 'tis called " The Willow Pattern," at Mortlock's
      in the Strand.

Other notices—if needed—Fancy easily supplies :
Doves as big as bustards, cooing, from Pagodas in
      the skies ;
Curious, frightful flowers, growing, upside down and
      inside out ;
Trees with fifty sorts of foliage—some with roots,
      and some without.

Everything as it should not be! Fish with feathers,
    birds with fins ;

Nature playing at cross-questions, ending ere she well
    begins !

Just as if the merry goddess (after dinner among
    friends)

Had made up this patchwork country out of all her
    odds and ends !

Just conceive the Spring amusements—how delightful
    they must be !

Junk excursions down Quang river ; sails upon the
    Yellow Sea ;

Picnic parties under Tea-trees, met to see some
    bird's-eye view,

For in lands without perspective, other prospects
    must be few :

Artists, struck with admiration (Chinese artists are
    not nice !)

At some charming mud plantation, tastefully turned
    up with rice ;

Mandarins in yellow buttons, handing you " conserves
    of snails " ;

Smart young men about Canton, in nankin tights and
    peacock tails !

Then conceive the dreadful dainties : kitten cutlets—
    puppy pies—
Birds'-nest soup, which (so convenient !) every bush
    around supplies.
But, enough ! "My soul turn from them !" Let the
    creatures take their fling,
Only—don't join that procession, going out to meet
    the Spring !

Oh, thou mocking tongue be silent ! Is there so much
    joy on earth,
Thou wouldst grudge the simple pleasures, that in
    Nature have their birth ?
Dost thou scorn the meek-eyed people ? dost thou
    deem that worship wrong,
That would welcome back God's blessings with a
    grateful heart and tongue ?—
That would greet the glorious summer, with its sun-
    shine and sweet air,
As a precious gift from Heaven, to be hailed with
    song and prayer ?
Oh, thou scornful heart, be humble ! If the dark
    untutored mind,

In its straitened happiness, such cause for grateful
    praise can find,

Shall the Seasons' change not waken, in thee, too, a
    kindly glow,

Half of thankfulness,—half pride,—for all the gifts
    thou hast to show ?—

For the green fields of Old England—for the Harvest
    hopes they bring ;

For that wealth of bud and blossom that comes out to
    meet our Spring ?

Oh ! when thy life-blood quickens, in the Years'
    delicious prime,

Cry aloud, "God bless the Spring-time, in whatever
    land and clime ! "

TO THE SEINE, NEAR ETIOLLES[1]

UNTRANQUIL River! by whose flow,
Dwell friends I love, yet leave to-day!
If I were *thee*—I'd linger slow,
Nor rush with headlong speed away!
Oh, lived we in th' enchanted hours
Which fed the Grecian poets' dreams,
When spirits dwelt in waves and flowers,
I'd be the Naiad of thy streams!
Then would I turn and twist about,
And make an " Island " of this scene,
I'd " cut me this small cantle out "
And keep it ever fresh and green!

[1] A country place belonging to the Comte de Ste. Aulaire, the Ambassador, with whose family the Author lived in close intimacy. She herself translated these lines into French verse.

I would belie those pedant maps,—
Those tyrant-laws, whate'er they be,
That force thee, with unceasing lapse,
To seek the far, unquiet sea !
And, from those hateful trammels freed,
I'd be a "lake" before their door,
Pure, peaceful—as the life they lead,
Reflecting "Heaven"—and nothing more !
But,—gentle River ! you and I
A kindred fate and sorrow prove,—
To wander 'neath a darker sky,
Nor linger long with those we love.
Yet, happier thou ! Thy fond farewell
Can never leave their friendly ear ;
Thy presence haunts them like a spell,
Still going, yet forever near.
Then, link my memory with thy voice,
And speak to them of me, sweet River !
And tell them,—had we both a choice—
We'd linger near these banks forever ;
Tell them,—like thee—if unrestrained
My heart and eyes might overflow !
Like thine—my course is preordained ;—
Like thee,—I murmur as I go.

THE DEAD LANGUAGE

TAKING sweet counsel, heart from heart,
    Walking life's by-road, with Love for guide—
All the good gifts he alone can impart
    Grew, like the flowers, their path beside.
Narrow their world, but sunny its airs,
    Full of small joys, that were great to them,
Transient sorrows and simple cares
    (Burrs on youth's glittering raiment-hem);
And innocent hopes, that loomed so large
    Thro' the purple mist of their morning-prime,
That a kingdom's fate or an empire's charge
    Had laid less weight on the busy time.
Living their life—dreaming their dream—
    Thus flowed the golden hours away,
Shining and swift as the lapsing stream
    In the sand-glass turned by a child in play.

They had a language that mocked at rules,
    A foolish tongue that was all their own ;
Its words had values unknown to schools—
    Dear for the sake of a look or tone.
Learned it was not, nor was it wise,
    Yet it had purport earnest and true,
Full of such playful metonymies !
    Figures—which love and hearer knew ;
Gay ellipsis—that left to the guess
    Tender half-meanings, metaphor bold ;—
Fond hyperbole—saying far less
    Than the heart hath held, or the kind eyes told ;
Strange pet-names that were nouns unknown,
    Epithets—mocking the love-charmed ears,
Verbs—that had " roots " in the heart alone,
    Jests—whose memories now bring tears.

For the " strong hours " came, that come to all,
    Bearing away on their stormy wings
All the poor treasures, great and small,
    Love had amassed as his precious things ;
All the rare joys, on the path they trod,
    And the cares that look so like joys, when past—

When one great grief—like the serpent-rod—
    Hath swallowed all lesser griefs at last :
All the rich harvest of mutual thought,
    The sweet life memories—reaped in vain,
And last—the language that Love had taught,—
    Ne'er to be uttered nor heard again.
One was taken—the other left ;
    Where was the use of that idle lore ?
Bury it deep in the heart bereft,
    Ne'er to be uttered, nor needed more!

What doth it matter ? solemn and sweet
    Is the communion the True Life brings ;
It will need no symbols where next we meet,
    The love that hath put away earthly things ?
How should we want these foolish words—
    Dear as they were to the mortal heart
Burthened with love, whose weakness affords
    No way else its strength to impart ?
Was it not *thus* we had longed to be—
    Heart and spirit and feeling bare,
Thought unto true thought springing free,
    As flame to flame in the fervid air ?

So shall our spirits meet, unbound,
    Freed from the clog of this stifling clay—
Knowing the depths we had sought to sound,
    Sure of the love we had tried to say.

So the heart reasons, and reasons well,
    Knowing its bitterness, owning its gain—
(Ah ! must the pressure-pain linger still,
    All that is left of a broken chain ?)
—Restless, rebellious, it "asketh signs,"
    Blind to the fire-cross o'er us hung,
And—deaf to the quiring angels—pines
    For one poor word of that lost Love-Tongue.

A LAMENT ON THE WEATHER

This little skit on the weather must have been written about 1831 or 1832.

My Seymour![1] I could sit and cry,
  So loud I hear you crow,
To think your spirits are so high,
  And the mercury so low!
Oh! Christmas is a merry time
  (Though *I* am but "So-so"),—
When nasty little urchins climb
  The trees for mistletoe!
When holly bushes fill the land
  With berries all aglow!
When tempting Christmas pies y'stand
  In pastrycook's window!
When children suck their dirty thumbs,
  So tempting is the show,
And ask for cakes and sugar-plums
  And parents answer "No!"

[1] The late Duke of Somerset.

When blacks fly down the windy flue
    On table, desk, bureau !
When noses turn from red to blue,
    And need the frequent " blow " !
When puddles make of every street
    An archipelago !
When grates throw out too little heat
    To toast the baker's dough !
And on the hob poor mortals long
    To sit incognito
With Shadrach, Meshach of the song,
    And eke Abed-nego !
When slides set out by rascals sly
    Poor fogies overthrow !
And Jews intone the dismal cry,
    " Old clo' !   Who'll buy ?   Old clo' ! "
When tradesmen send in " small accounts,"
    Though not accounted so !
When frozen pipes and pumps are founts
    Will liefer burst than flow !
When Mrs. S.,[1] with looks elate
    And patent clogs on toe,

[1] Mrs. Sheridan, the author's mother.

Between your house and Storey's Gate [1]
   Keeps trotting to and fro !
When N. [2] has his peculiar way
   Of walking through the snow !
When Uncle [3] just runs in to say,
   " I must be off, by Jo' ! "
When all these things are in this state,
   Above, around, below,
And even Spring itself suggests
   No better quid pro quo
Than East winds bearing on their breasts
   Fresh colds in embryo !
Then Nelly sits with feet on grate
   And wrestles with her woe ;—
She sits and sings, with hair uncurled,
   " There is, there is, I know,
Another and a warmer world,
   And there I mean to go ! "

[1] Lord Seymour lived in Spring Gardens ; Mrs. Norton at Storey's Gate.
[2] Mr. Norton.
[3] Mr. Charles Sheridan, second son of the Right Hon. R. B. Sheridan.

MEDITATIONS ON THE POOR LAW[1]

AN ELECTION SQUIB

Why should I support my neighbour
On my goods—against my will?
Can't he live by honest labour?
Can't he beg—or can't he steal?
Poor Rates make such sad confusion!
I, for my part, cannot see
How "John Thomson's" destitution
Gives him any claim on *me*.
"Smith" mayn't own a single penny—
Must I then *my* pound resign?

[1] Written, I think, when the author's brother, Mr. Sheridan of
Frampton, was standing for Parliament.

R

House and lands—" Brown " hasn't any,
'Tis no ground for taxing *mine.*
In the present social system
There must still be Poor and Rich;
Some *must* starve (may Heaven assist 'em)—
Then the only question's—which?
I would rather 'twere my neighbour,—
Not from any spite to him!
But the fact is—honest labour
Does not chance to suit my whim:
Stealing—too, is so immoral!
Begging's—a disgusting trade!
(I should feel disposed to quarrel
With a *Saint*—who begs his bread!)
From these facts—my own deduction
Is—that things are well enough:
That the Poor *should* live by suction
And the Rich *should* quaff and stuff.
'Tis a credit to the Nation
That such strict observance lasts,—
Keeping—without ostentation,—
We—the Feasts, and they—the Fasts!
At the Lord Mayor's—no pretension!
Turtle soup—cold punch (at *least*)—

Yet no sectarian pride ! no mention
Of the Saint whose day they feast !
At the Workhouse—still more quiet !
Nothing of parade—or show !
Grace—and water-gruel diet,
Wisely framed to keep them *low !*
All without the least elation,
Pomp, or Spiritual Pride,—
Fasting—as if sheer starvation
Were their object !—none beside !
What a fine religious Spirit
This displays—in high and low !
Both—their special gifts inherit,
Both—their special virtues show !
Who would wish for innovations
In the customs here made known ?
Where each in his several station
" Rallies round the Church and Throne ! "
Think not that, though clothed in ermine,
I don't *practise* what I sing :
For henceforward I determine
On rallying round—*everything.*
Round the Workhouse ! round the Poorhouse !
Round the altar ! " round my hat ! "

Round the Queen !—who (folks assure us)
Only can be saved by that !
And above all,—*round our purses !*
(You round yours—and I—round mine),
Here's—a fig for poor men's curses
Whilst we keep these rules divine.

AN INSULTED BOX

THE following lines were written on the spur of the moment, in a book kept at Glenquoich for the purpose of receiving visitors' "Complaints," in reply to the gibes and depreciatory comments of Mr. Edward Ellice, Sen. ("Bear Ellice"), on the size of the box the author brought to Glenquoich (his home in the Highlands), when it was being put on board the Yacht in which he came to fetch her at the mouth of Loch Hourn.   They were headed by a sketch of a lady contemplating a box.

WELL ! I have to complain of the numerous shocks
Which my feelings received with respect to my *Box* ;—
Imprimis, on reaching that wildest of lochs
In the Yacht, I was forcibly torn from my box,
Which remained all the night among torrents and
    rocks
In a place quite unfit for a civilised box ;
—And I somehow suspect from the state of the locks
They've been snipping and pawing my well-arranged
    box,

And probably wearing my lace befrilled sm——ks !

(The word is in Shakespeare,—the book's in my
     box.)

Since then, at Glenquoich, what with gibings and
     mocks,

I've not had one moment of peace with my box,

And none but the dullest of stones or of stocks

Could put up with these constant affronts to one's
     box—

For that Bear—as he's called (though he's more of a
     Fox),

Is constantly twitting the size of my Box !

What a heart he must have, who inhumanly docks

A woman's best joys—by curtailing her box !

Does he think we can dress in the skins of his flocks,

Like blessèd Arcadians, who needed no box ?

No doubt in the days of our grandmother's frocks

A woman might do with a smaller-sized box,

And a " Bloomer " perhaps, with a clean pair of
     socks

And a thin pair of (hem !) might dispense with a
     Box :

But I'd just like to see Lady Ailesbury's stocks

Of elegant dresses—packed up in my box,

And exposed to the rubs, and the shoves, and the
    knocks,
Which have very near finished both me and my box !
But I'll not bear it longer—by Savory and Cox !
(The Patrons of Boxes, who fitted my Box),
By Pluto and Erebus ; Saturn and Nox,
And all the dark Gods, who preside o'er *the* Box !
To-morrow at crow of the first village cocks
(For who at Glenquoich thinks of trusting the clocks ?)
I'm off by the steamer, past docks, rocks, and lochs,
To find in the Lowlands a place for my Box.

Your affectionate

PARADOX.

A VALENTINE

In this sad goblet full of tears
    (A melancholy beaker !)
I try to drown my hopes and fears
    In toasting Lady Rica.
Oh ! were it but a stronger drink,
    Or were my passion weaker,
It might have some effect, I think,
    And I'd forget thee, Rica !
But now, whate'er I do or say,
    My views of life grow bleaker,
And ev'n on this auspicious day,
    I hope for nothing, Rica !
I take no pleasure in my meals
    (They make me grow no sleeker) :

There is no use in food, one feels,
 That is not shared by Rica!
My taste for politics is gone;
 When I address the Speaker,
The word "Divide" recalls alone
 Division from my Rica!
At billiards I make endless flukes;
 At cricket I'm a sneaker;
I meet with nothing but rebukes,
 I meet not thee, my Rica!
My friends are ready with advice;
 They say, "Neglect might pique her!"—
Oh! who would buy at such a price
 One glance from thee, my Rica?
The "cup of bliss" (with sweets amid)
 For me is grown a leaker:
"Surgit amari aliquid"
 In all I drink, my Rica!
I once disliked being called a "muff,"
 But now I'm grown much meeker;
When Jones says "Pooh!" and Brown says "Stuff!"
 I feel they're right, my Rica!
I'm often wakened by a scream,
 And find I am the shrieker;

I see thee married in my dream,
 But not to me, my Rica !
But, oh ! if in my search for bliss,
 Your love would bless the seeker,
I'd cry : " Life holds no joy but this ;
 'Tis found, 'tis mine !   Eureka ! "

A VALENTINE

WHAT goose, from what fen,
Produced the blest pen
Which no mortal again
Shall employ for my Gwen?
Was it ibis or hen?
Was it ostrich or wren?
Or could it be, then,
Some wild denizen
Of the forest or glen;
Or, for aught that I ken,
Some quill such as men
May find, now and then,
By accident dropped in a porcupine's den?

And whence came the ink
(Which you see is bright pink)?
Is it wine from some chink
At the ruby-mine's brink,

Distilled link by link,
Which the little Elves drink
To Gwen's health, till they wink,
While the yellow gnomes swink,
As their hammers they clink,
And the rocks split and shrink,
And the dark caverns sink
Far deeper than Gwen ever dreamt of, I think?

Is this paper a thing,
A mere commonplace thing,
Such as stationers bring
Tied up in a string?
No: I've heard poets sing
That each gossamer swing
Which the gay fairies fling
O'er the bushes in Spring,
When gathered by Gwen, wherever they cling,
Are brought to the mills of the great Fairy King,
Where, mixed up with sunbeams and other bright
     things,
They Valentines make and new butterflies' wings!

OBERON.

PROLOGUE

TO THE PLAY OF "RICHELIEU"

Written for Countess Cowper's children when *Richelieu*
was performed at Wrest. Mr. and Mrs. Craven and
Mr. Henry Granville were the principal performers.

LADY EMILY.

THE big folks there are in a dreadful fright
Lest they should all forget their parts to-night,
So they have sent us on in hopes t'engage
Your kind indulgence by our tender age,
Just as one nation to another sends
Smooth-faced ambassadors to make them friends.

LADY FLORENCE.

But, sister, tell them what your play's about,
Some audiences are slow to find that out.

Lady Emily.

Indeed I hardly know—a foolish thing,
Something about a Cardinal and King,
A love affair, a duel, or a quarrel.

Little One.

I only hope your piece is strictly moral?

Eldest.

O that of course, but come, let's take our places,
How full your house is, and what pleasant faces!

EPILOGUE

TO THE PLAY OF "PATRONAGE" [1]

(EDITH *advancing.*)

So rich in patrons, and so blest with friends !
Methinks our artist's tale too gaily ends ;
For genius seldom on its heirs bestows
Aught of life's chances—save its wants and woes !
And such, his history—who, ere we part,
Bids Edith thank you, from a grateful heart !
The old, sad story—his ! the drooping wing—
The captive bird—too prison-sick to sing !
The fervid artist soul, that vainly pines
For his far home—beneath Italian vines !
But you have freed him ! at no distant day,
He goes, rejoicing, on his homeward way ;

[1] This play was acted on the 24th of December 1844, for the benefit of some poor but distinguished artist.

And should he in that lovely land recall
Our gloomier heav'ns, he'll own that, after all,
The light and warmth which fail our English skies
He found in English hearts!

(CLAVERING *to the audience.*)

                    And English eyes!
I must say that (*to* EDITH), you know, "the lover's
          part"
Gives one the habit of a tender heart,
And, with such fair excuse (*points to the audience*), in
          prose or rhyme
I'd play the lover—till the end of Time!
I'd ask no happier lot—if fortune please—
Than such sweet labour, paid by smiles like these;
And, from the patron's rank I held to-day,
Fall gladly to the state of—Protégé!

(ROCKELY *advancing.*)

"And now, that matter's settled"—let me crave
A moment's audience on a theme more grave:
Nothing (of course) improper, or unpleasant,
But, when on business, no time like the present!

(Confidentially to the audience.)

You, lovers of the Arts, may wish to see
My famous "Waterloo," and "Niobe!"
What say you to a strictly "Private View"?
('Twixt you and me) no one but me, and you!
For as to Eastlake,[1] and those other fellows—
(Don't say I said so), they're confounded jealous!
In Landseer's eye, too, that vile hue is seen—
But I confess, his horses are not green!
Now you're the sort of judges to my mind,
Quick to applaud, to venial errors blind;
To please such critics, is my sole ambition—
May I expect you at my exhibition?
Then smile assent! in this degenerate age
Genius is nothing—without—Patronage.

[1] President of the Royal Academy.

EPILOGUE

TO THE PLAY OF "ERNANI"

Written on the occasion of the amateur performance of
 Ernani at the St. James's Theatre on May 14, 1847,
 in aid of the fund for the relief of the sufferers by the
 Irish famine, and of the distress on the West coast
 of Scotland.

FRIENDS! for such are ye who have played friends'
 parts,
Whose hands have given kind earnest for your hearts!
Fain would I thank ye in their name whose grief
Needs but to ask and to obtain relief;
Who hailed ye brothers by the bond of woe,
And found no English heart that answered—"No!"
But sad thoughts lie behind these grateful words,
And my hand shrinks from such deep-sounding chords,

Lest I should pass the limits of my part
(To rouse the feelings—not to wring the heart)
I would remind ye that these hours of pleasure
Are not so wholly lost as some ye measure ;
That kindly purposes and motives right
Hallow such moments of else vain delight,
And pleasure's garlands when their bloom is fled
Shall bear sweet fruits of mercy in its stead.
And ye most gentle inexperienced eyes
That view real misery with a strange surprise,
And, lost in wonder as its depth appears
Incredulous, still question thro' your tears ;—
As stars that in appointed orbits move
Onward, tho' distant, in their light of love
To God's wide firmament their lustre yield,
Yet shed sweet influence on the peasant's field—
So your bright presence in these scenes to-night
On many a darkened hearth shall kindle light,
Shall fall like sunshine on the untilled soil,
Rouse the sad labourer to rewarded toil ;
And glow like spring on Scotland's barren shore,
And the waste plains of Erin—Green no more !
One word for us whose pleasant labours find
Indulgent critics generously blind,

Who blend together in their kind applause
The imperfect effort and its worthier cause,—
Take our best wishes !—be your dreams to-night
By hopeful thoughts of happier days made bright,
May no sad image on your memories dwell,
But thanks and blessings breathed in this farewell !

NOTE.—Her Majesty and Prince Albert, accompanied by Prince Lein-
ingen, and attended by the Countess of Charlemont, the Hon. Miss
Stanley, Lord Dufferin, the Hon. Colonel Phipps, and the Hon. Captain
Gordon, and Her Royal Highness the Duchess of Kent, honoured the performance with their presence. We also noticed Prince Louis Napoleon,
the Russian Ambassador and the Baroness Brunow, the Austrian Ambassador and the Count Potoski, the Countess Dietrichstein, the Countess of
Chesterfield, the Countess of Wilton, the Countess of Granville, etc.—
The *Times*, May 14, 1847.

PROLOGUE

Enter MR. CRAVEN, *in a hurry.*

LADIES and gentlemen ! here's all about it,
The Prologue's *lost*, and we must do without it.
Where can it be ?   I own I'm puzzled, quite—
I had it in this pocket safe last night !
It was the sweetest, neatest, cleverest thing !
So full of point ! so destitute of sting !
So neat, so terse, so elegant, so attic !
A thing at once domestic, and dramatic ;
It touched on all the topics of the day—
The last new fashion, and the last new play,
On all that interests, on all that pleases,
Papal aggression, and the Christmas pieces ;
The price of Stocks, the Industrial Exhibition,
The funds, the weather, and the odds on " Grecian."
In short, on every subject, great or small,
And not above five hundred lines in all !

Well, since it can't be helped, before I go,

I'll just extemporise a word or so!

Ladies and gentlemen! I look around and——

(*Voice behind.*)

("Mr. Craven! Sir! the Prologue's found!")

Well, this *is* luck, found *where*, if I may ask it?

(*Voice behind.*)

("'Twas at the *wash*, sir, in your dirty *veskit!*")

How providential! Stay, a dreadful doubt,

Suppose our Prologue should be all *washed out!*

(*Unfolds the paper.*)

No! no! all's right! *Now*, listen if you will!

(*Reads.*)

"Six shirts, two dozen——" zounds, the woman's bill!

The fates have willed it, and so you see

Our last resource is still extempore!

Kind friends, our play's a trifle, yet we ask

Help at your *hands*, in our delightful task!

Applaud our efforts, be ye friends in need,

And take the wish to please you, for the deed.

NOTE.—I forget to what play this was the prologue. I think it was one acted when we were staying with Lady Cowper at Wrest.

Mr. Craven was the husband of the Authoress of *Le Recit d'une Sœur.*—D. A.

TO HELEN SHERIDAN

THREE Helens in three distant ages born,
Greece, and thrice happy England did adorn.
The first in grace and loveliness surpassed ;
In wit the second, and in both the last.
The force of Nature could no further go ;
To make a third, she joined the former two.
Had Troy still been, more worlds had strewed her
      plain,
Had Charles still lived, he ne'er had roved again.
Where'er to gaze upon that form 'tis given,
Fiends own a heart, and infidels a heaven.

THE "SALDANHA"

BY THOMAS SHERIDAN

"RATHMILTON, *December 6th.*—His Majesty's ship *Saldanha*, one of our finest frigates, commanded by Captain the Hon. W. Pakenham, brother to the Earl of Longford, sailed from Cork on the 19th of November to relieve His Majesty's ship *Endymion* off Lough Swilly. Having reached the harbour, she again sailed on the 30th, with the intention of proceeding to the westward. On the evening of the 4th of December it blew the most dreadful hurricane. At about 10 o'clock at night, through the darkness and the storm, a light was seen from the signal-towers, supposed to be on board the *Saldanha*, passing rapidly up the harbour. When the daylight appeared the ship was discovered to be a complete wreck in Ballyna Stokes-bay. Every one of the 300 souls on board had perished, and all the circumstances of her calamitous loss had thus perished with her. The bodies of Captain Pakenham and about 200 of the crew are said to have been washed ashore and were interred in a neighbouring burying-ground."

"BRITANNIA rules the waves"—
Heard'st thou that dreadful roar?
Hark! 'tis bellowed from the caves

Where Lough Swilly's billow raves,
And three hundred British graves
         Taint the shore.

No voice of life was there—
'Tis the Dead who raise that cry—
The Dead—who heard no prayer
As they sank in wild despair,
Chaunt in scorn that boastful air
         Where they lie.

"Rule Britannia" sung the crew,
When the stout *Saldanha* sailed,
And her colours as they flew,
Flung the warrior cross to view
Which in battle to subdue
         Ne'er had failed.

Bright rose the laughing morn
(That morn which sealed their doom),
Dark and sad is her return,
And the storm-lights faintly burn
As they toss upon her stern
         'Mid the gloom.

From the lonely Beacon's height
As the watchmen gazed around,
They saw that flashing light
Drive swift athwart the night,
Yet the wind was fair and right
        For the Sound.

But no mortal power shall now
That crew and vessel save—
They are shrouded as they go
In a hurricane of snow,
And the track beneath her prow
        Is their grave.

There are spirits of the Deep
Who, when the warrant's given,
Rise raging from their sleep
On rock or mountain steep
Or 'mid thunder-clouds that keep
        The wrath of Heaven.

High the eddying mists are whirl'd
As they rear their giant forms,
See! their tempest-flag's unfurl'd,

Fierce they sweep the prostrate world,
And the withering Lightning's hurl'd
                Thro' the storms.

O'er Swilly's rocks they soar,
Commissioned watch to keep :
Down, down with thund'ring roar,
The exulting Demons pour ;—
The *Saldanha* floats no more
                On the deep !

The dreadful 'hest is past :
All is silent as the grave ;
One shriek was first and last,
Scarce a death-sob drunk the blast
As sunk her towering mast
                'Neath the wave.

"Britannia rules the wave !"
Oh ! vain and impious boast ;
Go, mark, presumptuous slaves,
Where He who sinks or saves,
Scars the sands with countless graves
                Round your coast.

NOTE.—The foregoing lines, which were republished in the *Athenæum* of July the 1st, 1893, were written by Mr. Thomas Sheridan, the son of Richard Brinsley Sheridan. He was in delicate health at the time, and was wintering with Lord Ponsonby at Ventnor in the Isle of Wight, about the year 1812. They were enclosed in a letter to Mrs. Mary Moncrieff of Pitcaithley House, Bridge of Earn. In the letter, Mr. Sheridan very modestly says, "The lines are of too lawless a character to bear the test of criticism. I have purposely left them with many blemishes, as I think that compositions of this description often lose in spirit what they gain by correctness."

IN MEMORY OF
THE LATE EARL OF GIFFORD

BY THE HON. MRS. NORTON (LADY STIRLING-MAXWELL OF KEIR)

FAREWELL! great simple heart, whose generous pulse,
Still beating feebler each succeeding day,
Fainted at last through anguish unto Death!

If the world knew how great had been its gain—
If the world knew how great is now its loss—
Easy it were to swell the vain lament,
Till the loud clamour of a popular cry
Waked answering grief in half-attentive men.

But thou wert for thy friends, not for the world;
So, as it is, thou goest to thy grave
In shadowy silence as a good unknown,
—A bark that hath swept past the headland heights,
None witting the rich argosy it bore.

To thee were known all themes of studious toil
Which men less learned have often made their boast,
The devious course of the enduring stars,
The mystery of their ethereal paths,
Their distances and magnitudes of light.

To thee, historic records, full of wars,
Long lines of conquerors and endless kings
Left lucid memories that gleamed across
Thy wise grave talk, and made the Past a guide
To future counsels for thy country's fate.
Their lessons sate upon thy thoughtful brow,
And many a generous and far-seeing plan
Proved thee fit servant of a troubled time,
And holding—for these strong progressive days—
The skill of statesmanship—without the craft.

To thee the earthly science half divine,—
The only one we fable shall pursue
Our souls beyond their sphere of grosser joys,
Music,—the echo sent from earth to Heaven,—
Was a familiar thing.   Mastered by thee,
As by the ancient masters of that art,
Was all the intricate linking of sweet sounds
And harmonies converging to a close.

To thee, untaught, came that which labour learns ;
And from the pictures of thine accurate eye
The modelled bust and sculptured triumph grew,
Surviving yet the hand whose work is done !

And, midst thy mute companions, those fair tomes
On whose for ever open page thy gaze
Attentive rested,—many a pencilled line
And marginal annotation still attest
The winged hovering of the living thought
Over the thoughts of sages dead—like thee !

Too little known thou wert !   The child that's reared
Amid a hundred daily household smiles

That flicker round his feet and round his head,
Making the tender daylight of his home,—
Grows sweetly bold, and garrulous in mirth,
And like the fair young knights of olden times
E'er the new shield hath motto or device,
Seeks the world's lists with gay defying pride,
Ready to challenge all, and all o'erthrow.
And thine, e'en from thy cradle, were the gifts
Of wealth and luxury and soft delights
And menial tendance due to noble names.

Not thine, hard toil for insufficient food,—
Nor tainted atmospheres 'mid whirring wheels,—
Nor strenuous tasks gone through for scant reward,
Far from the harvests of their native fields,—
Like alienated children of the Poor !
Thou wert the first-born of a titled house,
And all the toys of splendour which shine out
To dazzle the weak eyes of tempted men,
To make them miss the guidance of true paths,
And with a willing weakness sleep or stray
In the enchantment of Armida bowers—
All, all were thine—to breed a low content !

The greater merit had thy gracious soul,—
That held aloof from commonplace delights ;
And from the idle rest of common men
Departing early,—resolute in good,—
Filled up " the burden and the heat of day "
With labours self-imposed, and strict account
Of God's great trust—the fleeting treasure, TIME,
Fitting thenceforth each sunrise as it came,
Not with vain languors of a sliding day,
But with a dial of divided hours—
Each bringing such fair produce, that thy mind
Plucked from thy one life, fruit for many lives.

And all was done with such unboastfulness—
Such tranquil reticence of inner thought—
That like the dial-shadows, all those hours
Fled in soft silence, though their work remained.

Oh ! earnest nature !   Valued to the full
By those who knew thee,—how shall they lament
Who, being ever near thee day by day
Through the brief tenure of that modest life,
Saw,—with a loving wonder,—'midst them all
THEE only doubtful of thine own great worth ?

T

A sister's tears are thine—whose pity fell
Like dew upon the fever of thy pain ;
The stateliest scion of a beauteous race
And wife to him whom England's Hero left
Successor to the titles won in war.

And hers, whose younger loveliness is linked
With that man's son who ever foremost stood
In arts of peace and highest statesmanship,
And so bequeathed his children, equal each,
The proudest legacy a man can leave—
The self-earned glory of a stainless name.[1]

And brother's grieving hallows too thy tomb,
And other gentle sisters, far away,
When tidings reached them of the bitter death,
Reached through slow pain, for others risked and borne
With courage, such as decks the tented field,
And patience e'en like that by martyrs shown.

But one there is whose weeds are deeper yet,
Whose life was in thy life as thine in hers,

[1] Her Grace the Duchess of Wellington and the Lady Emily Peel,
sisters of the Earl of Gifford.

Who filled thy vacancy of homeless days
With answering energy of high pursuits
And intellectual hours.

                              The tears SHE gave,
The pain—the weariness—the ceaseless care—
The straining effort of the anxious day—
The dreary silence of the wakeful night—
All lavish treasures poured by grieving love
Over his dying bed—were all in vain ?

No—not in vain—though Death was still the end !
Nor grudging tongues, nor years of fading Time,
Can take away what dear love dearly bought.
The helpless thanks that shone in dying eyes—
Half thanks and half farewell ! The hopeful prayers,—
The fond relaxing hold of faithful hands
Which only so could loose their hold on life ;
And the most precious certainty that all
Of joy in health,—or comfort in sharp pain,—
Or pleasure in companionship of thought
Through the long loving, long remembering years

Was hers—hers only—hers for evermore—
Hers, so bestowed upon a thankful heart
Fond keepsakes buried with him in the grave.

Then fare thee well !   Farewell, great simple heart !
Certain to be forgotten by the crowd
E'er the first summer shall make green thy grave ;
Certain to be remembered while life lasts
By those who knew and loved thee, and who yet,
When other men are praised for truest worth,
For ready learning, or for natural gifts,
Shall turn and muse awhile with dreaming eyes
(As though in thought they saw thy vacant place)
And sigh and say—"Yea ! and long years ago
We had a friend—with all these gifts and more !"

A FEW THOUGHTS ON KEYS

Now,—this key was a Fairy.
History of Blue Beard.

IT must be a flinty heart that can read without a sympathetic throb one of those plaintive advertisements often seen in the second column of the *Times*, which offer lavish sums of valueless gold for the restoration of "a bunch of keys on a steel ring." Those simple words touch a keynote which finds an echo in every bosom not utterly destitute of feeling and cupboards.

Lives there the man so reckless, that he cannot recall to mind moments of exquisite suspense, hours of anguish, when life has been a blank and his keys have fled to that inscrutable Limbo, which in familiar household language is styled "nowhere." There are few amongst us who cannot realise the situation.

The wise and witty Sydney Smith instituted a

"Screaming Gate" at the verge of his Parochial
Demesne, for the purpose of allowing due scope and
expansion to the peculiar distress attending it; and
indeed, no family should be without some appropriate
"wailing place" of this sort, some monumental portal,
or limitary grove, sacred to memory, and the Dii
Viales who are said to preside over luggage. It would
save the breaking of many hearts and locks.

Although this particular misery is common to all,
yet for man's proper nature there are certain mitigations
and tender assuagements which his partner cannot
share, that soften, if they do not remove, the sense of
bereavement. He can at least kick his portmanteau
if he cannot open it; he can rip up and disembowel
his carpet bag; he can smash his despatch-box;—
above all, he can swear! A hearty D—mme has been
known to take the sting out of many such sorrows;
it enters into the category of what are called "resources
within one's self," and, as such, should be cultivated.

But, in the case of hapless woman, these safety-
valves for legitimate emotion do not exist. In her
keyless agony she is like a lioness robbed of her cubs,
yet denied the alleviation of a roar. Moreover, the
amount of misery entailed on the two sexes by this

loss admits of no comparison. Man has but a limited capacity of suffering, inasmuch as he is a creature of few keys. He probably possesses but *le strict necessaire* —let us say, a latch key, a watch key, a desk key, perhaps a cellaret key—mere bagatelles. Woman, on the other hand, especially woman of a methodical turn, is all keys. She absolutely bristles with them. Not to mention that congeries of cares—the domestic bunch, she has all sorts of outlying and isolated keys —keys *in partibus infidelium,*—colonial and collateral keys—keys that lock out, and lock in, and lock up everything lockable (especially keys which are in themselves susceptible of captivity!) *qui custodes custodiunt.* When that fatal complication takes place, it is impossible to sound the depths of a woman's keylessness ;—it is a slough of despond that hath no bottom !

Thoughtless persons look upon keys in a merely subjective point of view, as suggestive of and subordinate to locks. "Under lock and key" is the usual careless way of speaking, putting, as it were, the cart before the horse. Dean Swift, however, with his accustomed sagacity, restores the key to its proper place in the universal scale ; he gives it the due

relative importance in regard to the inferior thing—
a lock :—

> A messenger from Quilca[1] says,
> —" They've stolen the locks from off the keys ! "

His countrymen appear to have shared the common
prejudice, although, aiming in practice, as the sequel
shows, at rigid impartiality :—

> But then, to vex and plague me more,
> He adds—" They stole the keys before ! "

Persons of an analytic turn and discursive fancy
will overleap the true object of reflection ; they will
wander from the matter in hand—the key ; shut their
eyes upon its concomitant—the keyhole ; and, dis-
daining to linger even in that mediate region, the
press, cupboard, closet, cellar, or storeroom, will mount
(metaphorically) from shelf to shelf till they lose
themselves in bewildered contemplation of finite man's
infinite faculties of acquisitiveness and retentiveness.

The antiquarian, again, will busy himself with the
question,—When did man first begin to lock up ?
" When wild in woods the noble savage ran," of course
he carried no keys ; a stone rolled to a cavern's mouth

[1] The house of the Sheridan who was Swift's friend.

was probably the first rough expression of an art which has been so finely elaborated in later days. Boulders must have been precious stones in that golden age, when the rarity of property so simplified the duties and cares of possession !

The habits of the nomade patriarchs must likewise have presented difficulties in this particular, as is evidenced by the fact that when Rachel robbed her father Laban of his gods, her only means of securing them was to sit upon them.

The Greeks and Romans, too, must have had but sorry methods of guarding their possessions. Would Grecian Aristippus have strewn the Libyan sands with his gold, when his overburthened slaves found it too heavy for a hurried journey ? Would miser Cremes have buried his money in the earth, if either of them had possessed at home some decent lock-up place, or civilised strong box ? Who ever saw a Pompeian cellar key ? Rusty nails from that locality are to be met with in museums, but where are the keys that guarded their curious vintages ? Horace certainly uses the expression " *servata centum clavibus,*" but it is evidently a figure of speech in honour of his friend Posthumus's genteel establishment ; he never mentions the thing as in use in his own cosy bachelor house-hold. Indeed it puzzles one to guess how he managed about these matters. The Sabine *vin ordinaire* was probably left about in careless profusion, and it is possible that his Chian hogsheads may have been occasionally "on tap" in the Atrium, as pipes of claret used to be in hospitable Irish drawing-rooms fifty or sixty years ago; but how about all that "choice Falernian" and "hoarded Cœcuban"? Pitching and plastering the mouths of the vessels was but a poor expedient. What was to prevent the abstraction of a fat amphora or two if that ubiquitous "boy" of his had any taste for "care - dispelling Massic"?

But this is a digression. The uses of keys are no worthy subject for the true philosopher's contempla-tion; he looks upon the essences of things; he sees a key in its objective signification; he cares not for its qualifications as arbiter and agent of those vain characteristic attributes—"mine and thine"; he takes no interest in futile distinctions; he never locks anything up, knowing the inutility and peril of the act; it adds nothing to the security of property, but is apt to inspire others with too strong an interest in it; "nothing venture, nothing have" is his favourite proverb, but with a more enlightened signification than it generally conveys. He looks upon a key as a mystic entity of diabolical powers, a talisman, which can confer on inert matter, such as wood, iron, brass, leather, etc., the faculty of baffling and circumventing you in the effort to get at your own possessions. This is, in fact, the only sound view of the subject. When once the mind has recognised this truth, every single key on your bunch will assume a peculiar physiognomy, even as it possesses a distinct idiosyncrasy. One key will come into your family with a certain malicious glitter about it, a defiant swagger and sparkle that foretells the lifelong struggle you are destined to have with it. You see at once that it will "rather bend than break," and rather break than open your box, desk, drawer, or portfolio, as the case may be. Another will wear a dull and gloomy air, a "here-to-day-and-gone-to-morrow" sort of aspect, as good as an epitaph, and much more veracious.

House door keys have been seen of so truculent and forbidding a countenance that their very presence in the lock is supposed to have scared away the prowling depredator. One indeed has been known, on a remarkable occasion, to have "comprehended an auspicious person" with the sagacity of a Dogberry, and to have absolutely done good knightly service in the capacity of a life-preserver.

What family has not at times possessed some meek little tea-caddy, or perhaps cellaret key, which, however facile and effectual at other times, was liable, in any sudden exigency, to fall into so painful a state of hamper and embarrassment as no effort of its owner could soothe, or politely feigned indifference on the part of visitors, allay ?

What household but has its own legendary re-miniscences of keys strangely lost and mysteriously regained,—keys that have gone and hung themselves (for no human agency is ever traceable on these occasions) on wrong rings and wandered madly into wrong pockets,—impulsive keys that have been found apparently trying to open wrong locks of their own accord, and to have broken short off in the effort to recover themselves ? Industrious keys ! which, on some favourable occasion, have so "improved the shining hour" that wax has been found in their wards ! Precious keys (of tills and iron safes), each fondly supposed by its possessor to be as unique of its kind as the silver Decadrachma of Alexander the Great, yet suddenly discovered to have twin brothers as like as peas, and as experienced as their prototypes in the duties of their office!

The most careless observer will have been struck by a difference in the outward semblance of keys apparently subjected to the same external influences. Look, for instance, at the respective keys of your wine cellar and your coal cellar. What a bright, rollicking, jovial look the first wears, polished without effeminacy, forcible and yet insinuating, evidently habituated to your butler's cordial grasp and tenderly demonstrative of friction in his pocket. There is indeed a witching hour (about the fifth or sixth bottle, it is said) when this key assumes the figure of a miniature Thyrsus. The very wards seem to drip with "blushful Hippo-crene," ivy leaves to wreathe its stalk, and the handle curls round the fervent fingers with the cool tender freshness of vine - tendrils. In these subterranean regions "the atom darkness, in its slow turmoil," perhaps disposes the senses to such hallucinations; but, strange to say, no similar transfiguration attends the coal-cellar key. Visit that quiet retreat at what hour you will, no mysterious gnome peers at you from its

cavernous depth ; no swart Cyclop turns on " his
one eye in your face with the obtrusive radiance of a
policeman's lanthorn ; a harmless, unnecessary cat
perhaps pervades the gloomy precincts, but she is
but a cat ; Walpurgis Night itself could not invest
her with solemnity, and the key remains a key to the
end of the chapter,—a hang-dog-looking, melancholy
key it is, rusty, unamiable, antipathetic ; how unlike
" his wholesome brother " of the wine cellar, though
exercising his functions in such close proximity.

Observe, too, the engaging exterior of the Area-
gate key, exposed to all the vicissitudes of weather,
subjected to the temporary command of every scullion,
yet ever bright, brisk, alert, and shining, alive to
the meanest exigences of domestic organisation, cheer-
fully responsive to the call of butcher, baker, milkman,
and fishmonger, not superciliously deaf to the voice of
the humbler rag-merchant or sonorous dust-man.
How singular is its apt appreciation of the majesty of
Themis in the person of a policeman, with what oily
alacrity it turns in the impassive lock to give him
ingress, or discreet exit from the social seclusion of
your kitchen ! Thence, rising with rubicund visage,
he goes forth like a giant (no doubt refreshed) on his

sternly beneficent career. His march eastward is, in fact, a modest "triumph," not as madly clamorous perhaps as that of Indian Bacchus, but partaking in some degree of the god's privileges and attributes. Whispered "Evoes" from every area attend his steps, Pan is not entirely excluded from the pageant, the rattle of knife and fork will be heard, and the tinkle of the area-gate and other keys, instead of the clash of noisy cymbals !

The domestic latch key in full use at the height of the season is reported to have a worn and dissipated look. Those who are acquainted with its uses and habits affirm that it is apt to get muggy and confused about four o'clock in the morning, incapable of key-holes, and altogether effete and idiotic.

No doubt there is an appropriate horror in the aspect of a "skeleton" key; the name imports it. Secret murder is in the very sound. It has the hiss of caution, and the true burglarious rattle in it; there must be an evil harmony and coincidence between its countenance and its name; it leads the thoughts to another and a worse key—the Key of Newgate. Can the uninitiated realise *its* awful appearance? Viewed from the outside, no doubt its peculiarities are less impressive; but we can conceive an aspect whose steely glitter might have the effect of Medusa's head.

The Key of Bedlam is reported to work backwards (like a witch's prayer). Some say that it is always held by the ward end, and unlocks with the handle. Our information is derived from most respectable authority—the oldest inhabitant of the Institution.

The Lord Chamberlain's key has a moral influence superior to that of any key in the Kingdom, not excepting the Lord Chancellor's. It has the faculty of discrimination, and with the facility of a magic wand it separates the sheep from the goats in the fashionable herd.

But it would demand a greater space than these pages can afford to discuss the various attributes and powers of what may be called Public Keys, from the Foreign Office despatch-box key to the keys of the Chancellor of the Exchequer, which, we doubt not, are to be distinguished by a dignified reticence and an alacrity in locking up. What we would especially recommend to general observation is the generic tendency of all keys to spontaneous reproduction. This tendency is perhaps most remarkable in the *clavis domestica*, or key of private life whose prolific qualities may be tested by a simple experiment. A very small bunch of them left in any confined space during a few months' absence on the part of their owner, will be found, on his return, to have colonised the whole drawer. In fact, single keys should never be left under these conditions for any time ; they become family keys in no time. It is supposed that they sprout like asparagus in damp weather, or are produced like button-mushrooms in a hotbed. It is a singular fact that this reproductive faculty is to be found in no other metallic substance, however fashioned ; locks never multiply of their own head ; you may leave any number of sovereigns or half-crowns together, yet never find an additional sixpence among them, sometimes quite the reverse.

The awkward consequences which may arise from this property of the key of domestic life may be easily imagined. You may come some day in a transport of anxious haste to the receptacle of your more important keys, to seek for (let us say) the key of the medicine chest in some moment of an exquisitely emotional character, such as your best friend's having swallowed a bottle of blacking in mistake for ginger-beer, or your infant's having gulped down its mother's thimble !

Instead of the desired key, you find a mob of little nameless, objectless keys, staring you in the face, tripping up your fingers, and maddening you by their multiplicity and inane uniformity of aspect. Curiously enough these "tadpole" keys, as they may be called, have at first no special physiognomy; it is only when launched into practical existence and apportioned among the keyholes of real life that they grow to be as distinct in appearance and as diabolical in character as their elders.

Such is the essential nature of these "shining mischiefs," tricky, deceitful, capricious, never to be trusted out of your sight, full of irritating associations when in it, informed by some devilish intelligence that only leads them wrong, and provocative of evil impulses in others—

With all the rash dexterity of Wit,—

for purposes of annoyance, yet powerless to do even the small good for which they were intended. If man is wise, he will banish them from his pocket; if woman knows her own interests, she will lock them up for ever! If, however, the possession of great riches and their concomitant worries absolutely necessitate the employment of keys, let their hapless owner keep them well in hand, and allow no key to get the better of him. Let there be no "master-key" in his establishment, if he value his peace of mind. If he must use them, let him do so in moderation ; he will never want an occasion to abuse them. But the best thing that can happen to him is to lose them. When that fortunate, and not improbable, circumstance occurs, let him not rush madly into the second column of the *Times* newspaper, let him not provoke Fate by offering a reward for their restoration, but let him call "the Watch together, and thank God he is rid of knaves."

In concluding this slight notice of the properties of an agent only too powerful in its influence on human affairs, we cannot avoid taking a side glance at certain keys whose qualifications are universally alluded to in polite conversation and refined literature, but which have never yet been collected, labelled, and catalogued, as they ought to be.

We are constantly hearing of "the key to so-and-so's extraordinary conduct "—" the key to Miss Such-a-one's affections "—" the key to a certain person's machinations "—" the key of Lord Somebody's conscience "— "the key to everybody's secret thoughts and private affairs."

These things no doubt have a real existence. We cannot do without them ; they are an important part of those rather threadbare "properties" which belong to the world's stage (as it is generally called), and "Life's poor play." But has anybody seen them? Let somebody advertise for them. They are probably knocking about in that æsthetic "Green-room" of Commonplace to which we all know our way, from whence we draw those slashing wooden swords and tin bucklers that are so effective in all arguments,— those spangled coats and jerkins in which our poor thoughts occasionally strut so bravely,—those banners with grand inscriptions which look quite as well as opinions at a little distance ! There also may be found " all that useful lot " of hyperbolic essences—

> The entities of things—that are not yet !
> Subtlest,—but surest beings !—

such as,—the " wedge," whose thin end is always being introduced into our most venerable institutions ; —the " hinge," on which momentous affairs habitually turn ;—the hypothetical " leg," which nobody has got to stand on in all arguments ;—the "other side," to every question ;—in short, all the "material" for sensible conversation. These things are in constant requisition and daily use ; but, like the mysteriously circulating shoe in "Hunt the Slipper," their existence is only made manifest to the senses by the sounding rap with which we shuffle them round in the polite intercourse of good society.

It would be a good deed to fix, substantiate, and classify these useful but volatile possessions, that they may be always at hand when wanted in public speech or private conversation, more specially the mystic keys to which we have referred. What a handy bunch that would be !

(Sd.) C. L. AVIS.

FINESSE

OR

A BUSY DAY IN MESSINA

COMEDY IN THREE ACTS [1]

TIME 1811

[1] This piece was expressly written for Mr. Wigan, who, amongst his other great qualities as an actor, had a special talent for the part of a Frenchman speaking broken English. The farcical element was introduced to suit Mr. Buckstone, who was a leading member of Mr. Wigan's Company.

DRAMATIS PERSONÆ

BARON FREITENHORSEN (an eccentric Austrian).
DR. BERTRAND (a French émigrée).
ST. CLAIR (*alias* Sullivan, an adventurer).
COUNT FILLIPPI (a Neapolitan coxcomb).
CAPTAIN MORTIMER (an English naval officer).
MR. JOHN POPPLETON (a naval amateur).
JULES D'ARTIGNY (a young soldier of fortune).

THE BARONESS FREITENHORSEN.
LAURA BRANDON (her niece).
MRS. BOBBIN.
CATERINA.

Fishermen and Lazzaroni.   English Marines and Sicilian Police.

Time 1811.

Eight bars of Music before Curtain.

ACT I

Scene

The seashore before Messina, a rustic cabaret with benches, etc., in the background.

Enter COUNT FILLIPPI *and* ST. CLAIR *L.U.E.*

FILLIP.   And so you are but just arrived?

ST. C.   Straight from Palermo.   Safe, here? Eh? No eavesdroppers?   (*Looking round.*)

FILLIP. (*R.*)   No, no; no fear!   Come, open your budget; what news from the Court?

ST. C. (*L.*)   All's right there.   I bring full power to act, and all the necessary documents.   Everything we have done is approved of at headquarters.

FILLIP.   So it is; but, oh Lord, I do so long to get out of this doghole, Messina; it's all very well for *you*, St. Clair, who are always backwards and forwards between this and the gay Court at Palermo, advising Queens and earwigging Ministers; but here am I

reduced to act Deputy-Major in this out-of-the-way
place Messina! I that once set the fashion to all the
youth of Naples; let me tell you, men of parts are not
to be bottled up in provincial obscurity with impunity;
we ferment, sir, we explode!

St. C. Weak liquids are soonest liable to that
process.

Fillip. Ah, none of your sneering! I think I
may say, St. Clair, that I have some weight here.

St. C. Oh, enormous! (*Aside.*) The heaviest
ass in Sicily. (*Aloud.*) But now to business. When
are we to expect this young D'Arblay, General
Maitres's aide-de-camp, with the signed agreement?

Fillip. It's all arranged, the last despatch from
Maitres told us we might expect the young fellow
this very day.

St. C. This very day? I'm glad I returned in
time; but your uncle the Commandant's pigheaded
fidelity to the English and their own suspicions com-
bine to make it a difficult matter to bring a stranger
into the lines of Messina, without awkward questions
about his business.

Fillip. My dear fellow, these things only require
a little ingenuity. (*Takes* St. Clair *on one side L.*)

My trusty boatman, Antonio, brings him in the disguise of an English sailor, and directs him to my uncle's office, where our friends amongst the Council will meet in my private apartment. An agreement will be signed to deliver up to the French the Flotilla now anchored off Messina, and assist them to gain possession of the Citadel now occupied by our unsuspecting allies and protectors the English,—all our names will be signed to it, so it would be deuced awkward if it fell into wrong hands.

St. C. No fear of that; this young D'Arblay will be prudent for his own sake. Discovery by the English would be followed by instant trial and condemnation; greater names than ours are implicated. But this D'Arblay—you have his description—no fear of a mistake, eh?

Fillip. Here it is (*reads from paper*): "Three-and-twenty, 5 feet 10 inches, light hair, no whiskers,—brings a letter in Maitres's own writing (which I know), besides exchanging passwords."

St. C. And they are—— ?

Fillip. "You have been long expected." The answer "Sicily and Independence,"—the papers once exchanged, we shall get him quietly off after dark and before morning he will be on his voyage to Reggio.

St. C. Well, it's time we were at our posts; but stay, how goes on our little private plot; are you making any progress with the pretty heiress, Laura Brandon?

Fillip. Ask the lady; she and you must settle it between you; I wash my hands of the affair. Marry me if I must be married, but I've no turn for that sort of thing myself; it isn't in my line.

St. C. Come, come, don't affect indifference to £20,000 and the prettiest face in Sicily.

Fillip. As to the face, as the lady generally favours me with a view of her back hair, I haven't much opportunity of admiring it; and for her fortune, as my gambling debts to you and others will nearly swallow the whole, I can look on the acquisition with philosophy.

St. C. I don't deny that I take an interest in the matter.

Fillip. Interest! yes, 50 per cent, by Jove! By the bye, I never quite understood your position, St. Clair; if I didn't know you to be devoted to the Court and the King of Naples—Englishman as you are—one might fancy——

ST. C. As to that, I'm not of an encroaching disposition; I claim no particular country, and have a slight prejudice towards England, the place of my birth.

FILLIP. Indeed!

ST. C. My simple annals may amuse you, and as we are now so far committed that neither can safely betray the other, I'll trust you. My mother was a Frenchwoman; my father an Irish nobleman; there were slight informalities which precluded any claim on my part to his *Title* and *estates*, but his interest procured me a confidential situation as clerk in an opulent firm.

FILLIP. A good opening?

ST. C. I found it so. Unfortunately, I inherited my father's aristocratic tastes, if I was heir to nothing else. This predisposition, acting on a delicate organisation, produced a singular disease.

FILLIP. Indeed!

ST. C. Yes, a kind of a—nervous irritation (principally in the fingers), accompanied by a kind of —a—dizziness and confusion of ideas—on the subject of *property*, for instance.

FILLIP. Curious!

St. C.   Yes, it manifested itself in early youth in little *taking ways*, which, while they endeared me to my family (in one sense), often suggested fears of losing me, and at length terminated in a very serious complaint.

Fillip.   Ah! of the chest?

St. C.   Exactly, a material defect was proved to exist there; a consultation was held on my case by first-rate judges, and finally, several of my best friends (twelve of them) strongly advised me to *travel*.

Fillip.   Ah! I've heard that the air of England is sharp.

St. C.   Uncommonly sharp in cases of this kind.

Fillip.   And where did you go?

St. C.   I was conveyed to a lovely sheltered spot, called Botany Bay, where I was taken the greatest care of.

Fillip.   And you recovered——

St. C.   The use of my limbs sooner perhaps than was expected; but as I have always felt a delicacy about flying in the face of those friends who, I may really say, insisted on my leaving England, I have hitherto refrained from returning.

Fillip.   And you came hither?

St. C. Yes, curiously enough it happens that the· Baroness's first husband and Miss Brandon's uncle was the principal of the firm with whom I was connected, and the most active promoter of my foreign travel; that accounts for the interest I take in her, and her family, and I am now doing my best to get the niece and her fortune for *you* from the same disinterested motives. (*Looking off L.H.*) I see that old French Dr. Bertrand coming this way; that man is ubiquitous; I'm always tumbling over him. I sometimes fancy there is more than *chance* in the matter!

Fillip. Oh, nonsense! a good harmless old quiz! He hasn't an idea beyond his basket of rubbish, which he calls " botanical specimens."

Enter Bertrand *U.E.L. down C.*

Hah, Doctor, busy as usual I see! Culling simples, eh?

Bert. (*coming forward C.*) Serviteur, Messieurs! Eh, eh! you are so farceur, M. le Comte! Yes, eh, eh! I am *gulling* de *simple.*

Fillip. Ha, ha! so, and have you met anything curious in your way to-day?

Bert. Ouida! M. le Comte! I meet two very curious simples on my way.

FILLIP. Ha, ha, ha! and you have 'em safe in your little basket, eh?

BERT. Yes, M. le Comte; they are in the basket. (*Aside.*) Very much in the basket, hem!

(*Crosses to R.*)

ST. C. (*who has been looking off the stage U.E.L.*) It *is*, by Jupiter! I felt sure of it! Fillippi, yonder frigate, standing in, is the *Vigilant*, commanded by your rival Captain Mortimer. Some mischief's on foot! damn it! What brings him at this juncture? Fillippi, we must make sure of your position with the heiress; you must accompany me to the Baron's house this evening; luckily, I had made an appointment for you!

FILLIP. The devil you have; you might give a poor fellow time to breathe! Well, well, none of your black looks! I'm passive, let's get the business over, since it must be done; but I'm positively victimised! Farewell, Doctor.

(*Exeunt L. or E.*)

BERT. (*solus*). Serviteur, M. le Comte, ah, curl-pate Neapolitan! and you, you Irish vaurien, with your mocking tongue! Do you think to turn and return the old Bertrand like a glove, eh, eh? He holds you in his grasp—fast—fast; eh, eh! These poor puppets little think who holds the string that makes them dance—ay, and that man of destiny—that Napoleon Bonaparte—does he guess that in this little corner of the big world there lives an old man whose feeble hand can ruin his most cherished project? *This* is vengeance! This is happiness! No! (*sadly*) that word is not for me—vengeance, yes! but happiness—(*he sighs*). Well, to work! to work! I see a boat putting off from the *Vigilant;* Mortimer will soon be at my lodgings; but (*looking round*), where is my young gaillard that is to personate the spy, D'Arblay? He cannot mistake the place of meeting, I will go rest me on the bench; he must soon be here. (*Retires C, sits under the porch of cabaret R.*)

Enter JULES *U.E.L.*

Yes! there is the cabaret. This is the spot where I am to expect him. My heart almost fails me: to think that I shall see him face to face—speak to him, hear that beloved voice again, yet dare not reveal myself. Every gray head I have met has made my heart leap with expectation only to sink with disappointment! Ah, there is a figure that

x

resembles—yes, 'tis he! Years have sadly changed those dear, those well-known features; but courage, courage! I must be calm. Seven years since we parted, seven years. Suffering, and the Indian sun must have changed me; there is no fear that he should see a trace of his long-lost son in the young French-man whom he is sending to certain danger—perhaps death. Ay, and who would meet it gladly, rather than yield to another the right to serve, to save if need be!   (*Touches* BERT. *on shoulder.*)

BERT. Eh, eh, this must be my young unknown friend. Serviteur Monsieur! I think I may say "You have been long expected."

JULES. Dr. Bertrand, I keep my password—it may be needed!

BERT. You answer well!

JULES. These papers from our mutual friends in Malta will attest my mission here! (*Gives letters.*) This is the hardest part of my task!

BERT. C'est bien! and here I have the papers necessary for your enterprise. (*Gives paper.*) I am informed here dat you have reasons for concealing your name.

JULES. I have, sir, for the present.

BERT. Bien, bien, c'est votre affaire. You are young, my friend, to undertake this dangerous adventure in personating the real spy—le véritable D'Arblay; you are in danger from the two sides—c'est délicat, c'est délicat, you have well considered it?

JULES. Have no fear for me, sir; I have none for myself.

BERT. Well said, Monsieur—pardon, I had forgot.

JULES. You may call me Jules, sir.

BERT. Jules! ah! (*sighs*) that name was once dear to me; well, Monsieur, Monsieur Jules, you must proceed at once to the Commandant's office—and—have you parents alive?

JULES. My father lives, thank Heaven!

BERT. Ah! (*sighs*) you will proceed to—knows he of your enterprise, Monsieur Jules?

JULES. He is but imperfectly acquainted with my position.

BERT. Ah, well! you will enter this den of conspiracy; dose rascals will receive you with open arms; as the French spy, they will give you the signed agreement, and then we have them in our power. I need not recommend to you caution, for our sakes,

for your own, au revoir. (*Crosses L.*) You are your
father's only child, Monsieur Jules?

JULES. I am.

BERT. Ah! (*sighs*) when your meeting with these
traitors is over, come to my house, your movements
will be watched; but, eh, eh! I have a stratagem
by which I secure you a safe refuge, and exit from
Messina in case of suspicion or discovery.

JULES. There is no chance of that; at all events
I am ready to risk it in so good a cause.

BERT. No, no! there is no chance! The real
D'Arblay, whom you personate, can only arrive to-
morrow—this night you shall be in safety! Go now,
we must not be observed together. Ah, sapristi! I
had forgot it; no one can enter into Messina without a
pass; I will send it by Antonio; this little cabaret is
only frequented by Fishmans—remain there till he
arrives. Farewell.   (*Going.*)

JULES. Farewell, sir! (*He pauses.*) At this last
moment, far from any friends, upon a dangerous
service, I feel a strong desire for sympathy—for some
sign of interest—even from a stranger. Monsieur,
you will not refuse me a slight favour; stand for a
moment in the place of that beloved father whose

blessing I am not allowed to ask ; bid Heaven prosper me !

BERT. My dear boy, certainly ! que diable, you shall be prospered ! You do a good deed. Heaven bless you.

> (*He raises his hat and blesses* JULES. JULES *then kisses his hand, and exits into cabaret R.H.*)

BERT. (*wiping his eyes*). I am an old fool, eh, eh ! what is this fellow to me ? Pourquoi diable ! does he come asking a blessing ? have I the time to waste in blessing all the moutards that come in my way ? c'est ridicule ! allons ! I must find Antonio for this pass, eh, eh ! Poor lad ; he is going to put his head into the Lion's mouth,—a word—an imprudent look may discover him, and c'est fini—they shoot or hang him for certain ! But no, there is no fear ; I have so well managed, eh, eh ! Old Bertrand has a head ! It's a fine brave gaillard ! Ah ! he made me think of one who would have been just his age ! Allons ! n'y pensons plus ! a fine lad, I should be sorry he was hanged, mais c'est son affaire—c'est son affaire !   (*Exit L.H.*)

Enter CAPTAIN MORTIMER, POPPLETON, *and*
Coxswain, *as from boat U.E.L.*

MOR. I shall come off at ten this evening, and
tell Mr. Chambers I shall be heard of at Baron
Freitenhorsen's villa, if any message arrives from
General Maitland.

SAIL. Aye, aye, sir!

(*Exit, running against* POPPLETON *U.E.L.*)

POP. (*dusting his clothes anxiously*). Now then,
stupid, look where you're driving to!

MOR. Well, Poppleton, you seem to have recovered
from the effects of the voyage!

POP. Right as a trivet, sir! I find my sea-legs
the moment I touch dry land. But I say, sir, considering what a terrible time we had of it, don't you
think I stood it uncommonly well?

MOR. That depends upon what you call "standing
it." If lying on the broad of your back and begging
occasionally to be thrown overboard is standing it,
you've succeeded to a miracle!

POP. (*L.H.*) Captain, no quizzing! The fact is,
sir, it was such a topsy-turvy sort of life, I never
could make up my mind as to which end of me was

uppermost, so I thought it best to steer a *middle course* on the sofa, that I might turn up on any emergency.

MOR. (*R.H.*) Ah! I see, a sort of golden mean in the vicissitudes of sea life; well, Jack, we part company here. (*Shakes hands.*) I have business at the Commandant's office, and elsewhere. You, I suppose, are for beating up the quarters of your Sicilian friends —many acquaintances in Messina?

POP. Plenty, sir, plenty; that is to say, I don't exactly know them yet, but it won't be long before we make friends.

MOR. But seriously, Poppleton, don't let's have any foolish pranks here; circumstances make this rather an anxious time. I can depend upon my officers; I trust my passenger will be no exception to the rule. You know I promised my old friend, your father, to exercise a friendly authority over you; he hopes to sicken you of the sea, and cure a certain giddy love of adventure, which ill becomes the only hope of a rich commercial house.

POP. I give you my honour, sir, I will be discretion itself.

MOR. Well, well; and, by the bye, Jack, the Sicilian wines are *strong;* profit by the hint.

Pop. (*aside*). I must taste them. (*Aloud.*) I'll be the soul of abstinence, sir.

Mor. You see, Jack, a good sailor should be able to lay his course in all latitudes, keep a firm hand on the tiller, and a clear eye on the compass— Duty !

Pop. I say, sir, if one could box the conscience as one does the compass, eh ! the voyage of life would be a mighty easy affair !

Mor. Box the conscience ?

Pop. Yes, sir, just consider : there are thirty-two points on the compass, and only one Right and one Wrong. Don't you think it would be more ship-shape and convenient if a few delicate subdivisions were marked down, gently subsiding from " Quite right " to " Pretty well," " Middling," " So-so," down to due wrong ?

Mor. Ha, ha ! you would hardly do for a sea captain, Jack ; but you'd make a capital sea lawyer !

Pop. No bad berth either ; one might end by being master of the *rolls !*

Mor. Well, I must be off ; by the bye, Poppleton, the lines of Messina are strictly guarded—you have your pass, of course ?

Pop. All right, sir!

Mor. And, bless my soul, Jack, now I look at you, you're got up in great style—quite the "jovial tar," upon my word!

Pop. Hem! neat, sir, isn't it? Oh, I spare neither trouble nor expense; the costume is copied exact from Mr. Doubleshuffle's in *The Pirates of the Pyrenees;* one can't be too particular in sustaining the naval character of England—costume is half the battle! Do you suppose, sir, Nelson would have won Trafalgar in an apron and lawn sleeves? Observe the hitch in the trousers, sir; I took no end of lessons before Doubleshuffle thought me perfect in it!

Mor. You do him credit!

Pop. Twig the quid, sir, made me a little qualmish at first, but I flatter myself I chaw pretty well now.

Mor. (*laughing*). Oh, you're wonderfully perfect.

Pop. Nothing of the respectable City gent about me now—is there, Captain?

Mor. No, I give you joy, Jack, not an atom of respectability about you.

Pop. Thank ye, sir; and you *might* take me for a sailor, mightn't you, if you met me anywhere, eh?

Mor.   Well, perhaps, if I met you in the dark, and you held your tongue, I might.

Pop.   Oh, now you're quizzing, sir; but I'll bet you 50 to 1 I pass for a sailor all over Messina !

Mor.   Done, Jack, and I'll give you odds, 100 to 1, you don't take in a single individual.

Pop.   But we're upon honour, you know, sir. You won't betray me ?

Mor.   Not I, ha, ha ! keep your own counsel if you can !

Pop.   Never fear, aye, aye, sir !   Port your helm !
        (*Crosses, and exit dancing into cabaret R.*)

Mor.   Ha, ha, ha, a queer sailor, poor Poppleton !
                                        (*Going.*)

Enter BERTRAND *L.H.*

Bert.   I cannot find Antonio ; I must seek—ah, Mortimer !

Mor.   My dear Doctor !

Bert.   This, excellent Mortimer ? ah, je respire ; vous venez à point ! what you call the nick of time !

Mor.   Yes, my dear Doctor, here I am, as you

see ; but I'll be hanged if I know what I'm sent here for ; your letter was rather unintelligible to General Maitland and myself.

BERT. Eh, eh ! that is my principle ; it is best ever to write so as nobody shall read you, then there can be no mistakes.

MOR. Well, you'll explain now, I hope ? I know this much, that, owing to the gratitude of the boat-man Antonio (whose life you saved in a fever), you have been put in possession of the treacherous corre-spondence between the French General Maitres and those scoundrels, Fillippi and St. Clair.

BERT. Justement !

MOR. And that Maitres's agent is hourly expected to give and receive the signatures on each side, to the agreement to deliver Messina and the Flotilla into Maitres's hands.

BERT. C'est çà ! here is the last intercepted letter containing some trifling details. (*Giving letter.*)

MOR. What's this ? (*Reading.*) " And in case of resistance to massacre the English officers." The bloodthirsty scoundrels !

BERT. (*taking snuff*). Eh, eh !

MOR. Trifling details ; you take it coolly, Doctor !

BERT. Que voulez-vous? these are accidents that will arrive in the best-conducted revolutions.

MOR. Trifling details! The villains! Why, sir, I've several near relations in the little garrison here!

BERT. Allons donc! I think I am more nearly interested in the matter than you.

MOR. You! how so?

BERT. Diable! am I not their Doctor? Do I not physic the whole garrison? Kill my patients indeed! Is it to take away my professional privileges?

MOR. Well, what have you decided on doing? The rascals! I long to be at them!

BERT. Doucement, doucement! we must work like the mole, and until your Lord William Bentwick returns with the full power from England, what can you do against these Coquins?

MOR. True, true—hang it!

(*Walking about uneasily.*)

BERT. We can use nothing but *Finesse*—finesse— eh, eh?

MOR. Yes, yes, true; finesse is the thing; well, let me see, suppose I bombard the Citadel and send it rattling about their d—d ears, eh?

BERT. Jolie finesse ! 'tis a nice quiet operation, with Murat's ships within hearing !

MOR. Hang it ! well, then, suppose I send some of my blue-jackets to seize on these rascals and string 'em up to the yard-arm, eh ?

BERT. Allez vous promener with your blue-jackets; where is your authority to seize Italian subjects ? il est bête à manger du foin !

MOR. What do you propose, then ? This fellow's arrival will betray your deception, and the most important document, the signed agreement, will escape your hands.

BERT. Ah, ah ! vous croyez ! now comes my chef-d'œuvre ! Listen, I have employed some friends in Malta to send to me a young man to personate the spy D'Arblay—height, complexion, all is similar; the veritable spy is to arrive *to-morrow*. We have advanced the date by a day, and the false spy, mock D'Arblay, is even now *here*, about to enter this nest of conspirators and put the proofs we want into my hands. Hein ! said I not the old Bertrand had a head ?

MOR. Very ingenious; but what part am I to play ?

BERT. Send a boat at nine o'clock this evening

to that little landing-place, la Cas, under the high cliff.

Mor. The cliff on which the Baron Freitenhorsen's château stands?

Bert. Justement!

Mor. But that is within the guarded lines of Messina; the difficulty will be to get him there; and where will you conceal him in the meantime?

Bert. Eh, eh! here comes the *comique* of my drama. In broad daylight shall my good friend, this excellent Baron Freitenhorsen, convey my false spy, my mock D'Arblay, to his château.

Mor. Why, Bertrand, you have not trusted that maniac with the secret? and he a member of the council, and a devoted slave of the Neapolitan Queen?

Bert. Soyez tranquille! It is already a long time I have promise to give the Baron a splendid Egyptian mummy; he is to be fetched from my house to-day,—you comprehend what the case will really contain?

Mor. Ah! what?—this young fellow?

Bert. Justement! and also a light rope ladder; the case will be lock in the apartment of de Baron till I come; the window is but thirty feet from the

ground, and there is a subterraneous staircase leading
to the shore, donnez la clef at de bottom ; he find
your boat—here is the key.   (*Gives key.*)

MOR.   Well, my part's simple enough ; my boat
shall be there at the hour you name.

BERT.   This, excellent Mortimer ! it is late ; the
fishermen are collecting here ; join me soon at my
lodging, and remember—de la finesse ! de la finesse !

(*Exit L.H. or E.*)

MORTIMER (*solus*).

MOR.   Hum ! *finesse !*   I don't half like this
business ; here's this young fellow, one knows nothing
about, going in the guise of a game pie into the
house my dear giddy Laura inhabits.   It's just as well
she knows nothing about it ; she's so deuced romantic ;
and it's a novel position for making acquaintances.
Well, he won't be long there, for his own sake ; that's
one comfort.   I've time for one peep of her sweet face
before my visit to the Commandant, and I must make
the most of it.   (*Exit R.U.E.*)

Enter POPPLETON, CATERINA, *Fishermen sit laughing
and dancing U.E.R.*

POP. (*tipsy*).   Yes, my dear, you're right ;. I am a
jolly British tar, and no mistake.

CAT.   Ah, you—capitaine of ship ?

POP.   Captain—no, not exactly captain.   The
captain has a good deal of work to do, and I—I—see
that he does it, you know !

CAT.   Ah ! you Admiral ?

POP.   Well, no, not precisely admiral.   The fact
is, I'm sent to look after the admirals ; they're a lot of
giddy young fellows—always getting into mischief.
Well, now for another, what do you call 'em, tara-
diddle ?

CAT.   Tarantella ! tarantella !

(POPPLETON *and* CATERINA *dance a grotesque
Tarantella, during which* JULES *comes down
from cabaret R.H.*)

JULES.   No signs of Antonio and the promised pass !

POP.   Hilloah, messmate ! what cheer ?

JULES.   Sir !

POP.   Well, I said, "what cheer" ; don't you know
what that means, brother tar ?

JULES. Indeed, sir, I was not aware of the honour!

POP. Oh yes! brother tars we are; *my* name's Poppleton of the *Vigilant*; yours is——

JULES. Nameless of the *Inquisitive*.

POP. Hum! proud chap! (*Dancing up to* CATERINA, *dancing down to* JULES.) No offence, sir?

JULES. None, sir.

POP. We're keeping it up, you see; no offence?

JULES. I wasn't running you down, sir!

POP. (*dancing down to* JULES). No blame attaches to innocent mirth, I believe, sir!

JULES. I wasn't accusing your innocence, or objecting to your mirth.

POP. (*dancing down*). The bow can't always be bent, sir!

JULES. Pray unbend as much as you please, sir!

POP. (*testily*). I say, sir, one ought to know how to " desipere in loco."

JULES (*impatiently*). Once for all, sir, play the fool when and where you please, but allow me the liberty of my own thoughts. Deuce take the tipsy fellow, he seems resolved to quarrel! What can delay Antonio? (*Turns up the stage.*)

Y

(*Row amongst the Boatmen,* POPPLETON *noisy,*
kisses CATERINA.)

BOATMEN. Ah, Corpo di bacco—e mia moglie.
(*Points to* CATERINA.)

POP. Your Molly? stuff and nonsense,—she's my
partner; stand out of the way, young man.

(*Increased noise and quarrelling. Enter Military*
Police R.H. POPPLETON *carried off L.H.,*
struggling and protesting, his coat torn off his
back; he drops his pocket-book.)

JULES (*solus*). Stop! Hilloah! that tipsy fellow
has dropped his pocket-book! Stay! papers—here's
the young fool's pass,—"John Poppleton," passenger
H.M.S. *Vigilant*. I'll make bold with this for an
hour or so; every moment's delay is dangerous; once
in the Commandant's office, I can easily explain to
the conspirators by what means I passed the lines.

(*Exit.*)

(POP. *runs across from L. to R., followed by*
Soldiers, Fishermen, etc. etc.)

CURTAIN.

ACT II

Scene I

A room in the Baron's Villa.
The Baroness at her toilette—Bobbin assisting, Laura working.

BARONESS. There, there, Bobbin, don't worry with that brush. (*To* LAURA.) It's no use arguing, Laura! you know how contradiction disagrees with my sensitive nature. If you choose to disobey me, and marry your odious sea captain, not a shilling of your fortune shall go with you!

LAU. Well, aunt, I'm as firmly resolved not to reward poor Mortimer's disinterested affection by entailing poverty upon him, as I am determined not to marry that coxcomb, Count Fillippi! so it's a drawn game between us!

BOB. Bless her little 'art; she speaks like any almanac.

BARONESS. Bobbin!

BOB. Yes, mem! I took the liberty of blessin' her little 'art, if you've no petticular objection.

BARONESS. Be silent! (*To* LAURA.) I wonder at your folly, Laura; such a fine young man as the Count is! All your friends desirous of the match! The Queen of Naples gracious enough to interest herself about it (as our friend Mr. St. Clair informs me)! Your uncle the Baron advising it, and you, silly girl, the only one averse to it.

LAU. Really, aunt, it is hard I should be subject to the will of people to whom I owe no duty. The Queen of Naples is no judge of my affairs. Mr. St. Clair is an impertinent meddler in them; and as for the Baron, your husband, if my poor uncle had ever contemplated your own second marriage with a foreigner, he would not have left my little fortune dependent on your consent to mine.

BARONESS. Silly child! One would think it was cruel tyranny on my part to marry you to a good-looking young man, with high birth, Court favour, every recommendation except riches, and your fortune will supply the want. Why, there's nothing Count Fillippi might not pretend to!

LAU. I'm far from setting any limit to his *pretensions*, I'm sure!

BARONESS. Well, he'll be here in course of the day to plead his own cause, and I expect you to receive him discreetly as the person selected for your future husband.

LAU. As your guest, but nothing more. If I can't marry the man I love, I mean to live and die an old maid.

BARONESS. Well, my dear, perhaps a single life will be best for your happiness. There are drawbacks on connubial bliss, even in the best assorted marriages —heigho! (*sighs*).

LAU. Now, there, aunt,—if you ain't happy with the Baron, whom you married for love, can I be otherwise than wretched with a man whom I positively detest? Do consider my feelings.

BARONESS. *Feelings*, indeed, at your age! Don't presume, child, to set up feelings till you're forty. I shan't allow it! When a woman arrives at years of discretion (say forty-five, or perhaps *fifty*), she may listen to the tender promptings of her nature, but not till then, miss, not till then!

LAU. Forty-five or fifty?

BARONESS. And even then, alas! she may find she has lavished the hoarded honey of her heart upon some—individual, incapable of any adequate return.

LAU. And so, because you have put out your own heart at bad interest, you mean to make a "sinking fund" of mine?

BOB. What say you to a *tontine*, Miss? and the oldest inhabitant of the parish to get it at last?

BARONESS. Bobbin! don't presume upon my indulgent temper! you have a tongue that——

BOB. (*rapidly*). Yes, mem, thank Heaven! and it's well poor women has such resources within themselves, or what *we* should do in this mouldy old house, without a Christian soul to speak to except foreign*eers*, I'm sure I don't know! I declare I'm thankful when I'm startled by one of them blow-ups in Master's Labatory, when he's making his comical experiments! —'tis such a comfort to hear one's self scream—in English!

BARONESS. Bobbin!

BOB. (*rapidly*). For my part, I wish he would blow the house up, and have done with it (*aside*—and he's guy enough to blow anything up). But, la!

it's no use wishing; we shall never see poor, dear Bloomsbury Square again. And to think that Martha Bobbin should live to be buried among blue-bearded, macaroni-munching foreign*eers*!

BARONESS. Bobbin! (*To* LAURA.) You see, Laura, my impulsive disposition and sweet susceptible temper render it a difficult matter to make me happy—but you——

LAU. As to that, aunt, I can be quite as *susceptible* as my neighbours when necessary.

BOB. (*soliloquising*). Ah! I had a third cousin married to a foreign*eer*—poor thing!—a courier; *they* were always having rumpuses; and one fine day she was found dead in her bed with two black eyes and ever so many ribs broken!

LAU. And *you*, aunt, who have shown such disinterested romance in your own marriage, surely might have some sympathy for me!

BARONESS. Not at all, my dear! as I am such a creature of impulse in everything concerning my passions, I make it a point of conscience to study only my interest and convenience in other people's affairs. Heigho! giddy and guileless as I am, I have learnt some prudence.

LAU. A very vicarious sort it appears.

BOB. Ah! my grandmother's second husband's niece died of a broken heart, disappointed of her first infections, and married to a grocer as she despised, which it was to an Italian warehouse he belonged.

BARONESS. Bobbin! Moreover, Laura, even I might be happy here, if the exquisite refinement of my nature did not suggest little jealous doubts—little delicate suspicions of my beloved Baron's constancy.

LAU. Jealous! really, ma'am, when a man is near *sixty*.

BOB. Ah! Miss, little you know! My second cousin once removed was married to a helderly hair-dresser, quite a respectable man, who died of drinking, and then was discovered five other wives, all living, with large and small families, and no suspicions of the truth!—ah! *he* was a foreign*eer*!

LAU. (*laughing*). Why, Bobbin! your family seems to have been nearly as unlucky as Agamemnon's, and quite as ill-behaved!

BOB. Aggy—— who, Miss?

LAU. Agamemnon.

BOB. Ah, indeed! I shouldn't wonder! A *foreigneer*, of course, by the name.

BARONESS (*aside*). I sometimes fancy that Bobbin means more than her words seem to imply. If I could bribe her to watch the Baron! Hush! here he comes! Ah, Laura! what a forehead that is! how like the brow of Bacon!

Enter the BARON, *lost in thought.*

BOB. (*aside*). Uncommon like a pig's face!

BARONESS. Sir Isaac Newton must have had such eyes as those.

BOB. (*aside*). Then that 'ere Barrownight squinted preciously!

BARONESS. Laura, my dear, do you see a look of Socrates in the Baron?

LAU. What, the Philosopher with the jealous scolding wife, aunt?

BOB. Hum! I do see a likeness about the—the wife!

BARON (*aside*). Yes, Bertrand may assist me! (*Sits.*)

BARONESS. My love! I say, my dear Baron! How absent he is! But watch, now, how he will rouse himself if I touch on his favourite pursuits; he'll brighten like the polar star, new risen!

Bob. (*aside*).   A deal more like a pewter spoon, new rubbed!

Baroness.   My love, what was that you were saying of our bodies being made of air? Laura, attend—such a curious fact; we are all sylphs together!

Baron.   Aye, aye, we are but *spirits*—suffered to appear.

Bob. (*aside*).   And I wonder *it is* suffered. I'd have you locked up, you old goose!

Baron.   These, our outward semblances, are but tabernacles of condensed air.

Bob.   Ah, make me believe that 'ere! (*aside*).

Baron.   Our very garments are but forms of the same ethereal material.

Bob. (*aside, brushing clothes*).   Ah, I wish you had the cleaning of 'em!

Baron.   Has Dr. Bertrand yet called here?

Bob.   That 'ere tabernacle has been kicking his heels in Master's study this hour!

Baron.   Triflers! why was I not told of his visit?   I waste precious moments with you.

(*Exit hastily.*)

Baroness.   There, another secret interview; what can their conferences relate to? (*To* Bobbin.) Bobbin, follow me to my room. I feel an impulse to confide in her. (*Exit.*)

BOB. I say, Miss! (BARONESS *calls* "BOBBIN.")

BOB. Coming, ma'am! Oh, Miss, such a piece of news—— The *Vigilant's* come into harbour!

LAU. Oh, Bobbin, you don't say so?

BOB. Yes, indeed; and—eh, bless me! what's more, if there ain't the captain hisself a-coming up the Terrace walk!

LAU. Oh, you dear Bobbin! run, run, and bring him in. Ah! he's here!

Enter MORTIMER.

LAU. (*coldly*). Dear me, is that you, Captain Mortimer?

MOR. My own Laura!

BOB. (*mimicking*). "Is that *you*, Captain Mortimer?" the little deceitful hussy! It was "Oh, you dear Bobbin!" just now at the idea of his coming!

(BARONESS *calls* "BOBBIN.")

BOB. Coming, mem! (*Exit.*)

MOR. My beloved Laura! this moment makes

amends for the weary months I have been absent from you! to find you well! and constant?

LAU. Oh, constant enough, my dear Mortimer; in this solitude, you know, I have very little opportunity to be otherwise.

MOR. Opportunity! my dear girl, I see you haven't lost your merry mocking ways; you still like to tease your poor Mortimer.

LAU. No, no; but now, seriously,—suppose I do desire a little variety in our society in this dull place, it is more on your account than my own.

MOR. On *my* account, my love?—what, in my absence?

LAU. Yes, dear; it must be so annoying to you to have no means of putting my attachment to the test. For my part, I often sigh for an occasion of proving to you that amidst a thousand admirers I should still like you *the best*.

MOR. Well, my dear, that's very considerate of you; but, really, *I've* no wish of the sort.

LAU. No? that *is* surprising; why, you must be aware that any little harmless coquetry on my part would be exercised solely with a view to your happiness.

Mor. Well, I declare, it never struck me in that light.

Lau. Of course, I should flirt with them merely to prove that I preferred *you*.

Mor. In short, I am to consider every smile you bestow on a rival a personal compliment to myself?

Lau. Exactly so.

Mor. My dear girl, you are very kind; but, you see, I'm a plain-spoken sort of fellow, and I own I prefer a less *roundabout* method of expressing your attachment. But come, we won't speculate on these matters; I'm so anxious to hear if you've made any progress in gaining your aunt's consent to our marriage?

Lau. Not the least! She listens to no one but that horrid Mr. St. Clair; and they are bent on bestowing me and my little fortune on that odious Count Fillippi.

Mor. But have you reasoned with her?

Lau. Oh! it's " Diamond cut diamond " where two women argue; as we both talk at once to ensure having the last word, we neither of us benefit much by the other's logic.

Mor. Ah, Laura, if you would but let me claim

this dear hand irrespectively of her caprice! What is fortune in comparison with mutual love?

LAU. Nothing; but it makes a very pleasant addition; so we must still trust to time, and the chapter of accidents.

MOR. Well, well! And your new uncle the Baron?

LAU. Don't call him my uncle—my *aunt's husband*, if you please.

MOR. What could have induced that preposterous marriage?

LAU. Oh! Mr. St. Clair, who has constituted himself solicitor-general for the whole community! My aunt's romantic nature caught fire directly. But the Baron had all his wooing done for him—found himself married one morning, and has already forgotten the circumstance!

MOR. If you appealed to him——

LAU. Appeal to *him!* I might as well appeal to the thermometer, or expect sympathy from an air-pump!

MOR. I hear he is engaged in discovering the Philosopher's stone.

LAU. Quite cracked,—so are the windows! We

have an explosion once a week upon an average, and all aunt's fortune is going in sulphates and sodas!

MOR. Strange infatuation!

LAU. Strange indeed! and that Mr. St. Clair encourages him in all his vagaries.

MOR. The rascal!

LAU. Oh, *your* dear friend Dr. Bertrand is quite as bad! They're always closeted together, and a brisk interchange going on of invaluable rubbish. Pompeian pots and pans, rusty nails, fossil bones, and Roman brickbats!

MOR. Ha, ha, ha! very interesting.

LAU. Oh, by the bye, we're not so entirely at a loss for society as I said; we're expecting rather a distinguished visitor to-day.

MOR. A visitor?

LAU. Guess!

MOR. Oh, I'm a bad hand at riddles.

LAU. A Pharaoh! nothing less—a magnificent Egyptian mummy,—a present from the Doctor. Bobbin and I are in such a state of excitement! You know, in our present solitary condition, a mummy is quite an acquisition to the domestic circle!

MOR. (*aside*). Ah! I thought how it would be!

What a nose a woman has for a secret! If there *is* a thing you don't want them to know, they smell it out a mile off! (*Aloud.*) Ha, ha, ha! very ridiculous of Bobbin—silly creature—very natural; but *you*, my love, of course have no vulgar curiosity on the subject?

LAU. Vulgar curiosity! why, of course I have! I never saw one before!

MOR. True, my love, but to a person of your refined delicacy, a sight of that nature——

LAU. Refined delicacy! what has that to do with the matter?

MOR. Consider, my dear girl, this—this mummy fellow—is—in fact—hem—a deceased Egyptian; you wouldn't surely wish to—what do we know about him? I daresay he was some low fellow——

LAU. Ha, ha, ha! well, if I do pay him a visit, the intimacy can't make much progress, for he'll hardly *rise* on my entrance; but who knows, he may have been one of Pharaoh's lords-in-waiting.

MOR. Yes, of course, ha, ha! you are so amusing, my dear Laura. But seriously, my love, my feelings are so sensitive on the subject of feminine reserve, perhaps to a fault—that—that—really I can't bear the idea of your exposing yourself to the shock of seeing this—deceased Egyptian gentleman, especially as—the fact is—I have just heard the plague is particularly prevalent just now at Grand Cairo; and—in short, my love, you'll oblige me by not running such a risk. (*Aside*.) I'd no idea lying was so easy!

Lau. Ha, ha, ha! how very ridiculous! Why, you'd almost make one think this dried fossil of a man was a rival in flesh and blood. Now confess, you jealous wretch, you *are* a little afraid of his attractions!

Mor. (*aside*). Hang it, she's on the scent. Truffle dogs are nothing to women. (*Aloud*.) Jealous, my dear Laura, what nonsense; but your precious health, my dear,—your precious health!

Lau. Well, well, I'll be good. But it's hard to be denied one's Christian liberty of sight-seeing.

Enter Bobbin *hastily*.

Bob. Here's your uncle and Dr. Bertrand coming, Miss.

Lau. Go, go, my dear Mortimer! you may as well avoid his eye at present.

z

Mor. But I must see you again before I go this evening! My own Laura, you won't refuse me!

Lau. Yes, yes, this evening—when you like—ten o'clock—be on the Terrace—Bobbin will bring you in.

(*Exit* Laura C., Bobbin *pushing the* Captain *out.*)

Enter Baron *and* Bertrand.

Baron. This way, this way! here we shall be private; but first to make that certain (*locks the door*). Now, my dear Doctor, my dear friend (*brings chairs*), I will explain the nature of my astonishing discovery.

(*They sit.* Bertrand *takes out snuff-box.*) My dear friend, you do not believe in the perfectibility of man?

Bert. Eh, eh! is *that* your discovery?

Baron. Have patience! You think the present term of mortal existence too short for that purpose? But, Bertrand, when I tell you my life-long labours have been crowned with success; that I have the certain means of prolonging life indefinitely; that I have at last discovered the real *Elixir Vitæ;* what do you reply?

BERT. My dear Baron, I shall have the pleasure of drinking your good health in it.

BARON. That is not all! the most wonderful circumstance remains to be told; not only will it arrest life on the lips of the dying—but—(hist, Bertrand!) *it will bring the dead to life if administered within twenty-four hours of decease!*

(*A solemn pause.*)

BERT. Ah! ah! (*takes snuff*).

BARON. You do not seem so overwhelmed with astonishment as I expected.

BERT. Si fait! si fait! but I have a peculiar temperament; a sudden surprise affects me—gradually; I am very much startled, by *degrees!*

BARON. I see you are incredulous of its powers?

BERT. Pardon! if your dead man will only drink your potion I do not doubt its effect! In these matters, il n'y a que le premier pas qui coûte!

BARON. It is a remedy independent of all action on the part of the subject acted on. And now, think, my friend, what a glorious future lies before us! No more sorrow, nor sin, nor suffering! no more plodding in the vicious circle of mortal existence! Man shall no longer come into the world a wailing infant, to struggle through the same trials, fall into the same snares, mourn with the same vain repentance, and die of the same diseases as his fathers have done before him! No, there shall be an end of these things! First, *marriage* shall be done away with!

BERT. Diable!

BARON. Secondly, *births* shall be put a stop to!

BERT. Sapristi!

BARON. There shall be no more children, no more raw recruits in Life's Battalion! No; the virtuous and the learned shall alone be singled out from the common herd, and, by means of this elixir, preserved like precious *gems* from generation to generation, till (they alone remaining) a second golden age shall beam upon the renovated earth!

BERT. Only the virtuous and the learned! vous serez à l'aise! You will have elbow-room in your renovated earth.

BARON. But will not these be the inevitable results of my wondrous discovery?

BERT. My dear Baron, *en attendant* his perfectibility, man is so prejudiced I fear there will still be marriages and wailing infants and precious *fools* handed down from generation to generation in spite of your elixir! Have you made proof of its virtues?

BARON. I tried it on two sick persons—but, ah, Doctor! you are right, there *is* so much prejudice among men!

BERT. Ah, true! such an inveterate habit of dying!

BARON. So much obstinacy!

BERT. Such a want of *savoir vivre!*

BARON. It had no fair trial. But no matter; let the proof rest rather on its highest, most wondrous property, where there will be neither the prejudice of the sick nor the ignorance of the attendants to contend against; and here, my friend, *here* you can render me the most valuable assistance!

BERT. Voyons!

BARON. During two months that I have possessed this miraculous remedy, I have never been fortunate enough to lose either friend or relative, by disease or accident!

BERT. Ah, that is melancholy! It was enough to provoke an ardent Philosopher like you to *correct* fortune in that respect!

BARON. Yes, yes! I understand you—yes—to—

in fact to extinguish some existence that I may have the glory of restoring it. Ah, my friend, if I could find some one devoted enough to the cause of science as to submit to a temporary deprivation—eh? The simplest operation! a mere nothing—eh? Yes, believe me, *you* were the first person who occurred to me!

BERT. Ah, diable! (*Aside.*) Et il en serait capable! (*Aloud.*) My dear Baron, the preference is flattering; but, with my professional engagements, even a little temporary deprivation of life would be incommode.

BARON. Then again I thought of my wife——

BERT. A la bonne heure! Little services may be required of each other en famille——

BARON. But there were objections——

BERT. Ah, c'est beau! That is so fine (*patting him on the breast*), quelle délicatesse! You would not put yourself in a situation of so *great temptation?*

BARON. Eh? temptation?

BERT. To leave the operation *imperfect!* Yes, yes! I comprehend, I applaud you, this excellent Baron! But come, without resorting to the extreme measures, I can be of service to you on certain conditions.

BARON. My *dear* friend, only name them ! I ask but an opportunity of proving the value of my inestimable discovery !

BERT. Of course you require secrecy ?

BARON. It is of vital importance ; therefore have I confided in *you* alone !

BERT. You have done wisely. (*Aside.*) This excellent friend—he plays into my hand. (*Aloud.*) I have at my lodgings a *subject*—vous comprenez ?

BARON (*eagerly*). For anatomical purposes ? I see—yes ! and you cede it to me for this noble end ? Ah, my friend, this *is* a service ! But how your elevated soul will rejoice in the result ! Think of the glory to science—the advantage to society !

BERT. Hem ! The advantage to society is problematique ; the *subject* was not a patient of mine but of *justice*—he was hanged !

BARON. Hanged ! good heavens ! what for ?

BERT. (*taking snuff*). Eh, eh ! que sais-je, some little matter of highway robbery !

BARON. Highway robbery ! gracious powers ! a felon !

BERT. Que diable ! you did not expect to find *Archbishops* on my dissecting table ?

BARON. No, no, of course! But—highway robbery!—to be sure we don't know *the circumstances*.

BERT. Very true; no doubt there were faults on *both* sides.

BARON. We should be slow to condemn a fellow-creature unheard!

BERT. Sans doute; perhaps he acted from the best of motives. So you need feel no pedantic scruple in restoring this poor gentleman to a society that has taken such énergique measures to terminate the connection?

BARON. Dr. Bertrand, science is my idol! Every consideration gives way to the grave duties her worship imposes,—yes! I accept the responsibility; it will be an added glory! I will protect the renascent being from the assaults of temptation! I will lead his feet in the path of virtue; he shall be a *son* unto me!

BERT. Of course! au fait! any little error in his past career renders him the fitter subject for your Theorie of Perfectibility. He will be one of your "*gems*"—a shining ornament of your "Golden age." And now to arrange this affair with the secrecy we *both* desire.

BARON. True, true, my friend; how is this to be done?

BERT. The means are simple; to-day you were to have conveyed from my house the Egyptian mummy you desired to possess.

BARON. Ah, I see! An admirable plan; the case will contain——

BERT. The subject of our conversation. In your care, it will not be opened at the gates of the city, so the secret is safe. And now for my condition——

BARON. Ah! true—the condition!

BERT. My dear Baron, you know I am a Philosopher—un peu Voltairien! I believe what I *see* (more or less); you must allow me to administer your Elixir *with my own hands*, in your presence, soit; but at a certain distance! Eh, eh! you are too clever a chymist. There must be no galvanic tricks played upon your simple old friend!

BARON. Agreed! agreed!

BERT. How many hours are necessary for the effect?

BARON. Ten at the utmost.

BERT. Come to my house in half an hour. I

will try your experiment ; you shall yourself carry off the precious deposit, and at ten to-night I will be with you to test *together* the value of your discovery.

BARON. By that hour the labour of a life will be crowned with immortal success !

BERT. (*aside*). By that hour the good lad will be safe on board the *Vigilant*.   (*Exeunt.*)

SCENE II

The Town Mayor's Office in Messina.

MORTIMER, ST. CLAIR, *and* FILLIPPI, *rising and coming forward.*

MOR. Well, gentlemen, as the letter of which I am bearer contains details of the causes for complaint on General Maitland's part, I shall no longer detain you from its perusal. I can only hope that the explanations it demands, and which, no doubt, you are prepared to give, may prove satisfactory to the English Government.

ST. C. The efforts of the Sicilian Court are directed solely to that end ; your General will soon receive satisfaction in full.

FILLIP. Of all demands! the conversation assumes quite a commercial turn—he, he! The fact is, my dear sir, our debt of gratitude to your country is so heavy that we young spendthrifts can hardly give you a *Bill at sight;* but we shall pay you off soon; never doubt it!

MOR. And, no doubt, in coin as good—as your word. (*Aside.*) Scoundrels! (*Aloud.*) Am I to have the honour of bearing your despatch to the General?

ST. C. His letter contains propositions which must be laid before the council. Will your stay in Messina be of any duration, Captain Mortimer?

MOR. I sail by daybreak to-morrow for Palermo. If your despatch should be ready, I will call for it on my way to the Port at eleven o'clock to-night.

FILLIP. It shall be ready.

MOR. Gentlemen, I take my leave till then.

(*A noise at door. Enter Military Police with* CATERINA, *Fishermen, and* POPPLETON *tipsy, struggling and vociferating; he is without hat or coat; they let him go at* ST. CLAIR'S *sign.*)

POP. Come on, you dogs! one at a time, you cowards! and I'll let you know the weight of a British sailor's fist!

FILLIP. (*to* ST. C. *aside*). *British sailor!* Did you hear?

POP. Shiver my lee scuppers, if I don't! (*Sees* MORTIMER—*aside.*) Why, that looks like Captain Mort—mer! he, he! indeed I might say *two* Captain Mort—mers! ah! he, he! He was always *too many for me!* He mustn't see me, though; he'd be fancying I wasn't quite so—ber!

  (*Puts on* CATERINA'S *cap and endeavours to hide his face.*)

FILLIP. (*aside to* ST. C.) This must be our man! He avoids the Englishman's eye. Feigning intoxication, evidently.

ST. C. It would seem so! but, caution! he feigns uncommonly well.

(FILLIPPI *dismisses Police, Fishermen, and* CATERINA.)

MOR. (*aside*). Soh! Poppleton, steering very "*middling, by so-so,*" and a sheet in the wind already!

ST. C. (*getting between* MOR. *and* POP.) Well, Captain Mortimer! we mustn't detain you; no doubt your time is precious.

FILLIP. (*nudging* POP.) Be upon your guard.

POP. Eh? oh!

MOR. (*aside*). I thought it wouldn't be long

before he got into a scrape! He shall fight his own way out of it!

FILLIP. (*getting between* MOR. *and* POP.) Beautiful day, Captain Mortimer. My horses are at your disposal,—a ride in the country, perhaps?

ST. C. (*nudging* POP.—*aside*). Be cautious! he suspects you!

POP. Eh?—ah! I shouldn't wonder!

MOR. Well, gentlemen, good day! I thought for a moment that that gentleman in the light summer costume was an acquaintance!

FILLIP. Ah! indeed! curious, these resemblances! This gentleman is—ahem! a cousin of mine!

POP. (*aside*). Dear me! this is a friend in need, and with a most convenient talent for lying. (*Aloud to* CAPTAIN MORTIMER.) Did you mean me, sir? My name's Thompson, sir, at your service.

MOR. (*aside*). Upon my word, he's been "boxing his conscience" to some purpose! (*Aloud.*) Indeed, sir? a remarkable name for an Italian family!

POP. Very common here, sir! Thompsono dei Thompsoni! Eh, cousin?

MOR. No doubt; once more, farewell, gentlemen! Your servant, Signor Thompsono dei Thompsoni.

> (*Exit.* St. Clair *and* Fillippi *bow him out,*
> *then come on each side of* Poppleton.)

Pop. Remarkably friendly people! My dear fellows, you managed it cleverly. I was afraid at one moment he was going to smoke me; and that wouldn't have done at all—he, he! would it?

St. C. No, no! but now to business,—"*You have been long expected.*"

Pop. Well, sir, I hope I answer your expectations; but really I must object to your method of making acquaintances! Of course, I'm delighted to know you, but my coat needn't have been torn off my back in the process of introduction.

St. C. Come, come, sir! time presses. Have you——   (*Makes signs.*)

Fillip. We're quite alone, you see. Are the——   (*Makes signs.*)

Pop. I hope, gentlemen, you understand one another; otherwise here's a deal of fine conversation thrown away!

St. C. Pshaw! (*Aside.*) We're on the wrong scent, Fillippi!

FILLIP. (*aside*). By Bacchus! I'm afraid so! Well, he mustn't suspect. (*Aloud.*) A stranger, sir, I presume? You must taste our Marsala.

(*Retires up with* POPPLETON *to table.*)

ST. C. He's had enough already! I ought to have guessed that monkey couldn't be the man. Strange, that D'Arblay should linger thus!

(*Servant announces* Mr. JOHN POPPLETON.)

Enter JULES.

POP. (*drops his glass*). What's that?

FILLIP. The gentleman gave the name of John Poppleton.

POP. Oh! you call that *giving?* I call it *taking,* damme! (*To* JULES.) Why, you impudent rascal, if——

JULES. These papers, gentlemen, will explain my business with you—here also is my passport.

(*Gives* POPPLETON'S *pocket-book.*)

POP. The devil! my pocket-book, as I live!

ST. C. (*aside to* FILLIP.) The description tallies exactly—try the password.

FILLIP. *You have been long expected!*

JULES (*aside to* FILLIP.) "Sicily and Independence."

FILLIP. All's right. (*To* ST. C. *aside.*) This is our man——

POP. You impudent thief!

> (*Endeavours to collar* JULES. FILLIP. *and* ST. C. *prevent him.*)

ST. C. Come, come, young man, none of your drunken roistering here!

POP. I say, sir, *my* name's John Poppleton, and that's my passport,—this fellow's a cursed impostor!

FILLIP. You forget, Signor Thompsoni,—you were a cousin of mine just now!

POP. Oh, hang your relationship! It's the infernalist, coolest—— (*To* JULES.) I say you, sir, is there anything else of mine you've taken a fancy to? Don't be shy, you know.

JULES. You are very liberal, sir, but you don't seem to me to have much you could conveniently part with, at present, if I may judge from your costume.

POP. I won't stand this!—I'll——

ST. C. We can't have this tipsy fellow vapouring here all day. Come, sir, who are you? Account for yourself, or you must go to the guard-house.

POP. Don't I tell you—*that's my passport!*

ST. C. Nonsense, that belongs to Mr. John

Poppleton, yonder. It is for a single person; and though *you* may see it double, *we* don't! Consider yourself in custody, sir! (*They retire up talking.*)

POP. (*sinks on a chair*). Ah! my poor head! (*Laughs hysterically.*) Hi, hi, hi! rather a good idea! *My* poor head—as if I had a head, or anything else of my own! If it wouldn't be considered inquisitive, I should like to know who I am? But of course it doesn't signify! (JULES *comes down C.*) So, there he is—I mean there I am—(I'm getting a little muzzy); perhaps it will be safer to say, here *we* are! (*To* JULES.) I beg pardon, sir, but, if convenient, I should like to say a few words.

JULES. Well, sir?

POP. (*very drunk*). I feel a conviction, sir—I say, a profound *conviction*, that I am John Poppleton; appearances may be against me—but, I say, sir, that I cannot divest myself of that idea.

JULES. Come to the point, sir.

POP. I *am* coming to the point, sir. Well, sir, by the inscrutable decrees of this tribunal, it appears that you have succeeded to the titles and estates of the aforesaid—what's his name?—ah—John Poppleton (I shall forget my own name presently).

2 A

JULES.　You are wasting time, sir!

POP.　Don't think, my dear fellow, that I bear you any grudge; it isn't *your* fault, you know, that you are—me—and that—I am somebody else! No, no! I mean that you are—yourself, and that I'm nobody in particular. But since you *are* John Poppleton, Esq., please to do the name honour; don't let me hear of your disgracing yourself; I'll be hanged if I stand that. Above all, avoid drunkenness, my dear boy; it's a vice that brings a man to—all sorts of things—for instance, "the silent tomb!" I myself am about to enter the "silent tomb,"—an individual without a friend—or a name—or a coat (*weeps*), is best out of the way! I only ask that a plain stone may be put up to my memory—in the nearest Parish Church; no name in particular inscribed, and no questions asked. And some time, when you happen to go that way, you'll oblige me by dropping a tear—— Good-night, sir—I wish you a very good night——

(*Drops asleep with his head on table.*)

JULES.　Ha, ha! poor fellow! I'm afraid, gentlemen, we've been rather hard upon him,—but there was no other way to manage. What had we best do with him now?

Sᴛ. C. He'll be safe here, locked in—mustn't be let out till this evening, or he'll talk, and perhaps raise suspicions. But, my dear Fillippi, what the deuce made you claim cousins with him in Mortimer's presence ?

Fɪʟʟɪᴘ. You know we mistook him at first for this gentleman, and seeing Captain Mortimer's attention attracted to him, I thought a little proof was necessary to——

Sᴛ. C. Now, that's where you're always at fault ! Yours is such an impetuous, hand-over-head style of lying !

Jᴜʟᴇs. You forget, sir, that the Count was drawing on his *own* resources ; and, under those circumstances, a little off-hand prodigality is not amiss in youth.

Sᴛ. C. True, that makes a difference ; it certainly makes a difference ! This way, Mons. D'Arblay—this way !   (*Exeunt.*)

Scene III

Doctor Bertrand's lodgings in Messina.
Mortimer sitting at table; Bertrand walking about uneasily.

BERT. And you are *sure* it was your Mons. Poppleton?

MOR. My dear Doctor, I'm not blind! It was Poppleton—and rather more than half-seas over. I mean to leave him to his own devices; he's pretty sure to end in the guard-house!

BERT. And no one else there?

MOR. Not a soul. The curious part of the thing is, that they were hovering about him like a couple of old hens with a sick gosling, claiming relationship— and——

BERT. (*not listening*). Ah! sapristi! I would this hour were over—no sign of this young Jules?

MOR. Ah, Doctor, you'll have to come to my stupid, straightforward ways after all. I was devilish near calling them "*scoundrels*" to their faces just now. "Speak truth, and shame old Harry!" say I.

BERT. Allez vous promener with your old Harry! "Tell *the truth*"; la belle invention; one can always tell *the truth* when there is nothing else to tell; but why begin at the wrong end? why show your cards till the game is over?

MOR. Depend upon it, these *finesses* and stratagems and hocus-pocus doings never come to good; one screw loose, and the whole machine comes to pieces.

BERT. Eh? laissez donc; you John Bull! the "straight course" should always be the *second course;* it will keep—it will keep; 'tis a *pièce de résistance—after* the Entrées.

MOR. Well, give me fewer of your kickshaws, and more of the *beef!* However, I'm under orders,—take your own line.

BERT. Eh, eh! do you count for nothing the pleasure of the game? Ah, it is exquisite! figurez-vous! Here is two months that I do not sit down, that I do not eat, that I do not sleep, that I spend my days—my nights—in writing, copying, watching, spying! que je cuis dans ma peau! that I have no rest, no peace for this business!

MOR. Ha, ha! an odd kind of pleasure! For my part, I'd rather keep the middle watch every night for a winter's month in the Bay of Biscay! Ha, ha! it's all for the pleasure of paying off these rascals in their own coin?

BERT. And for other motives.

MOR. Ah! I know you have some old grudge against Boney! He can hardly have done you an ill turn, Doctor?

BERT. C'est possible! we will not speak of that!

JULES (*outside*). Thanks, gentlemen; I feel better already.

BERT. Ah! said I not so? he is here,—this fine lad!

Enter JULES.

Ce brave gaillard!—he has succeeded—I see it in his face!

JULES. The agreement, the signatures all are here! It was a disagreeable hour to pass, but 'tis over! And now to quit Messina! I am in your hands, Dr. Bertrand.

BERT. You shall see—you shall see; leave it to old Bertrand!

JULES. Captain Mortimer, I believe? I have to apologise for making free with the name of your young friend, Mr. Poppleton; it was absolutely necessary. (*To* BERT.) Antonio never appeared.

MOR. I hope, *now*, sir, we may be favoured with your own.

BERT. Eh! qu'est-ce que ça fait? what signifies it?

MOR. Much! that we should know whom we trust.

JULES. I risk my *life*, sir; let that suffice you.

BERT. It shall! it must! que diable! *I* answer for him; come, no time to lose!

JULES. Five minutes, sir, to write two lines to a dear friend, which I shall ask you to take charge of; then do with me what you will.

(*Sits at table behind.*)

MOR. (*aside*). He's such a deuced good-looking fellow! It's a foolish business, this visiting about at respectable houses, in a mummy case; it's a d—d foolish business! However, he'll make the best of his way out again, for his own sake; and Laura never need hear a word of the matter. (*Aloud.*) You seem sure of your man, Doctor; I can only trust you blindly.

BERT. You may—you may! Parbleu! if he is caught, will he not be hanged? My friends in Malta tell me he has good reason to hate the accursed Corsican Napoleon; why should we probe his heart? It is pain to speak of past grief; and yet—sometimes— *I* think it might be *comfort* too!

MOR. What you have suffered, Bertrand!

BERT. All suffer. I have had my share! Mortimer, I was not always this old caustic Bertrand that you know. I had once a happy home—a wife—a child—far away from here, in that old France that honoured God and loved her King! But the accursed Revolution swept all away—love, loyalty, and all good things. Then we, poor Emigrés, we found refuge in your noble country.

MOR. Refuge? aye, and welcome too, poor souls!

BERT. Yes, but I yearned for my old France! my house, my little Château in Picardie! When that bloody parody of Roman times was past we returned to France. I had worked, I had saved money in your rich England. I hear that my Château, Fontarêne, was to sell for little. I leave Paris with my little son,— we reach the dear old market-town, only three leagues from home—we ride—the people offer me a guide—*a guide to me!* was not every bush, every stone of that road painted on my heart?

MOR. No doubt; *home* is never forgotten!

BERT. I think so! But ah, all was so changed! I wander this way and that! A few paces off I see a poor farmhouse. I say, "Here we will ask our way." I enter the courtyard—I stand a moment—then— deadly sickness claws my heart! My little son cries,

"Father, what ails you? why do you turn pale?"
I answer not—I weep! Vous comprenez? *C'était
Fontarêne!*

MOR. What! that poor farmhouse your old
home?

BERT. My father's heritage! Burnt, blackened,
ruined,—only graves left for me and mine!

JULES (*aside*). Poor father! that scene still haunts
my memory.

BERT. Well, that dream was over! Years pass.
My little son grows into a fine youth. Ah! if you
had seen him; blue eyes, his mother's smile, blonde
curling hair; only fifteen years of age. Alas! the
cruel Conscription takes him from us! I make
reclamations. I implore generals and ministers,—the
Emperor himself! They answer, "La France a
besoin de ses fils!" My God! had I no need of mine?

MOR. My poor friend!

JULES (*aside*). He wrings my heart; but courage,
only a few hours more, and then!

BERT. They took him from my arms! Mor-
timer, that blonde head now lies in a nameless grave!

MOR. Take comfort! Say rather, the *bed of
honour.* Where *should* a soldier sleep?

BERT. Honour? (*Wildly.*) Do tyrants leave us ever the right to grieve? Honour? I am robbed of all! *My boy died the death of a deserter*, on the eve of Austerlitz! un infant de sixteen ans.

MOR. How? what mean you?

BERT. My poor wife was dying, from the day he left us. I took her to her birthplace, Strasbourg. At the last, she prayed so to see his face again. Fool that I was, I wrote—I told him all. I murdered my child——

MOR. My poor friend!

BERT. The leave he asked was refused. Mad with grief, he fled,—came but to kiss his dead mother's face and returned to his regiment! He was met near the camp by a patrol, brought in a prisoner, and within six hours——

MOR. Good God! why were not the circumstances made known?

BERT. His commandant himself interceded for him; but, "examples were needed!" I have seen the order,—"La Mort,"—signed *Napoleon.*

MOR. I can well understand the hatred you bear that man.

BERT. It is seven years now. I have learnt to

bear my fate. It is seldom I trouble my friends with my old griefs—eh, eh! mais on n'est pas toujours sage!

MOR. That's well, Bertrand, cheer up! Why, look here, you've made our young friend here as melancholy as a cat!

BERT. Eh, eh! 'tis a good lad. (*Aside.*) I should be very sorry he was hanged. (*Aloud.*) Come, is your letter finished?

JULES. One moment, sir.

BERT. En attendant, I will go prepare for your embalming. (*Exit.*)

JULES (*rising and speaking rapidly*). Captain Mortimer, you are a man of honour; I will trust you with my secret. I am Jules Bertrand d'Artigny, the son whom that poor old man has mourned so long *as dead!*

MOR. His son! how is that possible?

JULES. My commanding officer pitied my youth. He suppressed the order for my execution; an Austrian spy was shot in my place. The battle next morning gave me the opportunity of redeeming my honour; but, struck down by a Cossack lance, left for dead upon the field, and saved only by the compassionate care of a rude peasant, it was months before I recovered either memory or strength. By that time all trace of my dear father was lost.

Mor. Your story is almost incredible, yet (*shakes his hand*) I feel I may believe you!

Jules (*showing paper*). This commission under Lord Lake's hand I have held for three years in your Indian army. The testimonials which accompany it are among my dearest possessions.

Mor. But why withhold from your father the happiness——?

Jules. You forget the dangerous nature of the service I have undertaken. When it was proposed to me at Malta, I for the first time learnt my father's existence. The situation he was in determined my acceptance; but for worlds I would not complicate his perils by anxiety on my account. If I escape, my life shall be devoted to him; if I die—hush—he's here!   (*Sits down.*)

Re-enter Bertrand.

Bert. Allons vite! is your letter finished?

Jules (*rising*). It is, sir.

BERT. Eh, what is this? "For Dr. Bertrand in case of my death."

JULES. You know, sir, it's possible in a matter of this kind; so I am prepared with a "last Will and Testament" in case of accidents. Captain Mortimer is *witness* and you *executor!*

BERT. Bien, bien! 'tis a good precaution! But now for my scheme! All is—hark! steps on the stairs? it is the Baron! vite, vite, entrez là! the case is ready—in—in. (*Exit* MORTIMER *and* JULES.)

(*A knock heard.*) Entrez, entrez, mon cher Baron!

Enter the BARONESS.

(*Aside.*) Diable! his wife! at this inconvenient moment! (*Aloud.*) Ah! madame, quel honneur! To what do I owe this inestimable advantage? That *teint de rose* reassures me as to that dear health!

BARONESS. Dr. Bertrand, you were expecting my husband! don't deny it! the *second* interview to-day!

BERT. Mais, madame! C'est permis!

BARONESS. Don't interrupt me; you know my impulsive nature; the rapidity of my resolutions! I have formed one. I act upon it! I am determined *to confide in you!*

BERT. Oui!

BARONESS. Take a chair (*they sit*). Dr. Bertrand, I have reasons to think that some evil *female* influence is at work to ruin my domestic happiness.

BERT. (*impatiently*). But, madame——

BARONESS. A thousand trifling incidents confirm my suspicion. The Baron's constant preoccupation of mind, the slight attention he bestows upon a devoted wife, the absence of all those "petits soins" I might naturally expect from one who has so lately exchanged the title of lover for that of husband!

BERT. Mais——

BARONESS. By day he walks as in a dream; by night he is ever murmuring in his sleep of "Affinities" and "Attractions," and that sort of thing. You won't persuade *me*, Dr. Bertrand, that he is alluding to *mine?*

BERT. Certainement! c'est peu probable.

BARONESS. As to the absorbing nature of his chemical pursuits; that's all nonsense! Pots and pans, Dr. Bertrand, don't come between a man and his natural rest! *They* wouldn't supersede the wife of his bosom!

BERT. Sans doute! the wife is a more probable cause of uneasiness! But, madame, what I do in this matter?

BARONESS. Much! I am resolved to know the truth—*you* can assist me.   (*Rises.*)

BERT. Comment?

BARONESS. I know you are the only person in whom he has much confidence; question him adroitly on the subject, and let me be present at the conference unknown to him!

BERT. Ah, bah!

BARONESS. His appointment with you is for two o'clock; it wants but ten minutes to the hour; place me where you like (*goes to door L.*)—here, for instance!

BERT. Eh? pour l'amour de—— fi donc, madame! that is my bedroom!

BARONESS. Well, well (*goes to door R.*), *here,* then!

BERT. Diable! that is my dissecting room!

BARONESS. Tiresome! where you please! Behind this curtain?

BERT. But it is impossible, madame! Consider— betray professional confidence! it is unheard-of action!

BARONESS (*aside*). As I suspected! evidently *conniving* at the Baron's errors. (*Aloud.*) Take care, Dr. Bertrand, your refusal of so simple a service fills me with suspicion!

BERT. (*aside*). Eh? je m'en fiche! but he will be here directly! what to do? Ah! une idée. (*Aloud.*) My dear lady, my refusal proceeds from a simple cause. I have in the next room a poor patient in the last stage of small-pox!

BARONESS (*aside*). A pretence! (*Aloud.*) My dear doctor, your kind fears are unnecessary; *I have had it, severely!*

BERT. (*aside*). Diable de femme! she is capable of having had *the Peste!* (*Aloud.*) The fact is (you force me in my retrenchments, my dear lady)— but since you *will* have the truth—the fact is, in my little "*bicoque de garçon*" you run the risk to meet with—persons—vous comprenez? that I would not expose you to associate with!

BARONESS (*aside*). Hah! no doubt! (*Aloud.*) Don't make yourself uneasy, my dear doctor! A respectable married woman like me can afford to wink at——

BERT. Ah! cent mille tonnerres! (*Aside.*) She

would wink at the Devil! Is there no way of getting rid of her? Ah! tant pis! en avant les grands moyens! (*He plants himself before her.*) Hah! and *you*, a woman, cannot read the human heart? Hah! you are blind to the motive, qui vous saute aux yeux, that stares you in the face? Do you not guess why I would banish you from my house—from my eyes—from my *heart?* Have I so well hid myself— oh! my friend's wife!—that you divined not the passion that burns within this breast?

BARONESS. Gracious goodness!

BERT. (*seizing her arm*). Hah! frivole little trembler! have you dared to trifle with a passion *d'Homme!* passion bouillante! brûlante! enfin, *passion d'Homme?* have you dared to intrude yourself upon the sanctity of my hearth? Have you forced yourself into this virginale chamber (which will evermore be tapissée with the scorching souvenirs of your smile), and do you think that I can refouler the feelings of my heart? You know me not, Baroness—you know me not! I am (sans que ça paraisse) a man of the most fiery temperament, the most ardent passions—what you call a *Lothaaiire!*

BARONESS. Goodness gracious, Dr. Bertrand!

BERT. Ah, call me not by that formal appellation! Call me Alphonse, *your* Alphonse! Fuyons! mon ange! Let us fly, my Belinda—Sophia (what's her dam name—*aside*)—let us fly from this world of cold conventionalities—to a happier——

BARONESS. What a situation! Mercy on me! and my husband perhaps at the very door!

BERT. (*with increasing vehemence*). Let him come! Let him come! Let him find me at your feet! I have thrown my cap over the mills! Je ne me connais plus! Reason forsakes me! Je me sens capable de tout! (*Kneeling at her feet.*)

BARONESS. Oh, good heavens! he's quite distracted! (*Runs out.*)

BERT. (*getting up, and dusting his knees*). Ouf! Ce n'était pas sans peine! This woman is of courage, of a persistance. Oh! ce cher Baron.

Enter BARON.

BERT. (*embracing him*). Ah! what a moment of emotion! vous m'en voyez tout bouleversé! you have brought the precious Elixir?

BARON. Yes, yes!—we are alone?

BERT. Yes, I have prepared everything,—in the inner chamber,—give me the wondrous remède.

BARON. Behold! Oh, Bertrand! be careful of it! Think what is committed to your charge!

BERT. N'ayez pas peur! remain *here*, according to our compact. I will be careful and expeditive.

(*Exit* BERT.)

BARON (*solus*). It is an agitating moment. Perhaps I have been imprudent! I should not have entrusted it to any hands but my own. Such a temptation, such a strong temptation! But Bertrand is a tried friend; and, luckily the liquid is unpalatable —singularly unpalatable.

Re-enter BERTRAND *and two servants, bearing the mummy case.*

BERT. Take the precious deposit, my friend! (*Aside.*) Be cautious, remember police! Inquisition! we have everything to fear.

BARON. How can I be grateful enough?

BERT. The obligation is mutual!

BARON. Yes, you will share in the glorious result! You will be punctual?

BERT. At ten I will be with you.

(*Exit* BARON *with case.*)

BERT. (*watching them from window*). So! he is at the end of the street; he nears the gate! Ah! he parleys with the sentinel—no, no! They will not dare! Sapristi! the old bavard, why does he stand to talk? Ah! mon Dieu! they fumble with the case—no, no! Bien, bien! take it up! that's well. Victoire! he is through the gate! All's safe! Ouf! je n'en peux plus! (*Sinks on a chair.*)

END OF ACT SECOND.

ACT III

SCENE I

A room in the Baron's Villa.

Enter FILLIP. *fanning himself, and* ST. CLAIR.

FILLIP. I tell you what, St. Clair, I can't stand this sort of thing long; I'm perfectly exhausted! If I'm to make any amount of love to the young lady she must take lodgings for the purpose in town! To have to climb this infernal hill in a broiling sun every day—I should never survive to be married!

ST. C. Pooh, pooh! faint heart never won fair lady!

FILLIP. I tell you, I've too much on my hands at once, for the time of year! I shouldn't have minded a light summer attachment, but honourable love is an awful heavy business!

St. C. Oh, nonsense, you've energy enough for anything when you're roused!

Fillip. Well, keep rousing me, do! The interview with D'Arblay has taken a great deal out of me this morning. I declare, what with conspiring and perspiring, I'm getting as weak as a cat!

St. C. Such a fine athletic frame as yours is too! As the Queen observed to me the other day, "They'll make the handsomest couple in Sicily."

Fillip. No, really! did her Majesty?—I say, St. Clair, the thing must be done, mustn't it?

St. C. Of course. Hush! here they are!

Enter Baroness, Laura, *and* Bobbin.

Baroness. At least, child, you can listen to what he has to say!

Lau. I know the sort of thing by rote already. (*Aside.*) I wonder if the fool has it *by heart?*

Baroness. Welcome, gentlemen! we are charmed to see you. Bobbin, chairs!

St. C. Madam, this interview which you and your lovely niece deign to accord to my friend and me on the subject nearest his heart fills it already with gratitude and hope. (*Aside to* Fillip.) Come, put in a word yourself. (*Aloud.*) To be on this delightful footing——

(BOBBIN *sets chair violently down on* FILLIPPI's *foot.*)

FILLIP. The devil! delightful footing? I tell you, she's crushed me to a jelly!

ST. C. (*aside*). Don't be a fool! (*Aloud.*) His emotion, Miss Brandon, is, as you see, overpowering!

BARONESS. Such interesting confusion! Ah, Laura, it tells its own tale!

LAU. (*aside*). That's more than the gentleman himself can do!

ST. C. The ardour of his attachment makes him perhaps the worst interpreter of his feelings; it quite paralyses his faculties! (*Aside to* FILLIP.) Are you going to leave all the wooing to me?

FILLIP. (*in an indifferent tone*). As Mr. St. Clair observes, it quite paralyses my faculties.

BARONESS. You lucky girl! What a strong passion you have inspired!

LAU. Uncommonly strong,—it takes two men to express it!

ST. C. One glance of encouragement from those bright eyes will do much to break the spell. (*Aside to* FILLIP.) And be hanged to you!

BARONESS.   I'm sure my niece is sensible that——
(*Aside to* LAURA.)   You idiot! can't you say a word
for yourself?

LAU.   Your exertions, aunt, are quite enough;
as the gentleman is passionate by proxy I may be
sentimental at second hand.

ST. C.   Surely, madam, you can make allowances
for a certain timidity in one so new to the character
of a candidate for matrimony!

LAU.   For matrimony? surely, Mr. St. Clair, you
mean a candidate for baptism; you promise and vow
so much in his name.

ST. C. (*to* FILLIP. *aside*).   Her manner is decidedly
encouraging; come, man, pluck up a spirit! One
plunge and it's over.

FILLIP.   Madam! Miss Brandon, hem! As my
friend, Mr. St. Clair, observes—I am—quite overcome
—with the warmth——

ST. C.   Of his attachment, poor fellow!

FILLIP.   Of the weather; and, in fact, might I
trouble you—for a glass of——

ST. C.   Water! poor fellow! it's quite affecting!

FILLIP.   Of lemonade; eau sucrée—anything!

BARONESS. Bobbin, refreshments! Laura, your heart must be *stone* if you don't feel *this!*

ST. C. Poor fellow! 'pon my honour, it may sound ridiculous, but I really do so enter into his feelings, that—— (*Wipes his eyes.*) Such fervour! such affecting fervour!

(BOBBIN *with tray pushes table against* FILLIP.)

FILLIP. Devil take the woman! she's at it again! (*Exit* BOBBIN.)

LAU. There's a good deal of fervour in his *expression*—certainly.

ST. C. (*to* BARONESS). That nervous irritation is very significative!

BARONESS. Ah, very! All lovers swear! It's proverbial, "Lover's *oaths*," you know! I remember, before the Baron and I married, *he* used to use dreadful language; didn't he, Mr. St. Clair? You often shocked my delicacy by repeating it!

ST. C. Oh, awful! These foreigners, you see, madam, haven't our English *phlegm*.

BARONESS. Very true!

ST. C. Now, there's Fillippi, poor fellow, this very morning (speaking of Miss Brandon's complexion) says he, "St. Clair, I'll be eternally——"

BARONESS. Oh, hush, hush! Laura is quite satisfied without your repeating it; you're quite satisfied, Laura?

LAU. Oh, quite! (*Aside.*) I believe if the man were to sneeze they'd say it was a sign of the purest affection!

FILLIP. (*aside*). Capital ale! there's that at least in an English connection. (*Drinking.*)

ST. C. In fact, Miss Brandon, he's a perfect volcano—like his own Etna—ice *without*—but *within* a devastating fire that nothing can quench.

LAU. He appears to be *getting it under* at present.

BARONESS (*to* ST. C.) How well one recognises the signs of suppressed emotion! Ah, Laura, when nothing escapes the *lips*, how much is concentrated *within!*

LAU. To judge from appearances, a gallon at least!

ST. C. (*aside to* FILLIP.) The game's in your own hands, if you only put a little heart into it! Now, mark what I say, and down on your knees at the proper moment! (*To the ladies.*) But we will not waste these precious moments! Allow me to come to the point. You see before you, madam, one whose very *reason* trembles in the balance, so intimately is his happiness bound up with the thought of this union! One, whose ardent nature, bubbling and boiling like the lava flood of this favoured isle, may indeed burst the bounds of cold conventional formalism, in its efforts to find a vent for its irrepressible impulses. (FILLIP. *snores.*) And now prompts him to throw himself—hem—I say to throw himself.

(*Turns and finds* FILLIP. *fast asleep in chair.*)

BARONESS. Good heavens! has the poor gentleman fainted?

LAU. (*laughing*). His emotions, and the ale combined, have been too much for him.

ST. C. (*angrily aside to* FILLIP.) Deuce take the fellow! Here have I been making love for you till I'm black in the face, and you can't keep your stupid eyes open. (*Aloud.*) Sleepless from anxiety—for many nights, he naturally—— (*Enter* BOBBIN.)

BOB. Oh, ma'am! oh, miss! oh, I'm all of a tremble!

BARONESS. What *is* the matter, Bobbin?

BOB. Oh, ma'am, the Baron——

BARONESS. Gracious powers! what of the Baron? Speak!

BOB. Send away them foreigneers, or I shall burst.

ST. C. Madam, allow us to return a little later, when my poor friend shall have regained his composure!   (*Exeunt* ST. CLAIR *and* FILLIPPI.)

BARONESS. Now, Bobbin, speak!

BOB. Well, ma'am—well, miss—you know that 'ere outlandish Corpus that master brought up from the Doctor's to-day——

BARONESS. The mummy,—well?

BOB. Oh, ah! mummy, indeed! you know as how master locked it up in his study! Well, I happened just now to be going down the corridor, and as I passed the door I heard a noise, and it guv me such a turn (knowing as I did, it couldn't be master) that I felt like to drop, and indeed *did* drop—down on my knees, with my eye accidentally just on a line with the keyhole! Wasn't that curious?

LAU. Of *you?* very!

BARONESS. Well, girl, what did you see? I'm on thorns!

BOB. Well, ma'am—— Oh, them foreigneers!

BARONESS. For heaven's sake, go on! What did you see?

LAU. Yes! what of the mummy?

BOB. Say *mummery*, miss! mummery, ma'am! for that's what it is!

BARONESS. *What* is? You'll drive me distracted!

LAU. Don't keep us in suspense; what did you see?

BOB. I saw—sitting on master's couch—as bold as brass——

BARONESS—LAU. What? What?

BOB. A beautiful young——

BARONESS. *Woman!* I knew it!

BOB. Not at all! a handsome young——

LAU. Man! I foresaw it!

BOB. La! how quick she is at guessing! Yes, a handsome young man! and that's what master has been bringing in so gingerly, and locking up so particular! and sending us out of the way so slyly, and putting me to no end of trouble to find out the why and the wherefore, as is us poor hard-worked servants' natural privilege and perquisite!

BARONESS. What horrible mystery is this? Bobbin, are you certain that the young *person*— *was* a young man?

BOB. Well, ma'am, you know master says we're

all tabernuckles of convinced air, but this appeared
to me to be a *he* tabernuckle!

BARONESS. Bobbin! *again I say*, had that young
person *a beard?*

BOB. La, ma'am! how could I say for certing?
You don't suppose I kissed him—through the keyhole?

BARONESS. The crisis of my fate is at hand!
Bobbin, I will confide in you! I depend on your
vigilance. Don't lose sight of the Baron, and bring
me word whenever he returns to his study. (*Aside.*)
My plan is formed. I have the key of the condemned
door leading to that room from the other corridor:
I *will* know the worst!

(*Exit in agitation, followed by* BOBBIN.)

LAU. (*solus*). Oh, it's quite plain; he knew all
about it! and I, silly creature, swallowed every word!
"Refined feelings." The wretch! how well he
acted! "My health—my precious health!" The
deceitful wretch! "Plague at Grand Cairo!" I'll
plague him! Some jealous quirk has taken possession
of the silly man! He shall go through a little wholesome discipline to cure him of his tendency. Ah!
his step on the stairs. Now for a little offended
dignity.   (*Sits down and takes book.*)

Enter MORTIMER.

MOR. My own Laura! I fear I'm before the hour; but when that hour is to be spent with *you* I am apt to count time by the beating of my heart; and that—— How absorbed you are in your book, my love! May I ask the subject of your studies?

LAU. *Manners and Customs of the Ancient Egyptians*—uncommonly interesting!

MOR. No doubt, no doubt! but, my dear girl, you can read that at any time—whereas——

LAU. (*reading*). "How they embalm their dead." Through the nose! dear me!

MOR. (*aside*). What new freak is this?

LAU. (*reading*). "And sometimes" (how very curious!)—"sometimes insert jewels in the eyes!"

MOR. D—n their eyes!

LAU. (*rising*). Captain Mortimer!

MOR. I beg your pardon, Laura! but, really, this studied neglect may well irritate a heart already saddened by the thought that we may not meet again for months—nay, years!

LAU. Oh, ah! I remember! you leave Messina this evening?

Mor. Good heavens! what have I done to deserve this? I left you this morning so different— so affectionate! Dear, capricious girl, explain this change!

Lau. Well, the fact is, Captain Mortimer, that I have been reflecting on the hazardous nature of an engagement between two persons who have not perfect trust in each other!

Mor. My dear girl, I have the most——

Lau. Stop, hear me out! I appeal to you, whether, on *my* side at least, there has not been the most implicit, the most tender confidence! For instance, have I ever disguised your faults from you?

Mor. No, no, my love! I confess you have been always very candid on that point.

Lau. There, you see! Then, have I ever scrupled to complain of my aunt to you, abuse my best friends, and ridicule most of our mutual acquaintance?

Mor. No, no, my dear creature! to do you justice, you have been perfectly unreserved on that score!

Lau. There, you own it! and what is my reward? What does my candid, trusting nature meet with in return?—Base ingratitude, and (I say it advisedly) Machiavellian duplicity!

Mor. Laura! good heavens! what on earth——

Lau. Stay, sir! Descend into the recesses of your conscience, and ask yourself the reason of the deception you have practised with regard to that mummy case, and the individual concealed in it!

Mor. (*aside*). Oh, Lord! that cursed mummy! (*Aloud.*) Dear Laura, forgive me; and since you know the secret,—(*aside*) I've made a bad hit of my first lie (though how the deuce she got hold of it, I can't imagine!),—let me explain the circumstances!

Lau. (*aside*). Oh, there *is* a secret! I'd give my eyes to know it! (*Aloud.*) No, no, Captain Mortimer, henceforth the subject becomes hateful to me. (*Walks up and down, he following.*)

Mor. But only listen, Laura!

Lau. To treat me with such reserve! I, that hide no thought from you!

Mor. (*still following*). A political secret, my sweet girl, that couldn't interest you!

Lau. (*aside*). I wonder what—— (*Aloud.*) So discreet as I am—so little inquisitive!

Mor. Of course; I feared to implicate you in anything of the sort.

Lau. So devoted as I have ever shown myself—so loving!

Mor. (*following*). Ah, Laura! there it is—I was an idiot; but this young fellow being so handsome and gallant—the situation so perilous—and you, my love, so romantic; but, as you know all——

Lau. (*stopping*). Yes, well? as I know all?

Mor. Of course, I had best say no more about it!

Lau. (*aside*). There's the disadvantage of seeming too well informed. (*Aloud.*) Oh, pray go on! at least your *own* share of the transaction needs explanation!

Mor. Spare me the confession of my weakness, you are so intimately acquainted with my jealous temper——

Lau. That there is the less necessity for introducing it to me so often!

Mor. Ah, Laura! is not jealousy a proof of love?

Lau. But love is not a logarithm, silly man! Spare me the proof, and I'll take twice as much for granted!

MOR. Well, forgive me this once, and I swear by this dear hand never to be jealous again!

LAU. (*aside*). We shall see that! (*Aloud.*) Well, I'll be magnanimous and forgive the offence! And indeed, Mortimer, I can hardly regret a circumstance which has procured me such a very interesting acquaintance.

MOR. How? Who? What? This young Jules——

LAU. (*aside*). Oh! "*Jules*" is the name! (*Aloud.*) Exactly! he is indeed singularly pleasing; some might say irresistible! And though I feel I ought to resent the artifice by which he has sought to recommend himself to my notice——

MOR. Artifice! recommend himself! the devil! but, no, no! I'm a fool to credit it! Ha, ha, ha! my dear Laura, that's a good joke!—a very good joke of yours! But if the young gentleman had had the intentions you impute to him, don't you think he would have lingered awhile at the shrine of his divinity?

LAU. Of course! Oh, I have no reason to doubt he will prove a very constant worshipper!

MOR. Ha, ha, ha! Odd enough, he should have thought proper to take such an abrupt departure.

Lau. Departure? My dear Captain Mortimer, I think I may venture to say he has no thought of such a step at present!

Mor. Do you mean to say the fellow is here still?

Lau. Of course he is! Hark! how it's raining; could we think of his leaving us in such weather as this?

Mor. Death and furies! Is the man distracted?

(*Walks up and down.*)

Lau. (*following*). Now take care, Mortimer! here's another of your little tiffs brewing.

Mor. Oh, woman, woman! is nothing safe from the poisonous influence of thy cruel coquetry?

Lau. (*following*). What ridiculous objection can you urge against my cultivating so pleasant an addition to our acquaintance?

Mor. Nothing but the strongest encouragement could have induced him to risk so much for the pleasure of remaining a night under this roof!

Lau. Ah, you're at your logarithms again! I wonder you allow trifles to disturb you so much!

Mor. Trifles, madam! (*Stops.*) But you are right, quite right! it is a just estimate, no doubt!

The love of an honest heart! a brave man's danger! fame, honour, life itself! what are they but *trifles* when weighed in the balance against the heartless pastime of a woman's vanity. But I have done with you, Miss Brandon; I leave you to the enjoyment of your *rapid* conquests; my intrusive affection shall trouble you no more! From henceforth I withdraw my too presumptuous claims! Henceforward, you are free to make others as wretched as it has been your pleasure to render me! I bid you an eternal farewell!

LAU. Oh, by all means, sir! Far be it from my thoughts to desire to detain you. The flattering nature of your remarks on my character and disposition puts that out of the question! A little civility in addition to so much eloquence would perhaps be too much to require; but don't imagine, sir, that I am the least annoyed by anything you have said,—not in the slightest degree, believe me—ha, ha! I'm rather amused than otherwise. You'll have the kindness to return me my letters; yes, and my picture, if you please; I may want *that*; I daresay Count Fillippi, or some other friend, may attach some value to it!

MOR. No doubt; oh, no doubt! That image will bestow a fleeting happiness on many. *Value?*

Yes, the value of a challenge racing cup! Fit type of a heart which every cheat and cozener may pretend to, and whose possession neither merit nor integrity can secure!

LAU. Enough, sir! leave me, I desire! I suppose you will wish to have your own letters again?

MOR. Yes, yes; let me destroy every evidence of my past folly!

LAU. I have no wish to retain a memorial of it. There is nothing else, I think?

MOR. No, nothing! You cannot give me back my wasted youth, my trust in woman's truth, my dreams of happiness! Oh, cruel girl! of what have you not robbed me? But why do I waste reproaches on you? *He* shall answer me—*he*, the double deceiver! Farewell; I go (*coming back*) to retrieve the error of my too honest nature (*going*); I go (*coming back*) to chastise falsehood and presumption! I go (*coming back*)—I go, madam, and for ever! (*Exit.*)

LAU. (*sola*). Ha, ha, ha! so he'd never, never be jealous again! so it appears! "Heartless vanity," indeed,—ha, ha, ha! I never heard anything so ridiculous!—ha, ha, ha! I shall certainly die of laughing!—ha, ha, ha!

Enter BOBBIN.

BOB.   La, miss, whatever is the matter?

LAU. (*crying*).   Oh, Bobbin, I have been so foolish.   I have quarrelled with Captain Mortimer, all about nothing; and we've parted—and he's gone, and has taken—has taken——

BOB.   La, miss, *what?*

LAU. (*with a burst of sobs*).   His leave for ever!

BOB.   Deary me, is that all?   Well, you *did* give me such a turn; I thought it had been the silver spoons at least.   Bless you! it's well it's no worse. Lovers is hartful creechers!   They're always a-taking something or other; and as for *taking leave*, I never knew one of 'em as took his leave for ever, that he didn't come back again to see how the lady took it too!

LAU. (*sobbing*).   And you think he may return?

BOB.   Bless your little 'art! in course he will! Ah! I had a second cousin once removed as had been keepin' company with a soldier for fifteen year, off and on; and one fine day *they* quarrelled; and "Mary," says he, "it's twenty minutes to two," says he, looking at her watch.   "May be," says he, "this 'ere is the last hour we shall ever spend together!" and with that he pressed her to his heart and cut away like winkin'.

LAU. And she never saw him more?

BOB. Bless ye, my dear,—*often!* but she never clapt eyes on her silver watch again!

LAU. Pshaw, Bobbin!

BOB. Oh, miss, I don't say Captain Mortimer— he's too much the gentleman in course. But still, my dear, men *is* men, and lovyers is lovyers, and you can't be too much on your guard agin 'em.   (*Exeunt.*)

SCENE II

A room in the Château. (*Storm without.*)

Enter the BARONESS *dressed in white with a candle in her hand.*

BARONESS. The Baron is restlessly pacing the corridor. I passed him with a withering look; he must have been struck by my resemblance to Lady Macbeth! But the wretch is quite callous; he wished me "a good-night,"—ha, ha, ha! "Good-night to me!" After that, the man is capable of anything! He hasn't yet entered the study; he merely watches the door,—what is he waiting for? Ah, Freitenhorsen! this is a fearful crisis; a woman of my impulsive

temper is not to be trifled with ! Gently submissive
as I am when no one opposes my will, there is yet
the spirit of a *Medea* within me ! All I want is *certainty*.
I should be quite easy if I could but positively ascertain that I am the most ill-used and wretched of
women. If I could find out *whom* to hate, and where
to direct my vengeance, I should feel in a thoroughly
Christian temper ! It can't be Bobbin—poh ! that's
out of the question,—nor my niece ; he never looks
at her, and she's besotted with her sea-captain ! Ah !
there at least I have a little comfort,—I can prevent
that. I haven't an atom of malignity in my nature ;
I'm a perfect dove in disposition ; but I've a keen sense
of natural justice, and I own I do *not* like to see
other people insolently enjoying themselves when I'm
miserable. Now to my post of observation.

(*Exit.*)

SCENE III

The Baron's Study. (*Lights down.*)

JULES (*at table*). It must be near the hour of my
emancipation. I own I shan't be sorry when it strikes.
'Tis tedious work to wait here now that light is gone.

(*Clock strikes nine.*)   *Nine!* thank heaven!   (*Rises.*)
The boat must be at the appointed place; now for
the rope ladder.   (*Goes to window.*)   What a night!
but the lightning is convenient.   Yes, I see the gate of
the subterranean passage.   (*Arranges ladder.*)   That's
well!   (*Returns to table for papers.*)

            POPPLETON *heard without.*

Pop.   House a-hoy!

JULES.   Some one without.   (*Looks at the priming of
his pistols.*)   For his own sake, I trust it may not prove
necessary to show I am armed; but it won't be a slight
obstacle that shall stop me now,—so near success.
(*Looks out.*)   I see no one! at all events I must risk it.
                                    (*Descends from window.*)

Pop. (*without*).   House a-ho—o—o—y! hilloah!
thieves! murder!   (*A short pause—appears at window,
still without coat, wet and dirty.*)   A fine romantic
country! rope ladders hanging out of all the upper
story windows!   I can't make any one hear outside, so
this is the best way of alarming the house.   (*Jumps in.*)
I'm certain it was that cool chap that stole my pocket-
book, and called himself Poppleton!   He can't have got
far, so if some one will lend me a hand.   (*He tries both
doors.*)   Locked! now here's a nice situation!   If that

fellow *has* prigged anything (and it isn't unlikely, as I
know to my cost), the people of the house will be accusing me! I'd best get out again. (*Runs to window.*)
Dear, dear! such a night as it is! and I'm wet to the
skin already. (*Sneezes.*) Such a cold and sore throat
as I'm getting! and my poor head going round like a
mill-wheel! I'd best make sure the ladder's all right.
It's no joke sliding down 30 or 40 feet on a skein of
silk, like a garden spider! I was never much of an
acrobat at the best of times. (*Unhooks the ladder which
drops.*) Now there! well done, butterfingers! if I
haven't let the ladder drop! Here's a pleasant state of
things! I'm in for it! I'm regularly up a tree, and
no mistake. (*Sits disconsolately on sofa.*) I've had a nice
day's pleasuring, haven't I? My coat gone, my pocket-
book stolen! Locked up all day by those d—d fellows
on pretence of my having no passport! Turned adrift
—starving with cold this nice damp evening, and now
caught like a mouse in a trap, and like enough to be
taken up for burglary! Oh dear, oh dear! I don't
look much like the Pirate of the Pyrenees, do I? I
think Doubleshuffle would hardly know me, would
he? (*Yawns.*) And I'm so deuced tired too, I can
hardly keep my eyes open! Well, I may as well take a

nap while I can ; it'll look well on my trial when they do take me up for this burglary. (*Lies down.*) "He was found wrapped in peaceful slumbers,"—he, he! I haven't much of the stolen property about me,—he, he! that's another point in my favour! Dressed in a rope ladder —Doubleshuffle—Pirate of the Pyrenees—— (*Sleeps.*)

Enter BARON *with a lamp.*

BARON. I can bear the suspense no longer! Bertrand comes not, and the hour is already arrived! Oh! moment of inexpressible anxiety. If all should prove delusion! a dream! the dream of a wasted life! No, no; it cannot be! Science alone is true—all other things are shows and shadows! Science alone is immutable in her decrees! Yet it may be that I am but a blind, crazed worshipper of the veiled Goddess! Let me know the truth—yea! tho' it crush to atoms the hopes, the labour of a lifetime! (*Goes towards mummy case.*) Gone! (*Sees* POPPLETON *on sofa.*) Hah! triumph! he lives! he breathes! my destiny is accomplished! I pant for breath; the universe itself seems too narrow for my soul to revel in! (*Walks up and down in strong emotion.*) But, hush! let me be calm—calm and collected, as beseems the favoured votary of divine Philosophy! *This* is a paternity of which I may well be proud! What are common fathers compared to me? I have raised from destruction itself a miraculous posterity that shall hand my name down to ages yet unborn! He sleeps! (POPPLETON *snores.*) A warm breathing sleep,—a childlike slumber! I must wake him! With what transport shall I hang over the first innocent accents of this—his second existence!

(*Touches* POPPLETON.)

POP. (*asleep*). Devil take you! Do leave me alone!

BARON. Hum! past associations still linger.

(*Touches him again.*)

POP. (*asleep*). Burglary! ha, ha! but they can't *prove* it upon me!

BARON. Good heavens! dreaming of his late guilty avocations! I must rouse him. Awake, young man.

POP. (*rubbing his eyes*). Bless me, where the deuce am I?

BARON (*aside*). I must be cautious, lest memory too suddenly overwhelm him. (*To* POPPLETON.) Be composed, young man; you are safe—you are in my mansion—the Baron Freitenhorsen addresses you!

Pop. (*aside*). Oh, Lord! the mad Baron himself! (*Aloud.*) I really beg pardon, sir, for this intrusion; it was quite involuntary—I was——

Baron. Hush! be calm, do not exert yourself! Let the current of life have time to re-establish its equilibrium!

Pop. Pray allow me to explain——

Baron. No, no; for the present let there be no recurrence to the painful past!

Pop. (*aside*). Painful past! what the deuce does the old gentleman mean?

Baron. At all events, take your time—collect your thoughts. How far do they take you back? Do you remember your incarceration?

Pop. Incarcer—— Oh, ah! what—those fellows locking me up? To be sure I do! and if I don't pay off the scoundrels——

Baron. Hush, hush! these passions must not survive their cause. You call to mind the last sad scene—the fatal ladder?

Pop. To be sure, I remember the ladder—— Dear me, I see it all,—what? I had a dreadful fall, eh?

Baron. *Awful*—you remember *now*—be calm!

Pop. No bones broken, eh? (*Feeling himself.*)

BARON. No, no; only utter insensibility; some would call it *death*, but that's a vulgar error.

POP. Dear me, what an escape I've had!

BARON. You may indeed term it so! Had your neck been broken, even my art could not have saved you!

POP. Why, no; I suppose not! Dear me, my head's very dizzy. I haven't the least recollection of the last part of the business! Now, would you believe it, I fancied I had been asleep? Dear me— well, I could have sworn I came in by the—— But, bless my soul, my dear sir, I'm really very much obliged to *you!* Pray, allow me to shake you by the hand.

BARON (*aside*). A felon's hand! but I am above these prejudices. 'Tis a fine erratic energetic nature!

(*Shakes hands.*)

POP. Much obliged, 'pon my soul! It's very odd, but I could have sworn I came in by the wind—— Very odd, 'pon my soul.

BARON. Your ideas are still confused.

POP. Well, the fact is, it has been such a busy day with me,—what with the finale and all——

BARON (*aside*). Busy day! evidently a man of *iron*

nerve! The making of a magnificent character! (*Aloud.*) Do you think you could rise?

Pop. Well, I think I can. (*Gets up cautiously.*)

Baron. That's well; any uncomfortable, unusual sensations?

Pop. I've an odd kind of a hollow feeling *here!*

Baron. Of course, of course; you must need refreshment! I have it ready.　　　(*Goes out R.*)

Pop. (*solus*). Capital fellow this Baron! Mad? no more mad than I am; a little enthusiastic in manner perhaps, but I like it! I confess I like it! The only thing I don't understand is about my *fall.* (*Looking round.*) I could take my oath I came in by the window! Ah! I daresay it's his little eccentric way of making one welcome,—as much as to say, "'Taint the regular thing to come visiting through the window, or down the chimney; but here you are, make yourself at home,"—and I mean to!

Enter the Baron *with tray of refreshments.*

Pop. My dear sir, this is really—so very—— (*Helping him.*) I can't say how obliged I am—ha, ha! The fact is (*bringing forward table*), I've had nothing in the way of *eating* since daybreak but two water melons and a peppermint lozenge. But really—very well—since you insist! (*Seats himself at table.*) But, 'pon honour, I can't think of tasting anything unless you join me—I couldn't, indeed!

BARON (*aside*). To sit in convivial familiarity with a—— but this repugnance is unworthy of a Philosopher! (*Aloud.*) Be it so; we will share the first meal!

POP. Now that's hearty! Let's be comfortable. Here's your health! (*Clink glasses.*)

BARON (*aside*). There's a kind of trembling joy in all this. I look on my work with mingled awe and happiness. (*Aloud.*) You seem perfectly able to *swallow?* No unusual *tightness about the throat?*

POP. Well, now you mention it—hem!—there is a *leetle* soreness—not to be wondered at, considering what I've gone through in the course of the day—ha, ha! I'm sure I shall think I've got off cheap if I haven't a stiff neck for the rest of my life!

BARON (*aside*). With what a fine composure he alludes to his execution! A grand Titanic nature! Marvellous power of endurance!

POP. Capital wine, this! Here's to you again, sir! (*Clinks glasses.*) Ha, ha, ha! Do you know, I never thought when I was going up that rickety ladder that the adventure would end as pleasantly as it has done!

BARON (*aside*). Dear me, there is something awful in this daring levity! (*Aloud.*) The sensation must indeed have been terrible!

POP. Ha, ha, ha! but I felt that the great difficulty would be the getting down again!

BARON (*aside*). I ought to be above this weakness, but I feel a creeping horror of him stealing over me. (*Aloud.*) Of course you knew it was impossible!

POP. Oh! as to that, in our profession, you know, we are pretty used to that sort of thing.

BARON (*aside*). Used to it! Good gracious, one would think he had been hanged half a dozen times! (*Aloud.*) Used to the contemplation of such an event, no doubt!

POP. Ha, ha, ha! contemplation! (Might I trouble you for the mustard?) We haven't much time for that, you know; here's your health again! (*Aside.*) I shall win my bet after all; he takes me for a regular Jack tar!

BARON (*aside*). Alas! I fear there is much depravity to be eradicated in him! (*Aloud.*) Let

us not recur to the past—the future is all before us,—
let us consider now what had best be done with you.

Pop. Oh, as to that, I must be off with the first
light, or I shall get such a wigging from the
Captain!

Baron (*aside*). Captain! oh, Lord! There's a
whole gang of them! Oh dear! oh dear! (*Aloud.*)
I fear you must have led a very dreadful life, young
man?

Pop. Oh! it's nothing when one's used to it!
The *night work*, to be sure, is a little heavy; but we
take the watches turn about, and there's a good many
of us.

Baron (*aside*). Oh, Lord! there's a good many
of them—and they *take watches*—turn about! (*Aloud,
but in a faint voice.*) And when—you—take—watches
—and things of that sort—you take nothing else, I
trust; the act is not accompanied by vio—— no
blows, eh?

Pop. *Blows*, did you say? Lord bless you, it's
the very thing we like! a squall makes it all the
pleasanter. Blows! I believe you, *and great guns
too!*

Baron (*aside*). Heaven have mercy on me!

What a responsibility I've brought upon myself. (*Aloud.*) Unhappy youth, is it possible that after the awful trial you have gone through, you mean to turn again to these dreadful pursuits?

Pop. Bless your heart, of course I do! I've had my *swing*, you know, and now I must be back to business again!

Baron (*sits down faint*). He's had his *swing!* (*Laughs hysterically.*) It doesn't seem to have been an unpleasant operation. My brain begins to reel! Oh, science, science! but 'tis vain to look back! What I have done is irretrievable! My duty is plain; no sacrifice shall be too great to make for the chance of reclaiming him! (*Aloud.*) Listen to me, wretched youth; have I not claims upon your gratitude? But they shall be yet greater if you will only listen to the voice of duty and reason!

Pop. (*aside*). What the deuce is the old gentleman driving at?

Baron. Listen to me! you are aware that you owe your existence to me?

Pop. (*aside*). What next will he say?

Baron. Yes, boy! I may call you my offspring; —born to me of *Science*, divinest of brides!

BARONESS (*opens closet door*). Now I shall hear what they're saying!

BARON. By *her*, to whom I have been wedded from early youth, you are indeed my son! my only, my legitimate child!

BARONESS. *Wedded! legitimate son!*

POP. (*aside*). The old buffer is decidedly cracked!

BARON. All other ties are nothing in comparison, —I cast them to the winds!

BARONESS. Oh, the deceiving villain!

(*Shuts closet door.*)

BARON. What's that? Hush!

POP. What?

BARON. That noise! a door shut close to us,— some one may be listening—I must ascertain this.

(*Exit.*)

POP. I'd best take myself off before the crazy old party comes back. (*Drinks.*) Here's to the restoration of his wits! he has capital claret! Now for French leave,—where does this door lead? (*Opens closet door.*) Bless me, a lady!

(BARONESS *staggers out and sinks into his arms.*)

BARONESS. Support me, wretched woman that I am, under this heavy trial!

Pop. *Heavy* trial indeed!

Baroness. A sudden impulse leads me to confide in you—I obey it! I have no time to give or receive explanations. Suffice it to say that the veil is at last torn from my deluded eyes, and I know *all!*

Pop. (*aside*). It's a lunatic asylum, and I've opened the door of the female ward!

Baroness. Yes, the fearful truth—of which I have long had a mysterious presentiment—is at last revealed, and you see before you the most injured, the most unfortunate of women!

Pop. Dear me!

Baroness (*solemnly*). Is your mother living?

Pop. She is, ma'am, and pretty well; I'm obliged to you. She had a touch of rheum——

(Baroness *waves her hand.*)

Baroness. Hush! are you aware who it is who now addresses you?

Pop. Haven't an idea, ma'am! Perhaps the——

Baroness. The Baron's *reputed wife!* Do you not *now* comprehend my painful—my humiliating position?

Pop. (*aside*). Bless my heart! Here's a pretty confession! And what queer taste the old buffer has! (*Aloud.*) Ma'am, I really——

BARONESS. Hush! I hear him returning! Be silent on this interview! I shall see you again. You shall assist in the determination I have formed!

(*Exit.*)

POP. Well, I've come unawares into the bosom of a respectable family, and it certainly is making a clean breast of it! Here's the old rogue again!

Enter BARON.

BARON. 'Twas nothing. You've had time for reflection. I trust you will now determine as you ought. If you will solemnly promise to amend your life, I——

POP. Ha, ha, ha! ho, ho, ho! "Amend my life," says he! Faith, there's a pair of us want mending, if it comes to that, my old boy!

BARON. Old boy!

POP. You sly old dog. (*Poking him in the side.*) You took me in at first with your long sober face and your virtue and morality. But I'm up to you now, old fellow!

BARON. Up to me?

POP. Yes, yes; I see through you! Ha, ha, ha!

BARON. See through me, reprobate! I repeat,

my conscience will not admit of my turning you loose upon society again without——

Pop. *Loose*, indeed! Ha, ha! I wonder which of us two—— Why, you naughty old gentleman, look me in the face while I tell you what a little bird has whispered to me about a certain lady!

Baron. Little bird? Lady? What does the young ruffian mean? (*Goes to table, looks at bottle.*) Ah, I see! Drunk, drunk as a piper!

Pop. (*aside*). It's no use talking to him. Mad— mad as a hatter!

Baron (*aside*). If I can but get him quietly to bed. (*Aloud.*) Come, come; compose yourself. You need rest. We will discuss these matters to-morrow. Within you will find my own couch prepared. Sleep (if you can)! (*Aside.*) When shall I ever find rest again?

Pop. Well, come; don't let you and I quarrel after our pleasant evening together! Why, we were as thick as thieves just now!

Baron. Oh, science, science! in what an abyss of misery hast thou plunged thy votary!

(*Exit, and* Poppleton *C.*)

Re-enter BARON *with* POPPLETON'S *trousers, etc.;*
locks door C.

BARON. The demon sleeps! He is bottled up
for a brief breathing time. I shall have a little space
for my miserable reflections! He cannot break loose
and spread devastation around him without these
(*showing clothes*). The horror with which he inspires
me prompts me to actions foreign to my nature!

Enter BERTRAND *behind.*

BERT. (*aside*). Now to see how he takes the
subject's disappearance. Hem! his face is long and
all upside down. I trust he does not suspect me!

BARON. If I could quietly smother him?

BERT. (*aside*). Sapristi! he means me!

BARON. Break his neck down the cellar stairs and
bury him at the bottom?

BERT. (*aside*). Diable! he has énergique ideas!

BARON. Anything rather than let the fiend loose
again! Ah, Bertrand!

BERT. (*retreating*). My dear Baron!

BARON. Come hither, I have much to say to
you!

BERT. (*retreating*). Confide in your faithful friend!

BARON. What I have to say is as secret as the grave.

BERT. (*retreating*). Whisper it in my friendly ear!

BARON. Why the devil don't you come nearer then? Am I to whisper through a speaking-trumpet?

BERT. Hem! The fact is, my dear Baron, having been engaged in professional duties, and the typhoid fevers being very rife, I fear to risk your valuable health by nearer proximity,—dat is my principe!

BARON. Oh, my friend, I am in the most fatal dilemma! The fearful experiment has been only too successful. Alas! I have restored life to a monster of iniquity, and bitterly repent my act!

BERT. (*advancing—aside*). All is well! (*Aloud.*) What? the remedy has been too potent in its effects, eh, and the patient has escaped? He would not stay for the process of perfectibility? Peste! he is an ungrateful! mais que voulez-vous? if you give a thief his legs, he will steal away!

BARON. No, no; it is not yet so bad as that! I have confined the evil spirit,—I have him under lock and key!

BERT. (*in astonishment*). You have him?

BARON. Yes, yes; I have taken measures to prevent his escape; he can hardly outrage society without these! (*Showing trousers.*)

BERT. Ah! Mille diables! here is a dilemma! (*Aside.*) What could have delayed his escape?

BARON. But now, for Heaven's sake, assist me with your advice! I think of giving him up to justice and having him hanged over again!

BERT. (*aside*). Ma foi! the contingency is not improbable! (*Aloud.*) Consider, my friend, such a step will divulge your fatal secret! You will be aux prises with the police—with the Church!

BARON. Alas! what is to be done? This comes, Dr. Bertrand, of your choice of subjects! If you had sent me a decent member of society——

BERT. Que diable! on ne peut donner que ce qu'on a! Do you think I have a museum of saints and martyrs for you to try your experiments on? Decent member! if you do not like him, give him me again! (*Aside.*) Reste le seul moyen! (*Aloud.*) Give me my dead man; ça m'est égal qu'il soit en vie!

BARON. No, no; I abide the issue of my terrible experiment; my miserable course is now marked out!

Henceforth, inseparable companion of the demon I have evoked, we must wander together through a hostile world—he sinning—I repenting! Horrible union of opposing natures—fit punishment for the presumptuous fool who snatches down fire from heaven—to burn himself out of house and home!

(*Exit* BARON *in distraction*).

BERT.   Le vieux fou! what is to be done?

Enter MORTIMER *hastily.*

MOR.   Bertrand, all is lost! By some curst ill fortune the real D'Arblay has arrived sooner than we expected!

BERT.   How? arrived?

MOR.   He was in Fillippi's office as I left the town. They will have easily traced his substitute to your house; and St. Clair is too intelligent an enemy not to have divined already by what means he left it!

BERT.   Diable! and the young imprudent is even now in this house!

MOR.   I know it!

BERT.   Yet he knew the danger of delay!

MOR.   A woman's coquetry has blinded him to it;

he has risked life and liberty to remain longer near Miss Brandon!

BERT. Sapristi! what's to be done?

MOR. Instantly reveal all to Baron Freitenhorsen. You have influence over him—with all his eccentricity he is humane.

BERT. Eh, eh! to tell a man, "I have made one d—d fool of you," ce n'est pas le moyen to put him into good temper. No, no; pas si bête! There is no proof of *our* complicity; the young man's safety is his own affair!

MOR. It is his only chance; linger not, Bertrand! This young fellow's fate may hang on an instant's delay!

BERT. Le jeune fou; it is his fault, il l'a voulu! Diable! when I had so well arranged. It is his fault! He must suffer! (*Sits down.*)

MOR. Good Heavens! would you expose him to the vengeance of the conspirators? It is certain death. St. Clair has the will for any villainy, and no doubt is furnished with the legal power to effect it!

BERT. Eh! laissez-moi donc! Can I put sense into the old mad——or the young fool? We must think of ourselves—eh, eh! dat is my principe!

MOR. Bertrand, even I, whom he has so deeply injured, must stand by this unhappy youth at such a moment! And you, you know not what you do! (*In agitation, aside.*) No promise can hold good in such an emergency. I must reveal the truth! (*Aloud.*) Bertrand, you have a heart—you have suffered in your dearest affections! Suppose for an instant this youth were—your *own* son!

BERT. (*rises*). Captain Mortimer, what for do you evoke these souvenirs? If, in a moment of weakness, I have betrayed my long and endless—shame and sorrow—is it for you to wound—to insult me? What for do you name my son? He is gone! Who spared *him?* Who pitied me? Name him not,—there are things I will not forgive, even to *you!*

MOR. It is to spare you endless sorrow that I disobey you. (*Aside.*) Time presses! how shall I tell him? (*Aloud.*) Bertrand, I have read—nay, *known* of such strange things, of lifelong sorrows turned to sudden joys; friends, long wept as dead, brought back in safety,—from the lost battle,—from the lonely wreck! aye, even from the brink of the Deserter's sudden grave! I know, I say, of one, a poor lad, only sixteen, in Soult's. 7th Regiment of

Cavalry (nay, Bertrand, be calm !)—condemned, unheard, to die this shameful death !—the hour at hand—
the fatal file drawn out (*lean on me, Bertrand !*)—a late
compassion snatched him from his fate—a wretched spy
filled the grave dug for him—he lived—*lives !* I say——

BERT. Let me look into your eyes ! You are no
fiend to torture me with false hopes ?

MOR. Bertrand, have you courage to bear what I
have to reveal ? Read the sealed paper that poor youth
gave you—read and know the truth ! (BERTRAND,
bewildered, tries to read, but cannot.) Your hands
shake so ; let me see ! look here ! the signature "*Jules
Bertrand d'Artigny !* "

BERT. (*sinks on his knees*). Mon enfant ! and I
knew him not !—I knew him not !

MOR. (*reading*). " Father, if I escape with
life——"

BERT. (*starting up*). Ah ! God ! he is here—in
danger ! Why do we linger ? Help—call the Baron !
Save him, Mortimer—Alas ! too late, too late !

Enter ST. CLAIR, FILLIPPI, *and guard of Soldiers.*

ST. C. Yes, too late for further deception ! So,
you thought to outwit St. Clair ? Your stratagem was

ingenious ; your accomplice played his part well,—and he shall play it to the end !—even to the gibbet that awaits the spy and traitor !

MOR. Those terms apply to you and yours alone ! The youth risked his life to unmask your devilish conspiracy against the lives of your allies and benefactors ! —he has done his duty ! Tremble rather for yourselves, vile plotters ! We have the proofs of your guilt——

ST. C. (*ironically*). Whose guilt ? What proofs do you speak of ? I believe, Captain Mortimer, partisan spirit causes you to exaggerate the importance of certain trashy papers we have found at Dr. Bertrand's house—and destroyed.

MOR. Destroyed ! by whose authority ?

ST. C. The King's ! None of your vapouring here, Captain Mortimer ! Sicily is yet a Kingdom, though under your obliging protection !

MOR. You shall answer for your deeds, sir !

ST. C. In good time, no doubt ! But now, soldiers, advance ! Search that apartment ; bring forth the traitor who dared to personate Mons. D'Arblay !

BERT. (*rushing forward and with suppressed agitation*). Stay, stay, my good St. Clair, my good

Fillippi ! Hear me, I pray you ; we are old friends,—old neighbours, there should be no enmity between us ! This poor young man, he is no traitor ! Vous comprenez ? No, no ; no traitor ! It was a frolic—nothing more ! (*Laughs nervously.*) A foolish jest !—eh, eh ! These young mads, que voulez-vous ?—eh, eh ! my dear friends, we have all made mistakes ! Why should we black each other's face ? Captain Mortimer, we make no accusations ; my good Mortimer, we know nothing ! My good St. Clair, you will not press this matter ? We will forget !—we will forgive !—this poor young man ! un enfant ! a frolic ! nothing more ! Ah ! yes, these dear ladies——

Enter BARONESS *and* LAURA.

They will speak,—they will save him ! (*Aside.*) Ah ! Mon Dieu ! vous !

BARONESS. Mr. St. Clair, what is all this I hear ? Taking prisoners in *my* house ! This is taking liberties indeed ! You surely cannot presume to——

ST. C. Madam, this is a matter in which private friendship can have no claim ! Still (it may be a weakness on my part), but for *your* sake, I am willing to forget my strict duty—on certain conditions.

Mor. (*aside*). His strict duty! the scoundrel!

Bert. Ah, my friend, name them!

St. C. First, the young adventurer must deliver up the signed paper he has surreptitiously obtained, and leave Sicily within an hour!

Bert. He shall go,—he shall go!

St. C. Secondly, that Captain Mortimer relinquish his claims on Miss Brandon's hand——

Mor. Sir, had I the rights you suppose, no earthly power should prevail upon me to relinquish them; as it is, Miss Brandon is free as air from any claim of mine!

Bert. Ah, mon ami, my noble friend! Yes, yes; you are right—I applaud your prudence! Ah! marriage is an awful thing! J'en sais quelque chose! (*Solemnly.*) Ah! I have been married myself!

Lau. (*aside*). And he can thus coldly consent to lose me! Alas, I must *seem* equally indifferent!

St. C. My third condition is that Miss Brandon will listen to the wish of her friends and consent to become the wife of my friend, Count Fillippi.

Mor. (*aside*). His wife! Down, down, rebellious heart!

Lau. (*aside*). Now to try him! (*Aloud.*) Mr.

St. Clair must feel that I cannot at once pronounce
on so momentous a question ; it will require time,
even with affections as thoroughly disengaged as mine
now are—to——

BERT. Ah! ma chère enfant ! My dear young
lady, how wise you are. Yes, yes ; in a little while
you like him quite as well as this good Mortimer !
Après tout, what is marriage ?—a bagatelle ! association
of interest—voilà tout ! J'en sais quelque chose, moi
—— (*Carelessly.*) Bah ! I have been married myself !

ST. C. Miss Brandon must be more explicit.
If I consent to tear this paper (an order under the
King's hand to seize this impostor), it must be in
return for a promise under hers to be Fillippi's wife
within this month.

(*Goes to table L. and writes rapidly.*)

BERT. Yes, she will sign—we will all sign—we
will all marry !

LAU. Give me the paper !

MOR. (*aside*). Oh, heavens ! must I see this ?

LAU. (*aside*). He turns pale ! he loves me still !

ST. C. Here, madam, you have but to place your
signature and I tear the order !

LAU. Hold, sir ! to you I will not speak ! To

Heaven alone are your motives known!   But you,
Count Fillippi, if there is one spark of honour in your
breast, I appeal to it against yourself!   When I tell
you that my heart and soul is another's, will you still
desire this empty promise?

FILLIP.   I say, St. Clair!   By Bacchus! don't
you think we might let her off—eh?

ST. C. (*aside*). No more of this cursed trifling!
Do you forget your place at Court—the Queen's wishes
—your debt to me?   Draw back *now* and ruin stares
you in the face!

FILLIP.   Well, then, hang it! do the thing pleasantly.
Make it agreeable to her; tell her it's no wish of mine!

LAU.   Your answer, Count Fillippi.

ST. C. (*aside to* FILLIP.)   Tell her you trust to
time and your ardent affection to win her.

FILLIP.   Well, really, madam, we must trust to
time and our ardent affection; mustn't we, St. Clair?
I give you my honour I don't want to marry you; do
I, St. Clair?   But it's necessary, you see.   My friend
St. Clair assures me the thing must be done; mustn't
it, St. Clair?   But, 'pon honour, I wish to be agreeable.
I'll see as little of you as I can after marriage!

ST. C. (*aside*).   Drivelling fool!   (*Aloud.*)   Come,

madam, this is trifling! You have just declared your heart to be free,—you have discarded Mortimer——

LAU. When I said so, I wronged myself and pained the truest heart that ever beat for woman! Mortimer, forgive the shortlived levity that could make you a moment doubt my real affection!

MOR. Oh, Laura! on my knees——

ST. C. Beware, madam, a life hangs on your decision!

LAU. No good can be achieved by unholy means! A vow to love and honour such as *he* would be perjury indeed. (*Tears the paper.*)

ST. C. Hah! you brave it then! Guard, do your duty! Bring forth the spy, alive or dead!

(*Soldiers advance.*)

BERT. (*rushing forward, snatches a sword from one of the Soldiers, and plants himself before the door C.*) Search! but first trample on the old man's body! Find him, but through his father's heart!

(*Pause—Tableau.*)

ST. C. His father!

BERT. Je suis Bertrand d'Artigny! Gentilhomme Français, Messieurs! There is the good blood in my veins! This is my son—my Jules—my one child—

come from the grave where so long I weep for him!
None shall touch him! none shall harm him! my arm
is iron to defend him! See, see, his mother smiles to
me from heaven! Yes, our Jules! our one child!
Pauvre mère! ne craignez rien! There is strength in
this arm—the strength of fifty men!—ha, ha! the
strength of fifty.

   (*He faints away. They carry him to the front.
    Soldiers burst open the door C. and discover
    * POPPLETON *draped in a blanket.*)

ST. C. Curses! this fellow only here!

       (*Exit into inner room C.*)

POP. Here's a nice state of public morality,—
there's a regular conspiracy against my toggery. I
suppose I shan't soon have a shirt to my back!

MOR. Why, Poppleton, how came you here?

POP. Oh, through the window! how should I
come? And I am ready to leave it by the same
aperture——

Enter BARON.

If you'll make that old lunatic give me back my——

 BARON. Help! secure the demon! 'tis an escaped
convict, whom *I*, unhappy wretch, have——

Re-enter St. Clair *from within.*

St. C.   The fellow has escaped! (*To* Pop.) So, sir, you too are in this plot; but you shall find it a hanging matter, sir!

Baron.   Yes, yes; let him be hanged! But, oh, Lord, he'll think nothing of it! He's used to it, the reprobate!

St. C.   Remove the fellow (*to Soldiers*), and also Dr. Bertrand!

Mor.   By whose authority do you dare——

St. C.   The King's—I have his sign-manual to approve my acts. As for the spy and traitor Jules d'Artigny, he shall not long escape me!

Enter Jules.

Jules.   He stands before you! (*Sensation. To* Bertrand.) My beloved father, fear nothing!

St. C.   Ah! in my power at last! I arrest you, in the name of King Ferdinand!

Jules.   Your authority is invalid!

St. C.   How mean you?

Jules.   The King of Naples and Sicily is called Francesco; his father has signed the act of abdication.

The Queen is already on board H.M.S. *Endymion*, and will shortly be on her way to Austria, leaving the scene of her intrigues to English protection, and the base tools who served her to the fate they merit. This warrant empowers me to arrest the Count Fillippi and the returned convict, *Sullivan*, who, under the name of St. Clair, madam (*to the* BARONESS), has so long abused your confidence.

BARONESS. Sullivan! my poor dear late husband's confidential clerk!

JULES. The same! (*To the Marines*.) Remove these persons. (*To* ST. C.) Your fate will be determined before the proper tribunals. The proofs of your guilt are in the hands of justice.

ST. C. Curses on my folly that trusted anything to writing!—so near my full revenge, and now the cup dashed from my parched lip!

FILLIP. By Bacchus! this is quite as unpleasant as marriage!   (*Exit guarded*.)

JULES. I have no time to explain all. Suffice it to say that, owing to your care, I found the boat and marines at the appointed place; and, by a most lucky chance, General Maitland's messenger reached your vessel at the same moment with myself, bringing the news of Lord William Bentinck's arrival at Palermo with the fullest powers from England, and of the abdication of King Ferdinand. He placed in my hands the documents enabling me to defeat St. Clair's malice. Dear father, this is joy indeed! Mr. Poppleton, forgive the temporary inconvenience I was forced to put you to by borrowing your name (you seem still less in a condition to lend me anything else than when I last had the pleasure of meeting you!) I find you have been kind enough to return the compliment by personating me!

POP. Oh! pray don't mention it, sir; only this time it appears probable that I should have been put to more than *temporary* inconvenience, as there was some talk, I think, of *hanging* me in your stead!

MOR. Oh! but here is the Baron, who has a knack of arranging these matters, you know!

Enter BARON.

BARON. Go, scoffers! you set at nought the powers of science! You have tricked and deceived me! Never shall your lips taste of the glorious Elixir!

BERT. No, no; my dear friend! they shall not taste; they are ungratefuls. But you and I will have a cheerful glass together ; we will (what you call) hob-a-nob in immortality !

BARON.   Begone !   ɪ repudiate your friendship ! Science, divine science, shall alone console me !

BARONESS.   And *I*, my beloved Baron, I find I have wronged your faithful heart !   Henceforth we will live for each other alone, and forget the world in that blest seclusion !   Captain Mortimer, you know my nature—a sudden impulse leads me to withdraw my opposition to my niece's marriage.   Be happy with her !

MOR.   How can I thank you ?

POP.   Well, as you seem all to be getting whatever you want, if it wouldn't be considered " exigeant," I should be really obliged by the return of my——

BERT.   Egoiste ! there are things of more importance to be demanded first !   (*Coming forward.*)

To Audience.

If cunning plots are to avail us *here*,
These friends (*pointing to Audience*) must have a
        hand in them, I fear ;
Our secret spies, in Gallery, Box, and Stall,
Must organise " *une vraie entente cordiale,*"

A huge conspiracy 'twixt Stage and Pit!
And fair confederates in each box must sit!
But since *to please you* we conspire, 'twill be
What people call " *Sécret de Comédie.*"
N'importe! from this good Mortimer we'll learn,
Straightforward ways, without a twist or turn—
Since frank appeals find favour in your eyes,
We'll leave off stratagems, finesse, and lies.
We can afford—so near the curtain's fall—
To think——

MOR.   The straight course wisest after all?

BERT.   This good Mortimer!—yes!—AFTER all!

CURTAIN.

LIST OF WORKS

BY MEMBERS OF THE FAMILY OF SHERIDAN

1. **Sheridan, Rev. Denis,** born 1590-1610.

   Assisted Bishop Bedell in translating the Old Testament into Irish, first published in 1685, and known as "The Irish Bible."

2. **Sheridan, William,** Bishop of Kilmore, born 1635, died 1716.

   A Funeral Sermon on the death of Sir M. Eustace, 1665.
   St. Paul's Confession of his Faith, a Sermon, 1685.
   Several Discourses preached on particular occasions, 1704.
   Practical Discourses upon the most important subjects, 1720.

3. **Sheridan, Sir Thomas,** born 1646.

   A Discourse on the Rise and Power of Parliaments, of Laws, of Courts of Judicature, of Liberty, Property, and Religion, of Taxes, Trade, and of the Interest of England in reference to France,—in a letter from a gentleman in the country to a Member of Parliament, 1677.
   Some Revelations in Irish History, 1677.
   A Short Account of his Case before the late House of Commons, 1681.
   History of his own Time, written in France while at the Court of James II.,—in MS. preserved in the Royal Library at Windsor.

4. **Sheridan, Thomas, D.D.** (Swift's friend), born 1687, died 1738.

   Ars Pun-ica sive Flos linguarum, 1719.

The Folly of Puns, 1719.

Prologue spoke at the Theatre Royal in behalf of the poor weavers at Dublin, 1st April 1720, single sheet.

An Elegy on the deplorable death of Mr. Thomas Sheridan, 1722.

The Drapier's Ballad, 1724, single sheet.

Tom Pun-sibi Metamorphized, 1724.

The Philoctetes of Sophocles translated into English verse, 1725.

Tom Pun-sibi's Letter to Dean Swift, 1727.

The Satires of Persius, translated, 1728.

The Intelligencer (edited by T. Sheridan and J. Swift), 1729.

An Ode to be performed at the Castle of Dublin, being the birthday of Queen Caroline, 1728-9.

Sermon Preached in St. Patrick's on St. Cecilia's Day, 1731.

The Satires of Juvenal, translated, 1745.

A new Gingle on Tom Dingle.

5. **Sheridan, Thomas,** M.A., born circa 1719, died 1788.

An easy Introduction of Grammar in English, for the understanding of the Latin tongue, etc., 1744.

A Letter to Mr. Woodward, Comedian (a satire on his acting), 1747, single sheet.

A full Vindication of the conduct of the Manager of the Theatre Royal, Dublin, 1747.

The Play House Prorogued, Dublin, 1754.

Captain O'Blunder, or The Brave Irishman, a Farce, 1754.

Coriolanus, or the Roman Matron, 1755, adapted from Shakespeare and Thompson.

British Education; or the Source of the Disorders of Great Britain, 1755.

Petition to Parliament on the Subject of the Proposed New Theatre in Crow Street, Dublin, 1756.

An Humble Address to the Public (on the same subject), 1758.

An Oration pronounced before a numerous Body of the Nobility, etc. (on the subject of a new Scheme of Education), 1757.

An Humble Address to the Public, together with some considerations on the Present Critical State of the Stage in Ireland, 1758.

A Discourse, introductory to his Course of Letters on Elocution, 1759.

A Course of Lectures on Education, together with two Dissertations on Language, etc., 1763.

A Dissertation on the Causes of the Difficulties which occur in Learning the English Tongue; with a Scheme for publishing an English Grammar and Dictionary, etc., 1763.

A Plan of Education for the Young Nobility of Great Britain, 1769.

Lectures on the Art of Reading, 1775.

A General Dictionary of the English Language, 1780.

The Works of Dean Swift, arranged by T. Sheridan, 1784.

The Life of Jonathan Swift, Dean of St. Patrick's, 1785.

6. **Chamberlaine, Frances** (Mrs. Thomas Sheridan), born 1724, died 1766.

Eugenia and Adelaide, a Romance, afterwards adapted for the stage by Mrs. Le Fanu.

Memoirs of Miss Sidney Bidulph, a Novel, Dublin, 1761.

The Discovery, a Comedy, 1763.

The Dupe, a Comedy, 1764.

The History of Nourjahad, a Romance, 1767.

A Journey to Bath, a Comedy.

7. **Sheridan, Charles Francis,** born 1750, died 1806.

History of the Late Revolution in Sweden, 1778.

Observations on the Doctrine laid down by Sir W. Blackstone respecting the extent of the Power of the British Parliament, 1779.

An Essay on the True Principles of Civil Liberty, 1793.

8. **Sheridan, Richard Brinsley,** born 1751, died 1816.

Jupiter, a Play (in conjunction with N. B. Halhed).

Epistles of Aristænetus, translated from the Greek (in conjunction with N. B. Halhed), 1771.

Clio's Protest and an Epistle from Timothy Screw, 1771.

St. Patrick's Day, or the Scheming Lieutenant, 1775.

The Rivals, 1775.

The Duenna, 1775.

Songs from the *Tempest* with music by Thomas Linley, Jr.

The Critic, 1779.

Verses to the Memory of Garrick, 1779, afterwards published as

The Tears of Genius, a Monody on the Death of Mr. Garrick, 1780.
A Trip to Scarborough, a Comedy, 1781.
The School for Scandal, 1785.
Comparative Statement of the two Bills for the better Government of India, 1788.
Epistle to the Right Hon. Henry Dundas, 1796.
Speeches. 5 volumes, octavo, 1798.
Speeches, with Life. 5 volumes, octavo, 1816.
Epilogue to Semiramis.
The Impostor Unmasked, or the New Man of the People, 1806.
Our King, Country, and God, etc.
Speech on the Motion for Army Establishment, 1802.
Dramatic Works. Edited by Thomas Moore. 2 volumes, octavo, 1821.

9. **Sheridan, Alicia** (Mrs. Joseph Le Fanu), elder sister of Richard Brinsley Sheridan, born 1753.
    The Sons of Erin, a Comedy, 1812.

10. **Sheridan, Elizabeth** (Mrs. Henry Le Fanu), younger sister of Richard Brinsley Sheridan.
    The Indian Voyage, a Novel, 1804.

11. **Sheridan, Tom,** born 1775, died 1817.
    A Speaking Pantomime, songs by Charles Lamb.
    The Untutored Savage, a Farce, 1797.
    The Shooting Company, a Farce.
    (These plays are unpublished, and are in MSS. in the British Museum.)
    Epilogue to The Sons of Erin, by his aunt, Mrs. Joseph Le Fanu.
    Poem on the loss of H.M.S. *Saldanha*, 1812.

12. **Callander, Caroline Henrietta** (Mrs. Thomas Sheridan).
    Carwell, a Novel, 1830.
    Aims and Ends, a Novel, 1833.
    Oonagh Lynch, a Novel, 1833.
    Carwell was translated into French by Monsieur Levilloux, two volumes, Paris, 1830.

13. **Sheridan, Charles Brinsley**, born 1796, died 1843.

Thoughts on the Greek Revolution, 1824.

The Songs of Greece from the Romaic Text, translated into English Verse, 1825.

14. **Sheridan, Helen Selina** (Lady Dufferin and Countess of Gifford), born 1807.

Lispings from Low Latitudes, or Extracts from the Journal of the Honourable Impulsia Gushington, 1863.

The Irish Emigrant, 1845.

Katey's Letter, 1857.

The Charming Woman, 1835.

The Fine Young English Gentleman and other Songs and Poems.

An Essay on " Keys."

Finesse, or Spy and Counter Spy, a Comedy, performed 1863.

15. **Sheridan, Caroline Elizabeth Sarah** (Honourable Mrs. Norton, afterwards Lady Stirling-Maxwell of Keir), born 1809.

POEMS—

The Undying One, Sorrows of Rosalie, etc., 1830.

A Voice from the Factories, 1836.

The Dream and other Poems, 1840.

The Child of the Islands, 1845.

Aunt Carry's Ballads for Children, 1847.

The Lady of La Garaye, 1862.

NOVELS—

Wife and Woman's Reward, 1835.

Stuart of Dunleath, 1851.

Lost and Saved, 1863.

Old Sir Douglas, 1867.

POLITICAL ESSAYS—

Separation of Mother and Child by the law of Custody of Infants considered, 1839.

A Plain Letter to the Lord Chancellor, by Pearce Stevenson, 1839.

Letters to the Mob during the Chartist Riots, 1848.

Letter to the Queen on Lord Cranworth's Marriage and Divorce
Bill, 1855.

Laws for Women in the Nineteenth Century, 1854.

Letters on Education and Emigration.

MISCELLANEOUS—

The Dandies' Rout, 1820.

Tales and Sketches in Prose and Verse, 1850.

The Rose of Jericho, 1870.

Several Sets of Songs, with original music by their author; and
various works edited.

The Keepsake and Fisher's Drawing-Room Scrap Book; several
volumes edited.

16. **Dufferin and Ava, Frederick Temple**, Marquess of.

Narrative of a Journey from Oxford to Skibbereen during the year
of the Irish Famine, 1847.

Letters from High Latitudes, 1857.

Ancient Syria, a Lecture, 1865.

Contributions into an Inquiry into the State of Ireland, 1866.

Inaugural Address delivered before the Social Science Congress at
Belfast in 1867.

Irish Emigration and the Tenure of Land in Ireland, 1867.

Mr. Mill's Plan for the Pacification of Ireland examined, 1868.

The Three F's, a paper laid before the Irish Land Commission in
December, 1880.

Speeches and Addresses, 1882.

Speeches in India, 1890.

17. **Hamilton, Hariot** (Marchioness of Dufferin and Ava).

Our Viceregal Life in India, 1889.

My Canadian Journal, 1891.

18. **St. Maur, Earl**, born 1835, died 1869.

Spanish Church and Exchequer, a Magazine Article.

Ten Days in Richmond with the Confederate Army.

19. **Norton, Thomas Brinsley** (Lord Grantley), born 1831, died 1877.

Pinocchi (Pine Leaves), a collection of poems.

20. **St. Maur, Lady Guendolen** (Lady Guendolen Ramsden).

Letters and Memoirs of the Twelfth Duke of Somerset, 1893 (jointly with W. H. Mallock).

Speedwell, a Novel, 1894.

21. **Le Fanu, Miss Alicia.**

The Flowers, or the Sylphid Queen, a Fairy Tale, 1809.

Rosara's Chains, or the Choice of a Life, a Poem, 1812.

Strathallan, 1816.

Helen Monteagle, 1818.

Leolin Abbey, a Novel, 1819.

'Tales of a Tourist, containing the Outlaw and Fashionable Connections, 1823.

Don Juan de las Sierras, a Romance, 1823.

Memoirs of the Life and Writings of Mrs. Frances Sheridan, etc., 1824.

Henry the Fourth of France, a Romance, 1826.

22. **Le Fanu, Joseph Sheridan,** born 1814, died 1872.

The Cock and the Anchor, a Novel, 1845.

Torlogh O'Brien, a Novel, 1847.

The House by the Churchyard, 1863.

Uncle Silas, 1864.

Wylder's Hand, 1864.

Guy Deverell, 1865.

The Prelude, 1865.

All in the Dark, 1866.

The Tenants of Malory, 1867.

Haunted Lives, 1868.

A Lost Name, 1868.

The Wyvern Mystery, 1869.

Checkmate, 1871.

Chronicles of Golden Friars, 1871.

The Rose and the Key, 1871.

In a Glass Darkly, 1872.

Willing to Die, 1873.

Shamus O'Brien, an Irish Ballad, 1850.

Phaudrig Crohore, an Irish Ballad.

23. **Le Fanu, William,** born 1816.
   Seventy Years of Irish Life, 1894.

24. **Knowles, James,** born 1756, died 1840.
   An Appeal to the . . . Proprietors of the Belfast Academical
      Institution, 1817.
   Orthoepy and Elocution, or the First Part of a Philosophical and
      Practical Grammar of the English Language, 1829.
   A Pronouncing and Explanatory Dictionary of the English Language,
      1835.

25. **Knowles, James Sheridan,** born 1784, died 1862.
   The Chevalier Grillon, an Opera, 1798.
   Fugitive Pieces, a volume of poems, 1810.
   Leo, or the Gipsy, a Play, 1810.
   Brian Boroihme, a Drama, 1811.
   Virginius, 1820.
   Caius Gracchus, 1823.
   The Elocutionist, 1823.
   William Tell, 1825.
   The Beggar's Daughter of Bethnal Green, 1828.
   Alfred the Great, 1831.
   The Hunchback, 1832.
   A Masque (on the death of Sir Walter Scott), 1832.
   The Wife, 1833.
   The Beggar of Bethnal Green, 1834.
   The Daughter, 1837.
   The Bridal.
   The Love Chase, 1837.
   The Maid of Mariendorpt, 1838.
   Woman's Wit, or Love's Disguises, 1838.
   John of Procida, 1840.
   Love, 1840.
   Old Maids, 1841.
   The Rose of Arragon, 1842.
   Alexina, or True unto Death, 1842.
   The Secretary, 1843.
   Fortescue, a Novel, 1846.

George Lovell, a Novel, 1847.
The Rock of Rome, or the Arch Heresy, 1849.
The Idol abolished by its own Priest, 1851.
The Gospel attributed to Matthew is the Record of the whole original Apostlehood, 1855, etc., etc.

26. **Knowles, Richard Brinsley.**
The Maiden Aunt, a Comedy, 1845.
The Life of James Sheridan Knowles, 1872.

27. **Marshall, Maria Knowles** (Mrs. Plunkett Rice).
Several Novelettes.

LIST OF WORKS

OF ADAM BLACKWOOD AND HIS DESCENDANTS

Adam Blackwood, born 1539, died 1613.

Caroli IX. Pompa funebris versibus expressa, par A. B. J. C. (Adamum Blacvodæum jurisconsultum); Paris, 1574.

De Vinculo seu conjunctiones religionis et imperii, et de conjunctionum insidiis, religionis fuco adumbratis, libri duo; Paris, 1575.

Adversus Georgii Buchanani Dialogus de Jure regni apud Scotos, pro Regibus Apologia qua Regii nominis amplitudo et Imperii majestas ab Hæreticorum famosis libellis et perduellium injuria vindicatur; Poitiers, 1581.

Martyre de Marie Stuart, reine d'Écosse et douairière de France.

Sanctarum Præcationum Præmia, seu mavis, Ejaculationes animæ ad orandum se præparantis; 1598.

Inauguratio Jacobi magnæ Britanniæ regis; Paris, 1606.

In Psalmum David quinquagesimum, etc., Meditatio; Poitiers, 1608.

Varii generis Poematia; Poitiers, 1609.

Adami Blacvodæi, etc., Opera omnia; Paris, 1644.

Henry Blackwood.

Hippocratis Coi Prognosticorum Libri tres, ad veterum exemplarium fidem emendati et recogniti; Paris, 1625.

Caroli Servini Ludovici fili genethliacon. 1612. 4to.

Elogia in scholis medicorum in quatuor candidatorum medicinæ gratiam. Paris, 1608. 8vo.

Jacques Blackwood.

Aristides Gallicus sive virtuti ac probitati Guillaume du Vair. Paris, Morellus, 1619. 4to.

De Annæ Franciæ & Navarræ Regina restitutâ sanitate. Paris, Morellus, 1620. 4to.

Une poëme dédiée au Duc de Longueville. "ἐπιβατήριον."

THE SHERIDAN GENEALOGY

SO FAR AS IT REGARDS THE PRINCIPAL PERSONS MENTIONED IN THE SKETCH OF LADY DUFFERIN'S LIFE

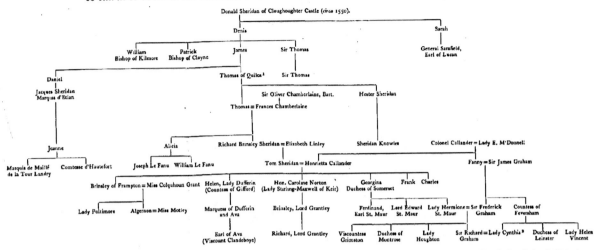

¹ There is some doubt as to whether Thomas Sheridan of Quilca was the grandson or the grand-nephew of Denis. I have followed the authority of the Rev. Mr. Brooke, father of the Rev. Stopford Brooke, who was a connection of the Sheridan family, and had carefully examined the point.

² Lady Cynthia, though the youngest of Lady Feversham's children, has been placed to the left for the convenience of noting her marriage with her cousin, Sir Richard Graham.

N.B.—On account of want of space some of the steps in the descents of the collaterals have been omitted.

THE SHERIDAN GENEALOGY

SO FAR AS IT IS KNOWN, DOWN TO THE TIME OF DONALD

SHERIDAN OF CLOUGHOUGHTER CASTLE

FATHER OF DENIS

Ostar O'Seridan, of Castle=d. of O'Rourke, Prince of Co.
Togher, married A.D. 1014   Leitrim.

Antony .   .   .   .   =d. of O'Neil, Prince of Tyrone.

Conor .   .   .   .   =d. of O'Donnell, Prince of Donegal.

Antony .   .   .   .   =d. of O'Farrell, Prince of Longford.

Conor .   .   .   .   =d. of the O'Conor Don.

Antony .   .   .   .   =d. of O'Reilly, Prince of Cavan.

Conor .   .   .   .   =d. of O'Rourke, Prince of Leitrim.

Antony .   .   .   .   =d. of O'Connor, Prince of Sligo.

Thaddeus .   .   .   .   =d. of E. O'Reilly of Cavan.

Audven .   .   .   .   =d. of T. O'Brady, Ballyhase in Co.
                         Cavan.

Donald .   .   .   .   =d. of the O'Neill.

                        Denis.

From the records of the Office of Ulster King of Arms.

EXTRACT FROM AN OLD RECORD IN THE BOOKS OF ULSTER
KING OF ARMS IN DUBLIN CASTLE :—

Sheridan
Seal.

"THE GENEALOGY OF THE NOBLE FAMILY OF O'SHERIDAN.

This noble family is descended from O'Connor Sligoe's second son,
who took the sirname Sheridan, he was married to O'Reilly's daughter
of the County Cavan, their only son Ostar marched into that country at
the head of an army, to assist his uncle O'Reilly against O'Rourke, who
invaded part of that County, and proposed no less than to possess himself
of the whole. In the year of our Lord 1013 Ostar Sheridan gained
several battles, O'Rourke not finding himself able any longer to with-
stand Ostar, concluded a peace and gave over all the lands he possessed
in the County of Cavan to Ostar O'Sheridan on condition that Ostar
married his eldest daughter, them conditions were accepted by all partys
and ratified in the year 1014, O'Rourke returned to his patrimony in the
County of Leterim. James is at present Chieff and first of the family.
The Mansion House of O'Sheridan was called Togher in the County
Cavan, he had many great possessions in said County and as far as to the
borders of Meath Westmeath and Longford too many to be here inserted.
There are three trefoils that furnish the arms about the Lyon. The
arms are a Lyon Rampant in a field argent furnished with trefoils, the
crest a stagg couched on a mountain."

NOTE.—There is some discrepancy among the authorities as to the
names of some of Denis's grandchildren, which my absence from home
has prevented me from investigating as closely as I should have desired.

CPSIA information can be obtained at www.ICGtesting.com
Printed in the USA
BVOW06s1440160114

342130BV00007B/92/P